T0319900

A Research Agenda for Lean Management

Elgar Research Agendas outline the future of research in a given area. Leading scholars are given the space to explore their subject in provocative ways, and map out the potential directions of travel. They are relevant but also visionary.

Forward-looking and innovative, Elgar Research Agendas are an essential resource for PhD students, scholars and anybody who wants to be at the forefront of research.

For a full list of Edward Elgar published titles, including the titles in this series, visit our website at www.e-elgar.com.

A Research Agenda for Lean Management

Edited by

ANDREA FURLAN

Full Professor of Management, Department of Economics and Management, University of Padova, and Scientific Director of the Lean Enterprise Center of CUOA Business School, Italy

DARYL POWELL

Adjunct Professor, Department of Business, Strategy and Political Sciences, University of South-Eastern Norway, Kongsberg, Norway

Elgar Research Agendas

Cheltenham, UK • Northampton, MA, USA

Published by
Edward Elgar Publishing Limited
The Lypiatts
15 Lansdown Road
Cheltenham
Glos GL50 2JA
UK

Edward Elgar Publishing, Inc.
William Pratt House
9 Dewey Court
Northampton
Massachusetts 01060
USA

A catalogue record for this book
is available from the British Library

Library of Congress Control Number: 2023952674

This book is available electronically in the **Elgar**online
Business subject collection
http://dx.doi.org/10.4337/9781035302918

ISBN 978 1 0353 0290 1 (cased)
ISBN 978 1 0353 0291 8 (eBook)

Printed and bound by CPI Group (UK) Ltd, Croydon, CR0 4YY

Contents

Figures

Tables

Contributors

Jiju Antony, Northumbria University, UK

Michael Ballé, Institut Lean France, France

Godefroy Beauvallet, i3, CNRS, Télécom Paris, Institut Polytechnique de Paris, France

Michela Carraro, Technical University of Munich, Germany

Fabian Dillinger, Technical University of Munich, Germany

Fabian Formann, ROI-EFESO Management Consulting AG, Germany

Andrea Furlan, University of Padova, Italy

Paolo Gaiardelli, University of Bergamo, Italy

Ambra Galeazzo, University of Padova, Italy

Rose Heathcote, Thinking People and University of Buckingham, UK

Peter Hines, South East Technological University, Ireland

Marte D. Q. Holmemo, Norwegian University of Science and Technology, Norway

Kai Magenheimer, ROI-EFESO Management Consulting AG, Germany

Florian Magnani, Université Aix-Marseille, CERGAM, Centrale Méditerranée, France

Giuditta Pezzotta, University of Bergamo, Italy

Daryl Powell, SINTEF Manufacturing and University of South-Eastern Norway, Norway

Gunther Reinhart, Technical University of Munich, Germany

Eivind Reke, SINTEF Manufacturing, Norway

David Romero, Tecnologico de Monterrey, Mexico

Henrik Saabye, Aarhus University and VELUX, Denmark

Rachna Shah, Carlson School of Management, University of Minnesota, USA

Guilherme Tortorella, University of Melbourne, Australia, IAE Business School, Universidad Austral, Buenos Aires, Argentina and Universidade Federal de Santa Catarina, Brazil

Desirée H. van Dun, University of Twente, Netherlands

Kodo Yokozawa, Yokohama National University, Japan

Matteo Zanchi, University of Bergamo, Italy

Foreword

Torbjørn Netland

In the dynamic realm of management practices, lean management stands out, not just for its longevity but also for its adaptability. Over time, it has transformed from a tactical tool for manufacturing efficiency to a holistic strategy that finds relevance across sectors and challenges. As one of the most popular business phenomena, lean management has continued to evolve both in terms of applications and content – and in our understanding of it. This exceptional compilation, edited by esteemed lean scholars Andrea Furlan and Daryl Powell, brings together contributions from renowned and emerging lean luminaries to provide a valuable compass for scholars into the next era of lean management.

This book is unique in its coverage of the subject. Rather than forcing a strict definition of lean management, Furlan and Powell acknowledge that the term "lean" has become ubiquitous and, by that, its definition elusive. As the editors note in their introduction, it is a concept that emerged not from theoretical dissections but from keen observations of Toyota's real-world practices. As lean quickly found applications outside Toyota, it had to change and adapt, not just to different settings but also across different times. While this book may not provide a definitive delineation of lean, it certainly offers an enriching exploration of what lean management embodies, its transformative potential for organizations, and the pivotal role of scholars in its continued study.

Comprising 14 diverse chapters, this collection is rich in its breadth and depth. Each chapter varies in length, methodology, lean interpretation, and presentation. Such a many-sided representation perfectly aligns with the book's purpose, because it encourages the multifaceted understanding of lean management that the editors emphasize. This way, the chapters also serve as varied examples for scholars in search of a methodological approach. This choice by the editors reminds me of Berger and Luckman's 1966 masterpiece *The Social Construction of Reality*, which argues that we understand the world through our actions and interactions with it. The way we understand a phenomenon is dependent on the tools we use to interpret it. Therefore, a variety of methods and approaches should give us a better understanding of lean management.

The very structure of the book mirrors the knowledge frontier of the field. Furlan and Powell elegantly split the chapters into five logical and cohesive parts: "Lean from bundles to strategy," "Lean and learning," "Lean and sustainability," "Lean leadership and behaviors," and "Lean and digitalization." These five headings are good starting points for future scholars searching to narrow down the scope of their research projects. All of them provide rich opportunities for exciting questions, and the chapters in this compilation can provide the tips needed to move forward. In particular, I would like to emphasize that we have barely started to understand the micro-foundations of lean implementation, and this book contains several human-centric chapters on topics from leadership to problem-solving behaviors that can spur new insights.

I wholeheartedly agree with the editors that the promise of lean remains enormous. The real-world benefits it can confer, from heightened productivity to contributions towards solving global challenges like the United Nations' Sustainable Development Goals, make it imperative for both researchers and practitioners to deepen their understanding of the subject. In this endeavor, Furlan and Powell's excellent book stands out as a lighthouse, illuminating a promising path forward for the next era of lean management scholarship.

Torbjørn Netland

Professor of Production and Operations Management, ETH Zurich

August 8, 2023

Introduction: On the need for *A Research Agenda for Lean Management*

Andrea Furlan and Daryl Powell

Though the term lean is by no means something new, its definition and research boundaries remain somewhat unclear (Hopp and Spearman, 2021). Lean production was first described by Krafcik (1988) as a means of achieving world-class quality and productivity in manufacturing and was later popularized in Womack et al. (1990) as a superior business system consisting of five integral parts: dealing with the customer, designing the product, running the factory, coordinating the supply chain, and managing the lean enterprise. Since then, lean has been described as the most popular and most misunderstood approach to business improvement of our generation (Netland and Powell, 2017).

Over the past three decades, lean production – now commonly referred to as lean management – has received much attention from academics and practitioners alike. Though there have been countless attempts at defining lean, academics have thus far been unable to agree on a common definition. This is in part due to the fact that, unlike other popular approaches, lean was not derived from theory, but from observing phenomena in practice at Toyota. The answers we seek therefore are not to be found in the definitions, but in the practice.

To avoid definitional conundrums, we choose to adopt the perspective of Netland (in Cusumano et al., 2021), who preserves a practical perspective and defines lean as a business phenomenon. The word "phenomenon" originates from the Greek word "phainomenon," which is the present participle of the verb "phainesthai," meaning "to appear" or "to be visible." The term "phenomenon" refers to any observable fact or event that is considered remarkable, extraordinary, or worthy of investigation. One of the characteristics of a phenomenon is that it evolves over time. It is not static.

Thus, interpreted as a business phenomenon, lean (and indeed our understanding of lean) does not remain static. It is something that continuously changes, even though it originated from observations of the Toyota Production System (TPS) during the second half of the twentieth century. As such, we continuously need new perspectives and theoretical lenses to re-orient our understanding of this phenomenon – an understanding that slowly but relentlessly changes over time, as we find new facets to it and new contexts for its application. Following this path, over the last couple of decades, research on lean has been very eclectic and pursued many directions. This evolution has been greatly fruitful but has led lean literature to become very fragmented.

With the aim of recovering a sense of unity on lean research, this book attempts to take stock of the perspectives and theoretical lenses that contemporary researchers are adopting to study lean. The five sections of the book provide a broad research agenda for lean management from which we can continue to observe and study lean. The five themes provide plenty of research opportunities for academics as well as key insights for practitioners. There are also strong interconnections among the different chapters, both within and across sections. These interconnections provide an overview of trending topics and research avenues, giving the book a sense of harmony and coherence.

The first theme of our research agenda for lean management, "Lean management: from bundles of practices to business strategy," focuses on definitional aspects of lean. As Rachna Shah observes in her chapter, an attempt to define lean once and for all might be fruitless since we are still uncovering aspects of lean that are less understood by contemporary researchers. The chapter starts from an examination of the seminal work "Lean manufacturing: Context, practice bundles and performance," published in the *Journal of Operations Management* (Shah and Ward, 2003) and concludes that the lean agenda today is richer than ever. New research opportunities unfold, for example, on the behavioral aspects of employees' involvement in implementing lean and on the relationship between lean and new technologies in emerging contexts like sustainable operations and not-for-profit operations. In the second chapter of the first section, Florian Magnani, Michael Ballé and Godefroy Beauvallet offer a view of lean as a strategy based on an emergent process of learning. The view of lean as a strategy departs from current research substantially. First of all, it positions lean in the realm of strategic management and not in operations management or related disciplines. Second, by focusing on learning, it does not distinguish the phase of strategy development from the phase of strategy execution. The authors urge scholars and managers alike to keep studying lean through the prism of strategy by adopting an emergent learning perspective. They argue that this will help to capture the essence of lean as a competitive weapon.

The second theme, "Lean and learning," builds on the learning perspective to give an original theoretical grounding to lean. Eivind Reke builds upon the notions of troublesome problems and threshold concepts to advance an interpretation of lean as an education system where the tools are instrumental to discover gaps in current knowledge, and learn knew knowledge, at all levels of the organization. The author urges scholars to pursue this line of research to deepen our understanding of how the lean education system can support lifelong learning inside organizations. Subsequently, the chapter by Henrik Saabye also revolves around the theory of learning by building a conceptual integration between lean and action learning. This integration provides an original methodological approach that can help scholars produce actionable knowledge that is equally relevant both for theory and practice.

The third theme, "Lean and sustainability: people, planet, profit," addresses the complex topic of the interdependency between lean and the triple-bottom line: planet, people, and profit. In the face of the environmental challenge, Rose Heathcote proposes gemba-inspired strategies to connect sustainable goals with realistic on-the-ground action by equipping and supporting employees to see and act on opportunities. Action learning research should inform future research to achieve this objective. Peter Hines and Florian Magnani further discuss how lean can be used to better understand the employee experience in a lean organization and trigger a self-development capability in employees. This is a timely matter given the current discussion about human-centered manufacturing and the great resignation. The authors also offer research per-spectives to continue improving the understanding of the human dimension's role in a lean organization. Such perspectives are further supplemented in the following chapter by Matteo Zanchi, Paolo Gaiardelli, Giuditta Pezzotta, and Daryl Powell, who present lean as a compensatory tool for neurodiverse people. The authors analyze the peculiar traits of the three statistically most prevalent neurodiversity conditions (Autism, Dyslexia, and Attention Deficit Hyperactivity Disorder) and explore how several lean practices might serve as a compensatory mechanism for neurodiverse people. In the final chapter of the section, Andrea Furlan considers the relationship between lean and resilience. Based on an empirical study of a sample of Italian firms, the author finds that there is a (weak) positive relationship between a firm's (economic) resiliency and lean. The chapter urges scholars to do more quantitative research that uses financial data on how different configurations of lean bundles can help to weather different types of disruptions.

The fourth theme, "Lean leadership and behaviors," deals with four topics that are at the crossroads between cognitive research, organizational behavior, and behavioral operations literature. Michela Carraro and Ambra Galeazzo investigate the organizational structure and infrastructure characteristics of a lean context that encourage employees to adopt proactive behaviors. Proactive behaviors are seen as the backbone of a successful lean implementation. Future research is needed to identify the macro-, meso-, and micro-factors that foster proactivity and disentangle their intertwined connections. Desirée van Dun offers a comprehensive overview and categorization of the various theories on lean leadership grounded on learning and other theories. The author drafts a research agenda that proposes a set of cutting-edge methodological approaches to further develop a true 3D (descriptive, dependent, and development) view of lean leadership. Subsequently, the chapter by Marte Holmemo is also about lean leadership. The author proposes three suggestions to improve future research: (a) finding characteristics of leadership that work in a lean management context, (b) narrow the scope of our research to focus on more precise concepts, and (c) emphasize the processual logic of lean leadership. The emotional and behavioral antecedents of kaizen are the focus of the next chapter by Kodo Yokozawa. In particular, the author focuses on the role of anxiety in driving individual and team proactive behaviors that support kaizen. The insights of the chapter shed light on managerial and leadership challenges to create a kaizen culture and provides original research avenues to strengthen this perspective.

The fifth and final theme of the research agenda for lean management, "Lean and digitalization," examines the controversial relationship between new digital technologies and lean. Daryl Powell, David Romero, Jiju Antony, and Paolo Gaiardelli present a state-of-the-art perspective on digital lean manufacturing (DLM) and present a description of the emerging concept of Lean 4.0 – its benefits and challenges. The final chapter by Fabian Dillinger, Fabian Formann, Kai Magenheimer, Gunther Reinhart, and Guilherme Tortorella studies the mutual tensions between lean production, digital technologies, and economic, environmental, and social sustainability. Drawing on the results of a Delphi study, the authors find complementarities between specific combinations of lean practices and digital technologies relative to the sustainability dimensions (and also some counterintuitive trade-offs). The fine granularity of the research approach adopted by the authors offers interesting ideas for future research on the topic.

Figure i.1 synthesizes the content of the book and visualizes the dominant topics that have emerged across the different chapters.

Figure i.1   A Research Agenda for Lean Management

The promise of lean management is still enormous. Those that have successfully adopted it have witnessed labor productivity soar, errors and defects cut in half, and product development times slashed. Lean thinking has also been shown to pave the way for digital transformation, as well as contribute to solving the United Nations' Sustainable Development Goals. Our hope is that each one of the 14 chapters, and the book in its entirety, will help researchers and practitioners to find new and original research ideas and to shed light on further unique aspects of lean management as a continuously evolving business phenomenon.

References

Cusumano, M. A., Holweg, M., Howell, J., Netland, T., Shah, R., Shook, J., Ward, P., and Womack, J. (2021). Commentaries on "The Lenses of Lean". *Journal of Operations Management*, 67, 627–639.

Hopp, W. L. and Spearman, M. S. (2021). The lenses of lean: Visioning the science and practice of efficiency. *Journal of Operations Management*, 67, 610–626.

Krafcik, J. F. (1988). Triumph of the lean production system. *Sloan Management Review*, 30(1), 41–52.

Netland, T. H. and Powell, D. J. (2017). A lean world. In D. J. Powell and T. H. Netland (eds), *The Routledge Companion to Lean Management*. New York: Routledge, pp. 465–473.

Shah, R. and Ward, P. T. (2003). Lean manufacturing: Context, practice bundles and performance. *Journal of Operations Management*, 21(3), 129–149.

Womack, J. P., Jones, D. T., and Roos, D. (1990). *The Machine That Changed the World: The Story of Lean Production, Toyota's Secret Weapon in the Global Car Wars That Is Now Revolutionizing World Industry*. New York: Simon & Schuster.

PART I

Lean management: from bundles of
practices to business strategy

1   Reflections on the "Lean Manufacturing Practice Bundles", twenty years on...

Rachna Shah

Introduction

In this article, I reflect on my 2003 article, "Lean manufacturing: Context, practice bundles and performance," published in the *Journal of Operations Management*. It was co-authored with Professor Peter Ward and received the prestigious Shingo Award for Research in 2003. In the paper, we examined the effects of three contextual factors – plant size, plant age, and unionization status of employees – on the likelihood of implementing 22 manufacturing practices. Further, we showed that these 22 practices were key facets of lean manufacturing and postulated that they could be grouped into four bundles that consist of interrelated and internally consistent practices. These bundles are just-in-time (JIT), total quality management (TQM), total preventive maintenance (TPM), and human resource management (HRM). We used data from *IndustryWeek*'s 1999 Census of Manufacturers Survey to show that implementing a practice was contingent on plant size, plant age, and union status. Specifically, plant size exerts a strong influence on implementation, whereas the influence of unionization and plant age is significantly less pervasive than conventional wisdom suggests. We also found that the four bundles explain about 23 percent of the variation in operational performance after accounting for the effects of industry and contextual factors, and plants belonging to process and discrete industries differed significantly in implementing JIT and TPM bundles, but not in TQM and HRM bundles.

Next, I describe the context in which the original article was written, highlight theoretical and empirical problems salient at that time, and comment on the likely reasons the article and my follow-up work has had a sustained influence in the field, particularly in the lean operations domain. Looking forward, I ask whether some of the issues, particularly definitional and measurement issues we discussed pose similar challenges today, and then go further to consider ways in which lean and the domain of operations management itself has changed.

Back then: the article and its inspiration

I wrote the first draft of the article as a second-year PhD student in the Management Science department (since renamed as the Department of Operations and Business Analytics) at the Fisher College of Business, at The Ohio State University. The article was written to fulfill a course requirement. The course was a PhD seminar taught by Professor Peter Ward and focused on Operations Strategy with a heavy emphasis on empirical research. Few people know this fact, and therefore it is important to highlight that the paper was not part of my dissertation. However, it proved instrumental in my decision to pursue lean production as the topic of my dissertation with Peter as my advisor. A few other events were critical to its development and are worth mentioning.

A confluence of opportunities

Organizational context

At the time (1999), the Management Science department at the Fisher College of Business housed the Center for Excellence in Manufacturing Management (CEMM, now called, the Center for Operational Excellence or COE). CEMM's mission was to serve as a conduit between the Management Science Department faculty and local businesses to facilitate learning. The corporate members were typically mid- to high-level operations managers. CEMM exposed its member managers to current research and the interaction informed department faculty of the critical business problems and issues facing managers in running their operations. Inevitably, many of the problems required process improvements. And, as part of its knowledge enrichment initiatives, CEMM regularly brought in world-renowned process improvement experts to participate in and lead CEMM activities.

I was fortunate to have received summer research funding from the center, and part of my responsibilities included helping to organize the CEMM quarterly meetings with corporate members and ensuring that they ran smoothly. The added advantage was that I got a front-row seat to observe and interact with a who's-who of world-class process improvement experts. This is where I first met Jim Womack[1] and John Shook[2], among many other contemporary luminaries of the lean world. These interactions provided an opportunity to hear first-hand their perspectives on how the term lean was coined and was meant to be used as a proxy of Toyota Production System, how US manufacturing plants and practices trailed their Japanese counterparts, and their strong belief that this new business phenomenon was going to be critically influential for US manufacturing.

Academic context

It is important to note that at that time (1999), there was little understanding of lean both among academics and industry. Although both *The Machine that Changed the World* (1990) and its follow-up book, *Lean Thinking* (1996) had been published[3] and spent some time on the *New York Times* best-seller list, there were almost no published papers in academic literature examining lean. At the same time, in the PhD coursework, including the Operations Strategy seminar, there were numerous published articles on JIT, TQM, TPM, time-based competition, and other similar management concepts. Many of these papers focused on defining and developing psychometric properties of these concepts, and a few others focused on empirically examining their impact on performance. Psychometrics was in vogue, and factor analysis and structural equation modeling using primary data collected using surveys were the methods du jour.

It was quickly apparent from the discussions at CEMM meetings that the academic literature seemed to be trailing the industry thinking and the questions being examined were narrow in scope. For instance, Jim W. and John S., the leading thinkers in the field, described lean as a cohesive, comprehensive approach to continuous improvement encompassing *the entire enterprise*. They used lean as a proxy for the Toyota Production System and frequently enumerated Toyota's resulting superior performance on multiple fronts. The corporate managers, despite their great interest and enthusiasm for it, were more guarded – they debated potential reasons why US manufacturing plants

---

[1]   Womack, J.P. and Jones, D.T. (1996). *Lean Thinking: Banish Waste and Create Wealth in Your Corporation*. Simon & Schuster, New York; Womack, J.P., Jones, D.T. and Roos, D. (1990). *The Machine that Changed the World*. Harper Perennial, New York.

[2]   Rother, M. and Shook, J. (1999) *Learning to See: Value Stream Mapping to Create Value and Eliminate Muda*. Lean Enterprise Institute, Cambridge.

[3]   *The Toyota Way* (Liker, 2004) had not yet been published and "Decoding the DNA of the TPS" (Spear and Bowen, 1999) was in publication process.

might not be able to implement lean. They argued that even if lean practices could be implemented, they doubted if the resulting performance would be as spectacular as it was at Toyota. In contrast, academic researchers were grappling with how lean was related to other existing concepts such as JIT and TQM. In absence of a reliable and valid instrument to measure lean, research was focused on examining the components and their performance impacts, in a piecemeal manner. In spite of these practical concerns, I was struck by the zealous nature of the discussions, the conviction that "lean worked, period," implying that lean was universally applicable and not subject to usual contingencies. I recall many intense and passionate discussions with Peter, Jim W., and John S. about the universal applicability of the lean production system.

Here, it is important to note that my background (growing up in India) and work experience (in management consulting) made me somewhat cynical about the academic research I was reading. My questions in most of the PhD seminars centered on "this is not likely to work in India" or "my (consulting) clients would not buy this." I believe that this healthy skepticism helped shape my early academic thinking and prompted me to explore "when, i.e. under what conditions will something work (i.e. produce benefits)" in most of my early seminar papers. My perspective found theoretical expression in the universalistic, contingency, and configurational thinking being discussed in the strategy literature,[4] and these views were instrumental in developing not only the lean-bundles paper but also my subsequent research.

Data availability

Access to appropriate data is the key to writing an empirical paper. And the data for the paper became available by a complete coincidence from *IndustryWeek*, a trade magazine with an illustrious publication history.[5] Interestingly, at the time I was working on the lean-bundles article, *IndustryWeek* was owned by Penton Publishing, which was founded by John Penton, who helped the US Census establish the Standard Industrial Classification (i.e. SIC) system. The central focus of *IndustryWeek* was, and continues to be, to identify and highlight upcoming innovations and trends in the manufacturing industry and

---

[4]   A special callout to Venkatraman (1989), Whetten (1989), and Meyer, Tsui, and Hinings' Introduction to the special research forum on configurations approaches (1993).

[5]   *IndustryWeek* has been a fixture in the US manufacturing community for over 125 years. It was founded as *Iron Review* in 1882; it became *Iron Trade Review* in 1888; and *Steel, The Metalworking Management Weekly* in 1930. It has been published as *IndustryWeek* since the 1970s, and as a monthly magazine since 2001.

provide a platform for management to interact and learn from each other. In order to identify the current trends, *IndustryWeek* conducted several different surveys, including the *IndustryWeek* Annual Census of Manufacturers which focused on assessing the state of US manufacturers and *IndustryWeek*'s Annual Best Plants Program, which helped identify the best manufacturing plants in the US. Fashioned similarly to the Shingo Best Plant Award, the *IndustryWeek* Best Plants Program included a 40-page survey that plant management filled out and a follow-up facility visit.

IndustryWeek had given Peter hard copies of almost ten years of Best Plants survey responses, which sat in a box in his office. During one of our meetings, Peter offered me the task of coding the survey responses and creating a searchable database in return for research funding for the summer between my first and second year in the program (which meant that I did not need to teach to receive summer funding). During the summer, I worked on coding the surveys and developing a database in MS Excel that would be easily searchable – *IndustryWeek* could develop a menu-driven automated version and sell it as a benchmarking tool to its subscriber base. Although prior to agreeing to doing it, I did not know how difficult and time-consuming the task would be, in hindsight, it was a great job for a junior student[6] – it exposed me to effective survey design, it helped me develop database construction skills, and it provided an opportunity to interact with *IndustryWeek* editors and the research design team frequently. This latter interaction was foundational in receiving the 1999 *IndustryWeek* Annual Census of Manufacturers survey response data for the lean-bundles paper. The survey included questions on many distinct aspects of a manufacturing plant including product-process characteristics, practices related to employees, manufacturing, information technology, and supplier-customers, and financial metrics. I used these data in several papers, including the lean-bundles paper.

Lean-bundles paper

Now, going back to the initial draft of the paper – it was a culmination of the discussions at CEMM, academic literature in operations and strategy seminars, and interactions with the *IndustryWeek* publication and research team. In the paper, I wanted to empirically examine perspectives of these various constituents, primarily surrounding the extent to which lean was being adopted in

---

6   Apparently, Peter had offered the survey-coding task to several other PhD students before me over the years. It is a running joke between Peter and I that no one was naïve enough to accept it.

the US manufacturing plants. My initial draft and the paper presentation in the seminar focused on this central idea – did US manufacturing plants face serious challenges in implementing lean because they were more likely to be unionized and were older in age? More specifically, was the implementation of a practice contingent on plant characteristics? For contingencies, in addition to union status of the employees and plant age, I included plant size based on the discussions informed by "innovation adoption and implementation" literature streams in the operations strategy and organizational theory/strategy seminars. Lastly, I also wanted to examine how the extent of implementation impacted plant performance. I was thrilled when the paper was received well by Peter and my fellow students in the seminar.

The paper went through several rounds of editing before it was submitted to the *Journal of Operations Management* in December 2000 – almost 20 months after I first presented the paper in the Operations Strategy Seminar. The paper came back with a "major revision" decision. I remember being very disappointed at the time because the review team's report was *very long* and raised numerous issues, some very critical and seemingly un-addressable. Peter, by now my formal advisor, not only helped me appreciate the gravity of receiving a revise and resubmit decision (back then, over 70 percent of the submitted papers failed to pass on to the second round), but also helped in navigating the revision process. We submitted the revised draft in April 2002. The paper was conditionally accepted in May and fully accepted in June 2002. Even in those days, it was rare for a paper to be accepted after one round of revision. And for that, I will be immensely grateful to the three anonymous reviewers and Professor Jack Meredith, the managing editor of *JOM*, for their excellent and helpful comments,[7] and my advisor and co-author Peter Ward for his guidance.

I want to share one other behind-the-scenes anecdote about the paper. By the time the paper came back with the major revision decision, I had made significant progress on my dissertation which focused on examining lean production more holistically.[8] In doing so, I had learned that the 22 manufacturing prac-

---

[7]   In those days, *JOM* did not have departments and the managing editor of *JOM* served as a reviewer. Our paper received three reviews plus the editor comments. The stated turnaround time was approximately 90 days.

[8]   My dissertation, titled "A configurational view of lean manufacturing and its theoretical implications," developed an empirically validated instrument to measure lean production and assessed how lean firms were different from non-lean firms in their environmental, organizational, and informational collection/distribution characteristics.

tices provided a very incomplete picture of the lean landscape. At one point, I wanted to withdraw the paper so a more comprehensive "tools and practices" view of the lean production system could be provided using data collected for my dissertation. I am truly thankful to Peter, who did not let me withdraw the paper – Peter's logic was simple: scientific knowledge is developed incrementally, and we should continue to examine theories and business phenomena such as lean, as they unfold. This logic has been very useful in shaping my own research and advising philosophy.

This submission-revision-resubmission exercise was an immensely useful experience. I learned that collectively, reviewers are likely to catch every problem in a paper. Every reviewer comment, whether substantive or not, must be addressed comprehensively. This may require reading existing literature, sometimes outside of your core domain, closely and critically. More often than not, the reviewer's comments are an outcome of the author's poor exposition because the author did not explain/describe their position clearly. Lastly, one need not agree with every reviewer comment. However, to disagree, one must have a solid foundation. For instance, for the lean-bundles paper, more than one reviewer suggested that we could split the paper into two separate papers – one examining the impact of contingencies on the extent of implementation of the 22 manufacturing practices and the other studying the performance impacts of the lean-bundles. However, both Peter and I thought that such a split would result in two weak papers. Fortunately, we were able to defend our position with the review team. I believe that our conviction has proven to be correct with time.

What explains the article's success? Why has the article been highly cited?

If citations are used to gauge an article's influence, then the lean-bundles article has been reasonably influential with over 4,000 citations as of April 2023. Why has our article been influential? Although it is not possible to say with certainty the drivers of interest in – and citations of – a paper, I speculate on four main reasons I believe our article has been highly cited. These are hidden in the title of the paper. Further, I think these reasons explain in general why papers are seen as "interesting" and are highly cited.

First, the article focused on a relatively novel business phenomenon – "lean manufacturing" was garnering immense interest from practicing managers and academic researchers but was not understood well by either community.

This made the topic both timely and relevant, with a higher potential for impact. As one of the first articles on lean published in a top-tier academic journal, it benefited from a first-mover advantage. In some sense, the article helped create a nascent scholarly "conversation" on lean manufacturing.

Second, the article challenged strongly held beliefs by US manufacturing managers about contextual contingencies that impacted the implementation of frequently used manufacturing practices in the US plants. A vast majority of managers believed that lean practices were difficult to implement in the US manufacturing plants because of the unionized workforce and aged plants. Existing literature also supported this view – a handful of industrial organization researchers had shown that unionized workforce and to some extent, plant age were a deterrence to implementing human resource practices, for instance. In contrast, the influence of plant size on implementation was well examined and found to facilitate implementation. Interestingly though, these contingencies were new to operations management researchers, and a few studies included size, and less frequently age, as a control variable during empirical analysis.

Third, the article examined both the determinants and the performance consequences of implementing lean practices. A quick review of the existing literature at the time showed that a vast majority of papers examined either the drivers and moderators of a concept or the performance consequences of the concept. The lean-bundles paper provided a more complete picture of the lean phenomenon by demonstrating the varying impact of unionization status, plant age, and plant size on implementation of lean practices, and then showing the impact of performance from their implementation. Further, in a post hoc analysis, the paper illustrated that lean bundle implementation differed between plants with different process types (Table 8, in the paper).

Lastly, and perhaps the most important reason why the paper has been influential is that while it examined a novel business phenomenon and challenged academic and practitioner conventional wisdom, it was grounded in existing literature, leveraged contemporary empirical tools to study the questions, and found results that had sufficient face validity to be believable. In one way, the article bridged theory and practice by using existing literature to address questions that practitioners were confronting related to a phenomenon of interest to managers. Specifically, we spent a significant amount of time selecting the 22 manufacturing practices that closely reflected the lean conversation and linking them to the existing literature (Table 1, in the paper). Such careful curation and theoretical grounding provided face validity to the set of practices, and subsequently deriving four bundles in the form of JIT, TQM,

TPM, and HRM (Table 4, in the paper) that were familiar to the audience using well-understood empirical methods, provided additional validation. The simple empirical approach, especially testing the impact of context on lean practice implementation (Chi-Sqaure Test, Table 6 in the paper), rudimentary by today's standards, was appropriate for the research question and fortunately for us, not a cause for rejection. Finally, the results, as a set, were within the realm of belief in contemporary literature. That is, although we found that unionized or older plants were less influential, the fact that size mattered as expected provided credence to the results. Interestingly, reviewers did not question this part of the paper much.

Going forward: the relevance of our ideas a decade later

Although research on lean has grown exponentially in the past two decades, several issues remain. First and foremost is related to the impreciseness surrounding its definition. While researchers continue to argue and debate about the exact definition of what constitutes lean, the central idea of the paper that lean practices are adopted in bundles has gained salience over time[9] and traveled across disciplines into healthcare, hospitality, and construction, among others. In studying the impact of lean bundles, researchers have demonstrated their impact on financial performance, quality and safety performance, and sustainability, among many other performance measures. While these papers may not have used the exact same definition of lean, it does not make the concept useless or less applicable. It merely suggests that there is a shared understanding of lean that reflects some universal practices associated with it. It is my perspective that phenomena that originate in business settings are difficult to define precisely because they not only evolve slowly but also the researchers' understanding of them grows gradually and incrementally. It is particularly true of lean – it not only evolved at TPS over time, but its journey to the Western researchers happened gradually and incrementally.

Thus, an attempt to define "lean" precisely requires us to consider that the concept itself may not have changed significantly over time and acknowledge that it is our understanding of lean that has changed in fundamental ways during this time. In stating this, I may be straddling the positivistic thinking that knowledge exists outside of the self and is measurable, and the construc-

---

[9]   A quick search for "lean bundles" in the title shows 205 references in Web of Science and over 100,000 references in Google Scholar.

tivism thinkers, who believe that knowledge is constructed by individuals in the process of interacting with themselves and their environment. If we follow this logic, to define lean we may need to consider who was observing, when the observation was made, and where the observation was made.

At the same time, I also believe that an attempt to define lean once and for all may be fruitless partly because we are still uncovering aspects of lean that are less understood by contemporary researchers. A case in point is the role of employees and cognitive thinking – both Ohno (1988) and Womack and Jones (1996) described the critical role of behavioral aspects of employees' involvement in implementing lean. This focus on human behavior is nearly absent in existing lean literature. However, incorporating it in future research as an important component of lean should not be taken to imply that the concept has "expanded" to usurp the current trend of "behavioral operations." It simply suggests a greater understanding of the phenomenon on the part of the researchers. Besides, it reflects the "social" dimension in the "lean as an integrated socio-technical system" (Shah and Ward, 2007).

Despite the ongoing debate about a decisive definition of lean, it is an exciting time for lean researchers. The past two decades, since the lean-bundles article was published, have witnessed radical shifts in the contexts within which US manufacturing resides. Technical advances like digitalization, artificial intelligence, and machine learning, and emerging contexts like sustainable operations and not-for-profit operations, provide interesting opportunities for lean researchers. I believe lean bundles can be used without any difficulty in these settings, and "synergy and complementarity" could provide valuable theoretical underpinnings. Historically in Japan, lean was meant for organizations whose supply chains were short and suppliers were collocated within 4–6 hours of the assembly plant. In the US, lean has been implemented in supply chains that span multiple continents and the work is geographically distributed among many supply chain partners. In this context, whether and to what extent lean bundles, particularly JIT, remain relevant is an interesting and open question. However, this also raises the question about a mismatch between the original context in which a business phenomenon emerges and the latter applications. It might be a useful exercise to outline relevant conditions under which lean bundles might prove to be effective.

Looking back, it makes me wonder whether the lean-bundles paper could be published in a top-tier journal today where the central focus is on "contributions to theory" and "establishing causality and controlling for endogeneity." Even so, I would encourage scholars to undertake research that describes and outlines the first principles of process improvement approaches by going back to the roots of lean production, where lean bundles is an important constituent part.

References

Liker, J. K. (2004). *The Toyota Way: 14 Management Principles from the World's Greatest Manufacturer*. New York: McGraw-Hill.

Meyer, A. D., Tsui, A. S., and Hinings, C. R. (1993). Configurational approaches to organizational analysis. *Academy of Management Journal*, 36(6), 1175–1195.

Ohno, T. (1988). *Toyota Production System: Beyond Large Scale Production*. Cambridge, MA: Productivity Press.

Shah, R. and Ward, P. T. (2003). Lean manufacturing: Context, practice bundles and performance. *Journal of Operations Management*, 21(3), 129–149.

Shah, R. and Ward, P. T. (2007). Defining and developing measures of lean production. *Journal of Operations Management*, 25(2), 785–805.

Spear, S. and Bowen, H. K. (1999). Decoding the DNA of the TPS. *Harvard Business Review*, 77(5), 96–106.

Venkatraman, N. (1989). The concept of fit in strategy research: Toward verbal and statistical correspondence. *Academy of Management Review*, 14, 423–444.

Whetten, D. A. (1989). What constitutes a theoretical contribution? *Academy of Management Review*, 14(4), 490–495.

Womack, J. P. and Jones, D. T. (1996). *Lean Thinking: Banish Waste and Create Wealth in Your Corporation*. New York: Simon & Schuster.

Womack, J. P., Jones, D. T., and Roos, D. (1990). *The Machine That Changed the World: The Story of Lean Production, Toyota's Secret Weapon in the Global Car Wars That Is Now Revolutionizing World Industry*. New York: Simon & Schuster.

2   Lean is a strategy

*Florian Magnani[1], Michael Ballé[2] and Godefroy
Beauvallet[3]*

Introduction

Lean has been variously described as a coherent set of manufacturing techniques (Shah and Ward, 2003), guiding principles (Liker, 2004), operational
practices (Karlsson and Åhlström, 1996), or an integrated socio-technical
system (Shah and Ward, 2007). The term "lean" was originally coined to
capture the difference in operating theory between Toyota and its competitors
in the 1980s. It was clear to the original research team that they were witnessing a new industrial paradigm, which has proved harder to capture than
originally thought. Looking at lean experiences and experiments outside of
Toyota has led to a richer understanding of what it encompasses (Ballé et al.,
2017). Previous research pointed out that lean encompasses different levels of
abstraction: from the philosophy (conceptual level) to its translation in terms
of operational practices (empirical level) (Marodin and Saurin, 2013).

The intention to capture the "essence" of lean gave rise to multiple theoretical
interpretations, leading to heterogeneous and wide-ranging models of lean
adoption (Anand and Kodali, 2010). Often derived from quantitative research,
such models can lack the contextual elements needed to help practitioners
adapt how they will adopt lean. Most models focus on the creation of a technical system of continuous improvement, without a clear idea of the potential
gains from a human perspective (Netland, 2013). Progress in research has
shown that lean has evolved from a set of production methods to a complex
and comprehensive organizational system, considering all stakeholders in the
organization, and changing fundamentally how to apprehend company strategy (Ballé et al., 2017; Marodin and Saurin, 2013).

---

[1]   Université Aix-Marseille, CERGAM, Ecole Centrale Méditerranée.
[2]   Institut Lean France.
[3]   i3, CNRS, Télécom Paris, Institut Polytechnique de Paris.

Lean frameworks can be classified into two main categories, namely "conceptual" and "empirical" frameworks. The more conceptual frameworks discuss the content of lean, i.e. what the elements of a lean system are (Karlsson and Åhlström, 1996; Shah and Ward, 2003), while the empirical frameworks discuss how to implement lean, including what should be the adoption steps and what feedback loops are in play to reinforce (or slow) adoption. About 30 frameworks were detailed and reviewed by Anand and Kodali (2010) based on their comprehensiveness, level of abstraction, and the degree of fit they present for adoption in an organization. The results showed that most of the frameworks examined were not constructed holistically, while many had rather high levels of abstraction. Recognizing lean as a strategy is a first attempt to connect these frameworks.

The central debate we want to discuss in this chapter is whether lean is a strategy or a set of operational principles to execute strategy determined elsewhere. Our contention is that lean is a strategy, and one based on learning that does not separate "strategic" thinking from execution (Ballé et al., 2019a). Our second contention is that this is the point of view of leaders known to be successful with lean (Ballé et al., 2019b; Byrne, 2012). This contention underlines the failure of any other interpretation of lean and its adoption (Secchi and Camuffo, 2019; Soliman, 2013).

In the first section of this chapter, the four levels of understanding identified in the lean literature will be presented. The second section is about the interpretation of lean as a strategy. And the third section shows how this strategy is implemented, primarily through the adoption process. Avenues for research will conclude this chapter.

Levels of understanding in the lean literature

Lean has been approached, both from philosophical or pragmatic levels and then from strategic or operational levels (Pettersen, 2009). This and other researchers' findings (Bhamu and Sangwan, 2014) highlight that lean is polymorphic, making its theoretical capture complex and applicable until research leads us to a new understanding. The concept becomes richer and more refined as we study it at different levels of abstraction.

Philosophical vs pragmatic levels

At a philosophical level, Shah and Ward (2007) conceptualized lean as an integrated socio-technical system, with the ambition of eliminating sources of waste by reducing or minimizing internal, customer, and supplier variability. The identification and elimination of waste are often reported in the lean literature (Liker, 2004; Ohno, 1988; Womack and Jones, 1996) but only serve one primary purpose: to show how to improve customer value by recognizing activities that add no value from the customer's perspective. Lean, however, is anchored on the human dimension of work: the alignment of managerial practices and the corporate value system, which are the legacy of the tacit knowledge of Toyota's leaders, managers, and employees (Hino, 2005).

At a pragmatic level, several studies have demonstrated significant disparities between the practical application of lean principles and their theoretical description in literature (Brännmark and Benn, 2012). Adler and Cole (1993) study lean at an individual level focusing on the role played by employees who are responsible for the quality produced, as well as the suggestions and implementation of improvements. Ensuring that employees operate lean practices daily is the most difficult task to achieve (Drew et al., 2004). This would mean paying systematic and continuous attention to operations, the work environment, behaviors, and infrastructure to adapt the adoption process.

Operation vs strategic levels

Moreover, lean exists at both an operational and strategic level (Hines et al., 2004): on the operational side, lean practices help identify and reduce non-value-added activities to encourage continuous improvement and help operationalize its strategic dimension. In this sense, lean is seen as a transformation of work, redefining the level of requirements to master and improve operational tasks (Losonci et al., 2011). The majority of the studies are carried out at this operational level, and notable research has already explained this level in great detail (Belekoukias et al., 2014; Negrão et al., 2017). At the strategic level, lean provides the foundation for managers to understand value from the customer's perspective and to focus internal collaboration on exploring and optimizing that value. In this sense, lean can be perceived as a set of strategic orientations that focus on understanding end customer value by achieving flow efficiency while ensuring quality levels, with resource efficiency as a byproduct (Modig and Åhlström, 2012).

Referring to lean as a strategy of course imports all the well-known complexities associated with the ambiguity of the term "strategy" (Mintzberg, 1987).

Distinguishing within "lean" layers in a manner similar to the "five P's", Mintzberg differentiation within "strategy" (strategy as plan, ploy, pattern, position or perspective) proves helpful:

- "Lean-as-system" encompasses all the tools and activities pioneered by Toyota and present in lean companies (from pull systems to kaizen-style continuous improvement activities) (Marodin and Saurin, 2013; Netland, 2013; Soliman et al., 2018).
- "Lean-as-pattern" reflects the intent of fostering collective learning and generating knowledge which must be present in all activities for lean efforts to be successful. It gives consistency to the behavior of lean-as-system practitioners and resilience to the systems they put to work. Maintaining lean-as-pattern alive is the main task of a class of actors specific to lean, the sensei (Ballé et al., 2019b).
- "Lean-as-competitive-advantage" is the often-vaunted situation of Toyota and of other companies whose lean mastery helps them in the market. It is the "silver bullet" of many lean consultants, their selling point, even though few companies have achieved lean-as-pattern at a scale comparable to Toyota's (Lewis, 2000).
- "Lean-as-perspective" is the collective intuition of lean practitioners and sensei about how the world works. It is visible in shared quasi-aesthetic judgments, such as "no liking inventory," and intra-daily routines and rituals, such as being willing to hear "problems first." The "lean paradigm" contrasts with Taylorism and financial management as the general theory of business. It informs the way lean practitioners create strategies at the firm level and "practice lean" in the field according to the three other definitions. The lean-as-perspective is epitomized by the first workbook of the lean community: *Learning to See* (Rother and Shook, 1999) which is discussed in more depth by Åhlström et al. (2021).

The multifaceted aspects of lean make it hard to grasp in a linear discursive structure, and therefore most researchers focus only on the form they are familiar with, without fully grasping the interactivity between the different forms that exist. Many debates about lean articulate – and sometimes mix – these four layers, similarly to debates about strategy. Future researchers are encouraged to express the point of view, the supported definition, the artifacts, or the framework chosen by the researcher and by the organizations studied, in order to better appreciate the results of the studies.

Highlights of the strategic interpretation of lean

Inviting researchers to illustrate the details of the organization being studied and the practices being observed will bring nuance to the results. This will also help in identifying the reasons for the organization's adoption of lean and the implicit strategy to achieve the expected results.

Previous efforts to describe lean as a strategy

In its simplest form, strategy is a way to achieve your goal, a path to victory. But isn't choosing a goal also strategy? Strategy is a young discipline, and few people agree on how to define it, or even if there is a way to define it. In the very early days of "strategy," Chandler (1962, p. 13) wrote: "Strategy is the determination of the basic long-term goals of an enterprise, and the adoption of courses of action and the allocation of resources necessary for carrying out these goals." Nevertheless, the overarching goal of business strategy seems to be a sustainable advantage to thrive under conditions of uncertainty. Uncertainty is relevant to the many moving parts: markets change, enabling technologies change, the company and its supplier networks change, and so strategy, which is meant to be a framework for medium- or long-term success, is by its nature always in flux. Businesses should both win the day to deliver promised value to customers and profits to shareholders, and evolve and adapt to changing, often difficult-to-see conditions. As discussed previously, Mintzberg (1987) provides five definitions of strategy: plan, ploy, pattern, position, and perspective. As Stacey (1996, p. 349) states: "The dynamics of successful organizations are therefore those of irregular cycles and discontinuous trends, falling within qualitative patterns, fuzzy but recognizable categories taking the form of archetypes and templates." This stream of decision successions appears to be consistent with sufficient time. This means that while some short-term control is possible through traditional techniques, long-term development avoids the kind of linear, analytical reasoning that underlies many of these techniques. Getting out of the management control aspect of the strategy is a challenge that lean literature intended to discuss.

Looking at the lean literature, numerous studies visualized the long-term objectives of lean initiatives, but few studies talk about lean as a strategy. Those that discuss lean strategy from a corporate level first identified lean as a strategic innovation, introducing fragility and flexibility in its system that provides dynamic competitive advantages (Helmold, 2020; Volberda, 2006). This strategic innovation reevaluates decisions related to capital allocation, mergers, acquisitions, partnerships, diversification scope, and coverage. Every choice is made taking care of stakeholders from the suppliers to the final customers to maximize the value and outcomes from an efficiency point of view and a human resource point of view (Smeds, 1994). Some studies found that lean strategy at the product level is driven by designing, producing, and selling the right product at the right time (Morgan and Liker, 2006). It has changed the way we have looked at innovation, with the introduction of incremental innovation that, over time, will be disruptive innovation. From a functional perspective, lean strategy focuses on cross-functional cooperation between research & development, production, supply chain, marketing, HR, and finance to pursue shared and mutual objectives (Singh et al., 2009). Finally, studies identifying the lean strategy from a business level depicted the planning, change initiatives, collaborative partnership, but most importantly the strong and robust alignment with the corporate level (Ahmadjian and Lincoln, 2000). This alignment is materialized by *hoshin kanri*, which strives to create strong links and alignment between management control of day-to-day activities (*hoshin*) and a compass for direction (*kanri*). Although studies have investigated lean strategy as one of the most successful management strategies for improving organizational performance (Chen and Taylor, 2009), researchers have found that lean strategy can positively contribute to organizational innovation moderated by human resource management, especially through knowledge management (Shin and Alam, 2022). The aim is to create a more knowledge-based organization (Nonaka, 1994) that will lead to organizational learning (autonomy and collective learning) anchored in organizational memory (i.e. culture). This knowledge-based organization is usually accomplished by reinforcing its dynamic capabilities.

There are multiple ways to achieve a lean strategy (Netland, 2013). What they all have in common is that they create dynamic capabilities to respond to internal and external uncertainties and organizational constraints (Pil and Fujimoto, 2007). These dynamic capabilities are defined as the ability of employees to integrate, construct, and reconfigure the competencies they hold to inform the transformations that result from their adoption (Teece et al., 1997). They are displayed throughout improvement, which relies on a set of interrelated meta-routines to incrementally improve existing products/ processes, and throughout innovation, which relies on a set of interrelated meta-routines to develop new products/processes (Furlan and Vinelli, 2018). These dynamic capabilities emerge as organizational competencies that denote existing learning patterns, as they ultimately modify the learning mechanisms themselves. These organizational competencies will evolve and stabilize into a new collective learning pattern that systematically generates new operational practices (Zollo and Winter, 2002). It should be noted that these dynamic capabilities emerge in the organization through the processes of acclimatization, commitment, and development of employees (i.e. the human dimension of lean).

Over time, a complex, intricate system will emerge from these dynamic capabilities. The system components and their connections were already explained in previous research through the lens of complex system theory (Saurin et al., 2013). The lean system emerging from these dynamics capabilities: (1) give visibility to processes, practices, and outcomes, (2) encourage diversity of perspectives when making decisions, (3) anticipate and monitor the impact of small changes, (4) design slack while anticipating its side-effects, (5) monitor and understand the gap between prescription and practice, and (6) create an environment to support and develop organizational resilience. We argue that the lean system commonly discussed is the outcome of a multi-layered lean strategy. This strategy encompasses generalized lean activities, lean behavior patterns, leveraging lean features (e.g. agility, quality) as a competitive advantage, and communicating within the company as a worldview compatible with lean tenets. Adopting lean incorrectly, without considering its strategic aspects, increases the inefficiency of an organization's resources and reduces employee confidence in lean usefulness (Ballé et al., 2017). The success and implementation of any particular management strategy normally depend upon organizational characteristics, which means that not all organizations can implement a similar set of strategies in their particular case (Shah and Ward, 2003). Therefore, applying the appropriate lean strategy at the appropriate time for the appropriate company for the right purposes seems crucial to leverage the benefits of its adoption. Consideration of organizational contexts such as organization size, and organization resource limitations has been noticeably lacking in research on the execution of lean strategies (Bortolotti et al., 2015; Marodin and Saurin, 2015).

The five strategic fits of lean: a framework

Marksberry (2012) and Samuel et al. (2015) insisted that organizations need to regard lean as a dynamic phenomenon and one which is constantly developing. This means that lean is viewed as a never-ending long-term commitment (Bhasin and Found, 2021). A word of caution is offered by Mårtensson et al. (2018), who suggest that companies applying lean tend to possess the knowledge of tools and techniques but frequently fail in direction, planning, and adequate project sequencing, i.e. the strategic aspects of it.

Based on our previous research, we argue that these dynamic capabilities are anchored in five "fits" (Ballé et al., 2017):

1. Customer fit: This is the most common fit. It focuses on understanding and satisfying the needs of the customer. It involves the identification of the customer's requirements and expectations and the provision of products and services that meet those needs and maximize value (Womack and Jones, 1996).
2. Market fit: This fit is the understanding and timely response to market demand. It requires monitoring market trends, identifying opportunities for growth or improvement, and developing products and services that are in line with customer needs quickly and efficiently (Morgan and Liker, 2006).
3. People fit: This fit emphasizes the importance of employee satisfaction, involvement, and empowerment at all levels of the organization. It involves first considering the preferences and needs of employees. It then involves creating a culture of continuous improvement, providing training and development opportunities, and involving employees in decision-making processes and knowledge-sharing activities (Alagaraja and Egan, 2013).
4. Technology fit: The focus of this fit is on the use of technology to improve processes and deliver better value to customers or employees. It involves the identification, selection, and implementation of proven technology solutions that support lean principles such as quality detection, visual management, and real-time data analysis (Mothersell, 2009).
5. Capability fit: This fit is the alignment of the organization's capabilities with its strategic goals and objectives. It requires an understanding of the organization's strengths and weaknesses, identification of areas for improvement, and making sure that strategic directions are consistent with the resources and capabilities needed to achieve them (Anand et al., 2009).

In an in-depth study of dozens of lean transformation efforts (Ballé et al., 2017; Medina and Charles-Lavauzelle, 2020), veteran researchers and company leaders in the lean field have shown that we can find at the root of lean thinking a radically distinct thinking process – leading to both distinct decision-making and operational realization. This distinct thinking is based on first *finding* problems with customers, workplace, and suppliers, then *facing* the challenges these problems represent to succeed in the market, to *frame* issues in a way that everyone in the company can understand what is at stake and so *forming* solutions from sharing individual insights, initiatives, and experiments. This contrasts with the traditional opposition of strategy and execution represented in leaders *defining* situations in the boardroom, *deciding* on options, *driving* them through the ranks, and then *dealing* with the unexpected consequences of their decisions.

Leaders who embody this 4F thinking could better appreciate how dynamic capabilities could emerge through the five fits discussed previously, and thus bring to light the lean strategy adapted to their organization. The lean strategy systematically integrates all activities affecting the products and services provided to the firm's customers, from product conception through the product life cycle, whether these activities are performed by the firm itself, or by external suppliers or channel members (Ahmed, 2021). It confirms the importance of vertical linkages – linkages that exist between a firm's value chain and the value chains of its suppliers and channel members (Yusuf and Adeleye, 2002). It also calls for the spanning of boundaries not only within a firm, but also between firms to engender a more competitive stance in the global marketplace. Then, the lean strategy consists of fine-tuning the way the organization will adapt to the changes in its environment. It combines transformational change where the organization is dramatically severed from its past ("framebreaking"), and adjustments to the structures, systems, or technology while retaining continuity with the past ("framebending") (Nadler and Tushman, 1989).

To foster all of these changes and adjustments, managerial and human resource management practices are also impacted (Shah and Ward, 2003) and consequently transformed. These modifications will then evolve thanks to cumulative dynamic capabilities (Hansen and Møller, 2016), including those related to the work system and those related to the improvement system, and creating a new set related to the second-level improvement system leading to innovations. Developing a system of continuous collective learning through solving the right problem in the right way at the right time, and every time, is at the heart of lean strategy. Learning was built into the purpose of Toyota's strategy, whereas most Western companies that have tried to implement lean have failed to include learning as Toyota did.

We have examined lean as a strategy, specifically through its five fits. The five fits help capture the key components to specify to consider a company's lean strategy. We argue that the five fits are part of a framework that can be applied to different contexts and that will produce an adapted and specific strategy.

Pathways toward a lean strategy

There can be multiple lean strategies, but they are all inspired by the framework we have presented. As a result, lean systems are specific to each company that adopts this framework (Netland, 2012). This uniqueness can be seen in the many ways to get started with lean.

Traditional adoption process

Looking at the operational declinations of the lean strategy, three models coexist: models constructed by academics; models resulting from consultants' interventions; and models resulting from organizations' adoptions. Most of the models built by academics are the result of quantitative research, thus mixing the specificities of each lean adoption in the considered organizations (Netland, 2013). Models resulting from organizational adoptions are generally empirical, technically biased, and, although influenced by contingency factors, these are rarely specified. Anand and Kodali (2010) while studying adoption models described their shared components: top management commitment, education and training of employees, management of social relations, and management tools (or manufacturing techniques). Whether such traits are specific to lean adoption remains uncertain.

Most strategic models describe top-down approaches, i.e. adoption is usually initiated by senior management and implemented by dedicated teams through projects, thus including a limited number of actors. In comparison, bottom-up approaches, based on the emerging initiatives of field employees (including their local managers), have been mostly relegated to the background. Womack and Jones (1996) showed that the top-down approach was inevitable in the initial phase of lean adoption. However, it is supposed to give rise to a bottom-up approach, equipping employees with problem-solving skills that ultimately transform the current organization into a learning organization (Liker, 2004). The field employees, accompanied by the proximity managers, through these daily activities of continuous improvement, participate in the local adoption of lean and continue to contribute to its adoption in the organization (Ohno, 1988; Shingo, 1981). Therefore, it seems essential to consider both top-down and bottom-up approaches together, to make explicit the strategic dimension of lean. Successful lean transformations use both approaches simultaneously: senior leadership adopts the orientation of lean (focusing on customer satisfaction, improvement of quality, lead times, and total cost reduction) while encouraging bottom-up kaizen from all workplace teams. Driving both top-down and bottom-up initiatives is unusual in Western management and hard to describe according to the traditional management paradigm, which leads researchers to choose one or the other perspective, thereby missing one of the unique components of lean: it is a top-down initiative that rests on bottom-up operational improvement (Ballé et al., 2017). Complementarity between top-down and bottom-up approaches can lead to better adoption sustainability and operational results: this can also add to the five fits an additional fit to monitor, the organizational fit (Galeazzo et al., 2021).

The analysis of models resulting from adoption by organizations shows that each company or factory has developed its approach to designing its strategy and resulting management system. Although these empirical models appear difficult to generalize, Anand and Kodali (2010) and Netland (2013) have shown that some commonalities can emerge. The general message that emerges is that a lean strategy, in its historical form, is adaptable to the circumstances, organizational factors, and contextual factors (Marodin and Saurin, 2015) of the organizations that adopt it. That reinforces the idea that each organization or company should appropriate their adoption process to their specificities and their environment.

Alternative adoption process

With a look back to the roots of lean, we discovered an alternative adoption process that possibly bypasses the organizational fit we were discussing previously. Fujimoto (1999) highlights the emergence of a multi-channel lean strategy. This explains the difference between the logic of the initial stage of adoption of the elements of the Toyota Production System (TPS) and their subsequent diffusion in the organization in the second stage. This initial logic has been extensively studied by researchers: Coriat (1991) describes it as a variety of small events and macroscopic conditions responsible for the emergence or, more generally, the self-activation of lean, i.e. a path-dependent logic (Cusumano, 1988). This strategy is not only the result of favorable initial conditions but is shaped through the evolution of the organization. Van Driel and Dolfsma (2009) propose carefully analyzing the timing and effects of the initial conditions that shape the strategy.

Individual and collective learning meta-routines, interacting with organizational episodes, enable a dynamic locking-in of the lean strategy: these metamorphoses form a process of adoption that is both voluntaristic and opportunistic. Among these, one meta-routine that has influenced the evolution over a long period is centered on transmission mechanisms: managerial policies on knowledge transfer through the circulation of personnel in the plants, and accumulation through the formal documentation of experiences, can explain the diffusion of the lean strategy at Toyota (Hino, 2005; Van Driel and Dolfsma, 2009). The company's dedication to this meta-routine still differentiates it from its main competitors: what Toyota does best compared to its rivals is not the rational calculations before each experimentation, but rather the systemization and institutionalization done after each experimentation (Fujimoto, 1999). The sequence of specific events, coupled with the meta-routines, can reveal the emergence of organizational characteristics generated by initial conditions, eventually giving rise to dynamic lock-in.

This lock-in is possible according to Knuf (1995) and Fujimoto (2012) through continuous transformational learning supported by a processual dimension (preparation, implementation, maintenance, evaluation) and by an interactional dimension (constant reflexivity of employees' perspectives). The operationalization of the lean strategy is materialized using the knowledge and skills of each employee to improve the existing system daily. On this point, even if organizations have adopted lean all over the world, few have truly followed Toyota in this respect (Saito et al., 2012). TPS capitalizes on the unique characteristic of Japanese culture with respect to employee commitment to organizational goals by incorporating other singular attributes of Western employees. Fujimoto et al. (2009) explain that the development of this dimension is done through education and skill building of each employee so that they can understand the state of the current system, and then improve it toward the future system. Saito et al. (2012) prefer to use the term "continuous learning system" rather than TPS or lean since it makes explicit the dynamic nature of the system.

The processual dimension of the continuous learning system is revealed when the incremental adoption phase results in the creation or reinvention of certain organizational features that support the adoption process (Knuf, 1995). Once a solid learning base is in place, the organization is ready to broaden adoption by creating communities of learners, moving from a focus on content (single-loop learning) to systemic learning (double-loop learning) (Barber, 2006). After learning how to work, through a succession of short learning loops, employees learn by working (Argyris, 1993), thus institutionalizing the initial learning. The evaluation phase is based on ongoing evaluations of the learning that accompanies the implementation of the strategy. Since this evaluation is specific to the organization's pace of adoption, it is designed locally by its members. Learning occurs by itself, through a stable social process centered on a permanent questioning of actions to develop the capacity to act of the members of the organization (Knuf, 1995).

Evolutionary learning capability as the key to lean strategy development

The lean strategy incorporates emergent qualities not known in advance related to the creative element in the human dimension (Ohno, 1988). Fujimoto (1999) exposes these through the evolutionary learning capability, which is both intentional and opportunistic in that the organization uses established routines to generate potential improvements, and at the same time, it can capture unexpected emergent improvements while intelligently institutionalizing them. These improvements seem to be possible only because of the human dimension of the system, i.e. its evolutionary learning capability (Cho, 1995). Importantly, this evolutionary learning capability is one of the dynamic capabilities we discussed earlier.

The Toyota environment is strongly influenced by the concepts of *monozukuri* and *hitozukuri* (Sugimori et al., 1977). It is often recalled that the focus on quality and continuous improvement is achieved through hitozukuri. Hitozukuri symbolizes the education of employees, but also a social and continuous process that allows employees to develop their skills, and to achieve recognition of their know-how and ability to solve problems in an atmosphere of mutual trust (Ballé et al., 2017). By empowering employees, they naturally deepen their practice and learn on their own to perform more effectively. This concept is often named in Western literature as the principle of "respect for people" (Sugimori et al., 1977). This principle is found in the Toyota Way and is characterized by the promotion of the best possible human relationships between employees, centered around mutual trust, transparency, accountability, motivation, and sound personnel recruitment and promotion policies. Womack and Shook (2011) argue that for Toyota, "respect for people" refers to the psychological process built through a series of meaningful dialogues between managers and their employees to help them identify dysfunction and empower them to act. It is about giving them meaningful activities to perform, ensuring that the environment is conducive to their execution, and then generating learning situations for employees. This construct implicitly captures the human resource development often referenced in the Toyota literature (Jayamaha et al., 2014), as an inherent part of the lean strategy.

Human resource skill development is grounded in a combination of individual learning through interactional deepening with managers in Toyota, or lean experts in adopting organizations (Cho, 1995). Learning does not come only from training or from an accumulation of information, but from interactions between employees. Hitozukuri aims to educate employees to continuously use their knowledge and wisdom to maintain stable process-related conditions and respond to anomalies in the organizational environment while capitalizing to improve its functioning. Finally, hitozukuri is akin to the continuous process of human development around actions and interactions among actors (Saito et al., 2011).

As a result, there has been a shift from seeing lean as purely a process-oriented strategy to lean as a people-oriented strategy (Jayamaha et al., 2014; Marodin and Saurin, 2013). Drawing on the work of Fujimoto (1999) and Saito (1995), the lean strategy is therefore based on a dynamic learning system that has evolved according to contextual constraints, but also according to randomized trials, successive capitalizations, and knowledge transfer mechanisms. This dynamic learning system is animated through the existence and development of an evolutionary learning capability operated by all employees embodied by the hitozukuri.

Conclusion and future research

In Western organizations, the key to prosperity lies in seeking to increase productivity. Previous research tells us that productivity can be the result of four factors: work (sought through organization and optimization), financial capital (sought through investment), human capital (sought through education, development, and use of skills) and technological progress (sought through innovation). Human capital, through lean, has a leverage effect on work (better organization, well-being, alignment), technological progress and financial capital (innovation acceptance and improvement idea generation). The lean strategy proposes and postulates that human capital is not acquired outside the company, but through educational activities daily, in the work environment, while working. This is exemplified by the hitozukuri principle that creates an evolutionary learning capability. Learning is, therefore, inseparable from production. Lean becomes a strategy for the acceptance and valuation of human capital to make better use of labor and financial capital, which consequently becomes a major competitive advantage. All employees accept that they can make mistakes. Above all, they are committed to identifying, understanding, and solving them. The lean system anchored in the strategy is designed to highlight these errors and give people the tools and skills to deal with them. At the same time, it develops their expertise, which ultimately delivers more value to the customer. This is achieved by specializing in one's field and by working in teams to spread expertise. This results in a more flexible organization, which can be used to implement a more adaptive and dynamic strategy.

The literature is consistent in its message that lean sustainability is characterized by four traits: scale (organization-wide), magnitude (influences the status quo), duration (can take years), and strategic importance. History shows that Toyota has the most adaptative strategy regarding contextual, economic, and environmental aspects of the competitive market but also regarding crisis management. Lean is viewed as a dynamic strategy, in comparison to static strategies clarified by Porter (2008), that is supported by a specific evolutionary learning capability intertwining value chain control with dynamic capabilities development (Soliman et al., 2018).

The first steps to understanding the lean strategy can be explained as follows:

1. Knowing what needs to be done better in the organization (learning to identify/see what is in one's interest to improve, starting with what will convince customers).
2. Developing problem-solving routines that will, with time, shape an improvement culture (learn to improve individually and collectively).
3. Investing the gains generated by problem-solving activities in what needs to be done better and in what needs to be started (learn to capitalize and innovate).

The lean strategy, through mostly its evolutionary learning capability, can also be viewed as a strategy-as-practice (Sage et al., 2012), i.e. something that people do rather than something that a firm possesses. Looking at the practical aspects of lean helps connects the macro- and micro-practices of strategizing (Jarzabkowski et al., 2007). It also stretches the way strategies are not only disseminated but appropriated, translated, and transformed by specific people, artifacts, and events, often in an unintentional way. To open the discussion, looking deeper into lean as a survival strategy, especially during these difficult times (Singh et al., 2009) can provide more details about its strategic features.

We would like to suggest avenues for future research. The first avenue is to keep studying lean through the prism of strategy. This was the main purpose of this chapter, and we specified future directions in this regard throughout our discussion. The second avenue would be to study in a more qualitative and contextual way the organizations by making explicit their strategy and the researcher's point of view to mitigate the interpretations. Researchers often use different interpretations of lean, sometimes implicitly, and therefore it is difficult to generalize the research results. It is about turning the feeling of knowledge into the actual creation of knowledge. The third avenue is to continue to strengthen the knowledge acquired about lean, moving from accumulation to assimilation of knowledge. It is our belief that this will be the best way to emphasize that lean is a new paradigm, rather than a mix of functionalist paradigms (as described by Hoss and ten Caten, 2013). This will reveal new questions to explore.

By doing so, future research could then reevaluate the interdependency of the lean strategies, the lean organization or systems resulting from it, and the impact of the interdependency on the outcomes. Paradoxically, this was a question addressed by early studies of lean, from the most positive (Womack et al., 1990) to the most pessimistic (Boyer and Freyssenet, 2000). The fact that this question endures – and not the issue of the "perimeter of validity" of lean, which was the other issue raised early by lean critics (Freyssenet et al., 2012) – testifies to the success of lean on the ground.

References

Adler, P. S. and Cole, R. E. (1993). Designed for learning: A tale of two auto plants. *Sloan Management Review*, 34(3), 85–94.

Åhlström, P., Danese, P., Hines, P., Netland, T. H., Powell, D., Shah, R., Thürer, M., et al. (2021). Is lean a theory? Viewpoints and outlook. *International Journal of Operations & Production Management*, 41(12), 1852–1878.

Ahmadjian, C. L. and Lincoln, J. R. (2000). Keiretsu, governance, and learning: Case studies in change from the Japanese automotive industry. *Organization Science*, 12(6), 683–701.

Ahmed, W. (2021). Understanding alignment between lean and agile strategies using Triple-A model. *International Journal of Productivity and Performance Management*, 71(5), 1810–1828.

Alagaraja, M. and Egan, T. (2013). The strategic value of HRD in lean strategy implementation. *Human Resource Development Quarterly*, 24(1), 1–27.

Anand, G. and Kodali, R. (2010). Analysis of lean manufacturing frameworks. *Journal of Advanced Manufacturing Systems*, 9(1), 1–30.

Anand, G., Ward, P. T., Tatikonda, M. V., and Schilling, D. A. (2009). Dynamic capabilities through continuous improvement infrastructure. *Journal of Operations Management*, 27(6), 444–461.

Argyris, C. (1993). *Knowledge for Action: A Guide to Overcoming Barriers to Organizational Change*. San Francisco: Jossey-Bass.

Ballé, M., Chaize, J., and Jones, D. (2019a). Lean as a learning system: What do organizations need to do to get the transformational benefits from Toyota's method? *Development and Learning in Organizations: An International Journal*, 33(3), 1–4.

Ballé, M., Chartier, N., Coignet, P., Olivencia, S., Powell, D., and Reke, E. (2019b). *The Lean Sensei: Go See Challenge*. Boston: Lean Enterprise Institute Inc.

Ballé, M., Jones, D., Chaize, J., Fiume, O., and Ehrenfeld, T. (2017). *The Lean Strategy: Using Lean to Create Competitive Advantage, Unleash Innovation, and Deliver Sustainable Growth*. New York: McGraw Hill Higher Education.

Barber, J. C. (2006). From the working class to the learning class. *National Productivity Review*, 13(4), 461–466.

Belekoukias, I., Garza-Reyes, J. A., and Kumar, V. (2014). The impact of lean methods and tools on the operational performance of manufacturing organisations. *International Journal of Production Research*, 52(18), 5346–5366.

Bhamu, J. and Sangwan, K. S. (2014). Lean manufacturing: Literature review and research issues. *International Journal of Operations & Production Management*, 34(7), 876–940.

Bhasin, S. and Found, P. (2021). Sustaining the lean ideology. *Management Decision*, 59(3), 568–585.

Bortolotti, T., Boscari, S., and Danese, P. (2015). Successful lean implementation: Organizational culture and soft lean practices. *International Journal of Production Economics*, 160, 182–201.

Boyer, R. and Freyssenet, M. (2000). *Les Modèles productifs*. Paris: La Découverte.

Brännmark, M. and Benn, S. (2012). A proposed model for evaluating the sustainability of continuous change programmes. *Journal of Change Management*, 12(2), 231–245.

Byrne, A. (2012). *The Lean Turnaround: How Business Leaders Use Lean Principles to Create Value and Transform Their Company*. New York: McGraw-Hill Education.

Chandler, J. A. D. (1962). *Strategy and Structure: Chapters in the History of the American Industrial Enterprise*. Washington, DC: Beard Books.

Chen, H. and Taylor, R. (2009). Exploring the impact of lean management on innovation capability. *PICMET '09 – 2009 Portland International Conference on Management of Engineering & Technology*, pp. 826–834. doi:10.1109/PICMET.2009.5262042.

Cho, F. (1995). Toyota production system. In K. Saito (Ed.), *Principles of Continuous Learning Systems*, Vol. 1. New York: McGraw-Hill.

Coriat, B. (1991). *Penser à l'envers: Travail et organisation dans l'entreprise japonaise*. Paris: Christian Bourgois Editeur.

Cusumano, M. A. (1988). Manufacturing innovation: Lessons from the Japanese auto industry. *Sloan Management Review*, 30(1), 29–39.

Drew, J., McCallum, B., and Roggenhofer, S. (2004). *Journey to Lean: Making Operational Change Stick*. New York: Palgrave Macmillan.

Freyssenet, M., Mair, A., Shimizu, K., and Volpato, G. (2012). *Quel modèle productif? Trajectoires et modèles industriels des constructeurs automobiles mondiaux*. Paris: La Découverte.

Fujimoto, T. (1999). *Evolution of Manufacturing Systems at Toyota*. New York: Oxford University Press.

Fujimoto, T. (2012). The evolution of production systems. *Annals of Business Administrative Science*, 11, 25–44.

Fujimoto, T., Shimokawa, K., Womack, J., and Miller, W. (2009). *The Birth of Lean*. Cambridge, MA: Lean Enterprise Institute, Inc.

Furlan, A. and Vinelli, A. (2018). Unpacking the coexistence between improvement and innovation in world-class manufacturing: A dynamic capability approach. *Technological Forecasting and Social Change*, 133, 168–178.

Galeazzo, A., Furlan, A., and Vinelli, A. (2021). The role of employees' participation and managers' authority on continuous improvement and performance. *International Journal of Operations & Production Management*, 41(13), 34–64.

Hansen, D. and Møller, N. (2016). Conceptualizing dynamic capabilities in lean production: What are they and how do they develop? *Engineering Management Journal*, 28(4), 194–208.

Helmold, M. (2020). Lean management as part of the corporate strategy. In M. Helmold (Ed.), *Lean Management and Kaizen: Fundamentals from Cases and Examples in Operations and Supply Chain Management*. Cham: Springer International, pp. 45–55.

Hines, P., Holweg, M., and Rich, N. (2004). Learning to evolve. *International Journal of Operations & Production Management*, 24(10), 994–1011.

Hino, S. (2005). *Inside the Mind of Toyota: Management Principles for Enduring Growth*. New York: Productivity Press.

Hoss, M. and ten Caten, C. S. (2013). Lean schools of thought. *International Journal of Production Research*, 51(11), 3270–3282.

Jarzabkowski, P., Balogun, J., and Seidl, D. (2007). Strategizing: The challenges of a practice perspective. *Human Relations*, 60(1), 5–27.

Jayamaha, N. P., Wagner, J. P., Grigg, N. P., Campbell-Allen, N. M., and Harvie, W. (2014). Testing a theoretical model underlying the "Toyota Way": An empirical study involving a large global sample of Toyota facilities. *International Journal of Production Research*, 52(14), 4332–4350.

Karlsson, C. and Åhlström, P. (1996). Assessing changes towards lean production. *International Journal of Operations & Production Management*, 16(2), 24–41.

Knuf, J. (1995). Changing organizational cultures in the lean manufacturing environment. In K. Saito (Ed.), *Principles of Continuous Learning Systems*, Vol. 1. New York: McGraw-Hill, pp. 57–82.

Lewis, M. A. (2000). Lean production and sustainable competitive advantage. *International Journal of Operations & Production Management*, 20(8), 959–978.

Liker, J. (2004). *The Toyota Way: 14 Management Principles from the World's Greatest Manufacturer*. New York: McGraw-Hill.

Losonci, D., Demeter, K., and Jenei, I. (2011). Factors influencing employee perceptions in lean transformations. *International Journal of Production Economics*, 131(1), 30–43.

Marksberry, P. (2012). *The Modern Theory of the Toyota Production System: A Systems Inquiry of the World's Most Emulated and Profitable Management System*. Boca Raton, FL: CRC Press.

Marodin, G. A. and Saurin, T. A. (2013). Implementing lean production systems: Research areas and opportunities for future studies. *International Journal of Production Research*, 51(22), 6663–6680.

Marodin, G. A. and Saurin, T. A. (2015). Managing barriers to lean production implementation: Context matters. *International Journal of Production Research*, 53(13), 3947–3962.

Mårtensson, A., Snyder, K., and Ingelsson, P. (2018). Interlinking lean and sustainability: How ready are leaders? *The TQM Journal*, 31(2), 136–149.

Medina, R. and Charles-Lavauzelle, B. (2020). *Learning to Scale: The Secret to Growing a Fast and Resilient Company*. Sèvres: Régis Medina.

Mintzberg, H. (1987). The strategy concept I: Five Ps for strategy. *California Management Review*, 30(1), 11–24.

Modig, N. and Åhlström, P. (2012). *This Is Lean: Resolving the Efficiency Paradox*. Halmstad: Rheologica Publishing.

Morgan, J. M. and Liker, J. K. (2006). *The Toyota Product Development System: Integrating People, Process and Technology*. New York: Productivity Press.

Mothersell, W. M. (2009). The role of technology and people in the diffusion of lean production in the automotive supplier industry. *International Journal of Automotive Technology & Management*, 9(3), 290–315.

Nadler, D. A. and Tushman, M. L. (1989). Organizational frame bending: Principles for managing reorientation. *Academy of Management Perspectives*, 3(3), 194–204.

Negrão, L. L. L., Filho, M. G., and Marodin, G. (2017). Lean practices and their effect on performance: A literature review. *Production Planning & Control*, 28(1), 33–56.

Netland, T. H. (2012). Managing strategic improvement programs: The XPS program management framework. *Journal of Project, Program & Portfolio Management*, 3(1), 31–44.

Netland, T. H. (2013). Exploring the phenomenon of company-specific production systems: One-best-way or own-best-way? *International Journal of Production Research*, 51(4), 1084–1097.

Nonaka, I. (1994). A dynamic theory of organizational knowledge creation. *Organization Science*, 5(1), 14–37.

Ohno, T. (1988). *Toyota Production System: Beyond Large Scale Production*. Cambridge, MA: Productivity Press.

Pettersen, J. (2009). Defining lean production: Some conceptual and practical issues. *TQM Journal*, 21(2), 127–142.

Pil, F. K. and Fujimoto, T. (2007). Lean and reflective production: The dynamic nature of production models. *International Journal of Production Research*, 45(16), 3741–3761.

Porter, M. E. (2008). *Competitive Strategy: Techniques for Analyzing Industries and Competitors*. New York: Free Press.

Rother, M. and Shook, J. (1999). *Learning to See: Value Stream Mapping to Add Value and Eliminate Muda*. Boston: Productivity Press.

Sage, D., Dainty, A., and Brookes, N. (2012). A "strategy-as-practice" exploration of lean construction strategizing. *Building Research & Information*, 40(2), 221–230.

Saito, A., Kozo, S., and Cho, F. (2012). *Seeds of Collaboration: Seeking the Essence of the Toyota Production System, an Appreciation of Mr. Fujio Cho, Master Teacher*. Monterey, KY: Larkspur Press.

Saito, K. (Ed.) (1995). *Principles of Continuous Learning Systems*, Vol. 1. New York: McGraw-Hill.

Saito, K., Salazar, A. J., Kreafle, K. G., and Grulke, E. A. (2011). Hitozukuri and monozukuri: Centuries' old eastern philosophy to seek harmony with nature. *Interdisciplinary Information Sciences*, 17(1), 1–9.

Samuel, D., Found, P., and Williams, S. (2015). How did the publication of the book *The Machine That Changed the World* change management thinking? Exploring 25 years of lean literature. *International Journal of Operations & Production Management*, 35(10), 1386–1407.

Saurin, T. A., Rooke, J., and Koskela, L. (2013). A complex systems theory perspective of lean production. *International Journal of Production Research*, 51(19), 5824–5838.

Secchi, R. and Camuffo, A. (2019). Lean implementation failures: The role of organizational ambidexterity. *International Journal of Production Economics*, 210, 145–154.

Shah, R. and Ward, P. T. (2003). Lean manufacturing: Context, practice bundles and performance. *Journal of Operations Management*, 21(3), 129–149.

Shah, R. and Ward, P. T. (2007). Defining and developing measures of lean production. *Journal of Operations Management*, 25(2), 785–805.

Shin, D. and Alam, M. S. (2022). Lean management strategy and innovation: Moderation effects of collective voluntary turnover and layoffs. *Total Quality Management & Business Excellence*, 33(1–2), 202–217.

Shingo, S. (1981). *Study of "Toyota" Production System from the Industrial Engineering Viewpoint*. Tokyo: Japanese Management Association.

Singh, B., Garg, S. K., and Sharma, S. K. (2009). Lean can be a survival strategy during recessionary times. *International Journal of Productivity and Performance Management*, 58(8), 803–808.

Smeds, R. (1994). Managing change towards lean enterprises. *International Journal of Operations & Production Management*, 14(3), 66–82.

Soliman, M. (2013). Lean transformation guidance: Why organizations fail to achieve and sustain excellence through lean improvement. *International Journal of Lean Thinking*, 4(1), 31–40.

Soliman, M., Saurin, T. A., and Anzanello, M. J. (2018). The impacts of lean production on the complexity of socio-technical systems. *International Journal of Production Economics*, 197(C), 342–357.

Stacey, R. D. (1996). *Complexity and Creativity in Organizations*. San Francisco: Berrett-Koehler.

Sugimori, Y., Kusunoki, K., Cho, F., and Uchikawa, S. (1977). Toyota production system and Kanban system: Materialization of just-in-time and respect-for-human system. *International Journal of Production Research*, 15(6), 553–564.

Teece, D. J., Pisano, G., and Shuen, A. (1997). Dynamic capabilities and strategic management. *Strategic Management Journal*, 18(7), 509–533.

Van Driel, H. and Dolfsma, W. (2009). Path dependence, initial conditions, and routines in organizations: The Toyota production system re-examined. *Journal of Organizational Change Management*, 22(1), 49–72.

Volberda, H. W. (2006). Strategic flexibility creating dynamic competitive advantages. In A. Campbell and D. O. Faulkner (Eds.), *The Oxford Handbook of Strategy: A Strategy Overview and Competitive Strategy*. New York: Oxford University Press, pp. 939–998.

Womack, J. P. and Jones, D. T. (1996). *Lean Thinking: Banish Waste and Create Wealth in Your Corporation*. New York: Simon & Schuster. Second revision (2003).

Womack, J. P. and Shook, J. (2011). *Gemba Walk*. Cambridge, MA: Lean Enterprise Institute Inc.

Womack, J. P., Jones, D. T., and Roos, D. (1990). *The Machine That Changed the World: The Story of Lean Production, Toyota's Secret Weapon in the Global Car Wars That Is Now Revolutionizing World Industry*. New York: Simon & Schuster.

Yusuf, Y. Y. and Adeleye, E. O. (2002). A comparative study of lean and agile manufacturing with a related survey of current practices in the UK. *International Journal of Production Research*, 40(17), 4545–4562.

Zollo, M. and Winter, S. G. (2002). Deliberate learning and the evolution of dynamic capabilities. *Organization Science*, 13(3), 339–351.

PART II

Lean and learning

3   The lean education system

Eivind Reke

Introduction

There is an ongoing discussion among academics that seeks to pin down and capture a once-and-for-all definition of "lean production." This discussion has surfaced a few different perspectives that have clarified both a gap in interpretation of the term and what different researchers attribute to the term. In a recent paper, Hopp and Spearman (2021) set out to close this gap by settling on four distinct lenses of lean: the flow lens, the process lens, the network lens, and the organizational lens which also recognizes the fact that people are part of the organizational fabric. However, their description of the organizational lens still narrows down to people's role in mechanically removing waste from a process. As a reply to this definition Cusumano et al. (2021) agree somewhat, waste removal is important, yet disagree with the notion that efficiency is the end goal of lean, but rather to improve the overall value creation of a system consisting of a multitude of socio-technical elements. Indeed in their conclusion, Cusumano et al. recognize the cognitive roots of lean and suggest that it has been under-researched compared to the technical manufacturing aspects that have come as a result of its cognitive roots. Capturing the meaning of lean production has so far proved elusive. However, there seem to be a couple of clear directions for future research: (1) the Hopp and Spearman direction of waste reduction and efficiency, (2) the Cusumano et al. socio-technical direction that seeks to understand how organizations implement, adapt, and support lean in the form of practice bundles, and leadership practices (cf. Hines et al., 2004; Shah and Ward, 2003, 2007), (3) and a third direction which we will explore in this chapter, the less researched cognitive view of lean. That interprets lean as a system of learning and development that allows people and organizations to develop their learning path to better product planning and development, better production, and better management (Powell and Coughlan, 2020; Powell and Reke, 2019). As such this chapter seeks to develop a theoretical foundation for researchers to further explore a view of lean as a learning system for developing people and thus organizations in line with the original premise of "respect for people" (Sugimori et al., 1977). To do so, an overview of current research on lean as a learning system is presented, followed by an introduction to a novel interpretation of the Toyota Production System (TPS) as an education system underpinned by the theories of threshold concepts, troublesome knowledge, and problem-based learning. Afterward, a description of the organizational application of the education system is presented, followed by a conclusion with suggestions for further research.

Lean as a learning system

The International Motor Vehicle Program commenced its work of benchmarking automakers across the globe in the late 1970s and early 1980s, and the researchers participating in the program would soon find themselves in an uncharted territory as some of the first Western scholars given the chance to look inside a company that was quietly going its own way – the Toyota Motor Company. On the back of the oil crisis in the 1970s, Toyota and its fellow Japanese automakers had successfully entered the US and European markets, first with imports and from the 1980s with cars built in plants in the US and Europe. The plants outside Japan also laid to rest the hypothesis that Toyota's rise was on the back of lower wages and a weak yen, and even if their thinking and practices were different it would be impossible to implement with American or European workers and managers. As we now know, this led to the release of the book *The Machine That Changed the World*, in which Womack et al. (1990) presented lean production to the wider world as a full business system: (1) how to manage the company, (2) how to develop products, (3) how to make products, (4) how to manage the supply chain, and (5) how to sell products. The book compares this new business system with the prevailing business system it was outcompeting at the time – the system of mass-production built on the foundations of Sloan, Taylor, and Ford in the US.

Going back to the study of Toyota, there is a fair bit of evidence to support the learning system hypothesis. Ohno Taiichi himself referred to both kanban and standardized work as frameworks that helped surface problems and promote kaizen (Shimokawa and Fujimoto, 2009). Fujimoto concludes in his seminal work *Evolution of Manufacturing Systems at Toyota* (Fujimoto, 1999) that Toyota's approach to manufacturing was based on their learning capabilities, guided by the TPS. Although there is a growing realization that learning is a core part of lean (Netland and Powell, 2017), it is often reduced to just learning the lean tools (Netland et al., 2021) or learning a set of leadership practices (Netland et al., 2019). This is fine, but it will never get practitioners to realize lean's strategic potential to "halve the bad, double the good." Rather, we should see lean as a system for accelerating learning and personal development. After all, the original Toyota starting point is to "develop people first" (Ballé et al., 2010). In a recent study of a supplier development program in Norway, it was found that companies that developed a learning-to-learn capability as opposed to just learning the lean production tools achieved greater success with their lean transformation (Powell and Coughlan, 2020). Interestingly, this aligns well with how Toyota veterans describe both the goal and the purpose of what we now call lean production. Nempashi Hayashi describes TPS as a process development system for achieving "genka teigen" (cost reduction) through developing human capital (Hayashi, 2018), Nate Furuta describes how factual self-assessment, problem-finding, and problem-solving leads to learning and development of both people and business (Furuta, 2022), and Isao Yoshino describes its (TPS) fundamental importance to developing leadership skills (Anderson and Yoshino, 2020).

Looking outside of production and into product development, the same misconceptions are evident. Too much research has been devoted to how lean product development can create a more efficient product development process, rather than studying how lean can help develop more knowledgeable designers and engineers, which in the end should lead to a more effective and efficient product development process (Morgan and Liker, 2019). Learning in product development is not learning product development tools, it is learning about customers, products, and production processes to design better products (Ballé et al., 2016). The idea of putting people at the center of the organization also applies to strategic thinking, where lean pivots from separating strategy from execution – thinking from doing – to accepting challenges and committing to change (Ballé et al., 2017).

The idea of the TPS as an education system was first introduced during the research for the book *The Lean Sensei* where the authors explored the role of the sensei and how the sensei approach differed from the traditional implementation approach and what the implications for that were (Ballé et al., 2019; Reke et al., 2020). During this research, it was discovered that the sensei was not looking at what tools to fit to which process, but rather was applying the lean tools to teach executives how they could discover for themselves the strategic problems they were facing, and how exploring these problems further could lead to breakthrough ideas and innovation. These problems arise from misconceptions, and misconceptions arise from troublesome knowledge. There are certain things we don't fully understand or don't see about our own customers, product, business model, production system, or other systems that make up an organization. So what is troublesome knowledge?

Threshold concepts and troublesome knowledge

Troublesome knowledge is linked to subject-matter-specific concepts that education researchers call "threshold concepts." A threshold concept is a concept that once grasped will open new ways of thinking about something that was previously inaccessible. Like a portal the learner has to pass, threshold concepts allow the learner to progress and view a subject in a transformed way (Meyer and Land, 2003). In other words, grasping a threshold concept, and passing through the threshold can sometimes alter the learner's worldview. For lean practitioners, this could be grasping the difference between flow and resource efficiency. Once a learner understands the concept of flow efficiency, they'll never look at efficiency the same way again. However, all subjects have threshold concepts – logistics, quality, economy, finance, psychology, medicine, engineering, physics, and so forth – and many of these subjects are just as important to an organization as process efficiency.

Threshold concepts are central to the mastery of a subject and can be recognized by their characteristics (Cousin, 2006):

1. They are **transformative** because once understood they lead to a shift in understanding and sometimes worldview. For a lean practitioner, this could be the shift from doing standardized work to others instead of engaging people in their work and not fully grasping Toyota's fundamental advice: "to make products, first we develop people" and "good thinking, good products."
2. Once a concept is understood a learner is unlikely to forget it, so threshold concepts are **irreversible**. As previously mentioned, once a lean practitioner grasps the concept of one-piece flow they are unlikely to revert to thinking that producing in large batches is the most effective production method.
3. Threshold concepts expose hidden interrelationships in a field or phenomenon. For example, one cannot produce in one-piece flow if one doesn't produce right-first-time or with an unbalanced production.
4. A threshold concept is likely to be bounded. There are clear boundaries between such concepts. Even though flow and quality are connected, they represent at the same time different subjects that require different types of knowledge to fully understand them.
5. Threshold concepts involve "troublesome knowledge," knowledge that may seem counterintuitive, incoherent, and alien to the learner. Before a lean practitioner understands that stopping at defects, or stopping when work is finished is more productive than producing continuously, it seems

completely irrational to stop a machine or production line at every defect or when production targets are met.

Returning to the fundamental problem of interpretation of lean production, it could be argued that the misinterpretation of lean production by both Western practitioners and academics alike is connected to our deeper understanding of the different concepts of lean. Viewing lean tools as a way of achieving efficient operations in certain manufacturing conditions is a far cry from the potential it was first presented as having, a new paradigm thinking about all aspects of running a company. It is not the first time in human history that progress in any field is slow as it takes time to replace old truths with new knowledge (Arbesman, 2013). The problem of interpretation can also be found in Piaget's notion that new knowledge can either be assimilated, adapted to what a person already knows, or new knowledge can be accommodated when a person recognizes that the new knowledge does not fit with previous knowledge and must make space (figuratively speaking) for new knowledge.

In learning theory, this could be described as the difference between surface learning or mimicry (copying and applying the quality control tools of lean, such as andon) and the liminal state that a learner experiences before they grasp the threshold concept in full (realizing that the quality tools are scaffoldings for discussing quality with operators frequently, deepening the technical understanding of both operators and managers alike). As with any subject, it is possible to get stuck in mimicry and not go through the state of liminality that occurs as a threshold concept is more fully grasped (Meyer and Land, 2005). The question then becomes, how can the learner be assisted in moving past the stage of mimicry and move towards fully grasping the threshold concepts of lean production?

Problem-based learning

Problem-based learning is a technique that was developed in the 1950s and has since been frequently used in medical studies to better prepare students for clinical settings and has grown in popularity across disciplines in both higher education and elementary education (K-12) (Hung et al., 2008). As such, the fundamental idea behind problem-based learning is to allow students to learn using real-world problems. As a theory of learning in lean, it is promising, with a similarity to the QC group structure and team structure often found in lean. According to Hung et al. (2008), these are the usual steps followed in a problem-based learning process:

1. First, students will engage and reason through the problem, attempt to define the problem and set learning goals by identifying what they already know, what hypotheses they can come up with, what they need to learn to better understand the problem, and finally which activities to carry out to learn.
2. The students will then complete their study individually before presenting reports to the group.
3. The students share what they've learned with the group to test their hypotheses, confirm correct ones, reject wrong ones, and if necessary, generate new ones.
4. Finally, students summarize what they have learned.

Comparing this process to typical lean problem-solving or improvement processes built on plan-do-study-act, we can see clear overlaps and similarities. For instance, these improvement processes all typically start with understanding the current conditions and clearly defining the problem. This is also where lean tools come into place in the lean education system. The tools are not themselves for improving the production process or the product. The tools act as scaffolding for people to better understand the problem or the challenge at hand. In the classic situation where the tool "doesn't work here," the tool is doing precisely what it should. It is scaffolding the fact that the process can't deliver what it is supposed to and allows people to investigate more precisely the reason for this. Of course, in a company setting the learner will not finish the assignment on their own, but work together as a group. However, the breakthrough insight often comes from individuals who mull over the problem on their own and then present their ideas or hypotheses to the group. So in the same manner that students present their reports to the group, the participants in a QC (for example) will present their reports to the group and from there test hypotheses, confirm correct ones, reject wrong ones, and if necessary, generate new ones. Finally, the improvement or problem-solving case is summarized and shared across the company in a report, for example, an A3.

Comparing the problem-solving and improvement methods usually associated with lean gives us a good starting point to look at the threshold concepts of lean and what could be considered troublesome knowledge. This brings us back to the Toyota Production System.

The lean education system

Developed over a period of probably 20 years or so from the early 1950s, the TPS was not formalized as such until later. Sugimori et al.'s (1977) seminal paper was the first description of the TPS in an English language academic journal, and the first internal document produced by Toyota that describes the full system was released internally in 1973, only four years before the above-mentioned article. According to several anecdotal sources, Ohno himself resisted writing it down fearing that it would lead to misunderstandings and misinterpretations. Which indeed it has. Peter Senge tells the story in *The Fifth Discipline* (Senge, 2006) of meeting with American automaker executives who had just come back from visiting Toyota plants and telling him: "They didn't even show us the real thing. I know what a car plant should look like and what they showed us wasn't it." This highlights the paradigm shift of looking at lean production as tools and methods to implement for producing something to seeing lean production as a path to improve the overall business through a process of learning and discovery.

TPS serves as an excellent starting point for this process, and its threshold concepts act as useful frameworks that help guide and address different parts of any organization, not just manufacturing. It is not complete, but it should serve as a solid foundation for discovering challenges and problems in any organization, in any industry. It allows people to engage with the real world, the Gemba, and discover the specifics of the business. It acts as an aid to progressively understand problems better by framing the TPS as lean conditions to strive for and to think upside-down and ask where and why are we not achieving these conditions?

Starting with customer value, the first condition is "Completely satisfy every customer in terms of safety, quality, delivery, and cost performance." This gives us the challenge of asking "Where are we not satisfying customers?" The tools tell us where to look for answers to this question. The second condition is the "Jidoka-condition: separate man and machine with intelligent automation and don't make, don't pass defects." Again, we look for places where we are passing defects, where we are making defects, and where humans must babysit machines so that they don't make and pass defects or overproduce. The third condition is "Just-in-time, the flexibility to make only what is needed when it's needed, and in the right amount that is needed." The tools act as scaffolding to help us discover the problems that stop us from reaching this condition and point us to where our processes are too rigid. Each condition represents a troublesome problem that the learner can grapple with and learn more about through problem-based learning, and the threshold concepts associated with them are the conceptual frameworks that form the education system.

If we go back to our journey through the TPS we arrive at *heijunka* or load capacity. The lean ideal would be for the production to be perfectly balanced and at a steady load capacity. Since this is not always the case, we can apply the heijunka tools to discover what we need to learn to better balance our production and better utilize our capacity. Standardized work as a lean condition means training everyone to master the relevant know-how for their job as it is today, and then kaizen is everyone, every day improving and developing new know-how. Finally, we strive for fully autonomous teams with complete ownership of their workplace (the concept of 5S), and individual autonomy where every person contributes with problem-solving when things are not working as they should. Finally, the last lean condition is support systems that work, and the related threshold concept is total productive maintenance (TPM). In this day and age, this should include all systems including IT systems such as enterprise resource planners (ERP), manufacturing execution systems (MES), design systems, sales systems, and similar. In other words, not just the machines on the shop floor.

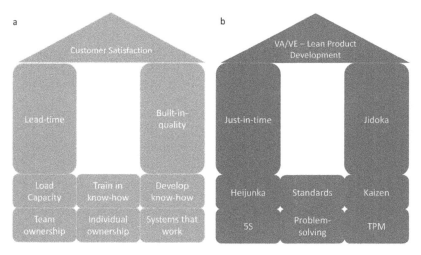

Figure 3.1   Lean conditions/troublesome knowledge and threshold concepts

Reke et al. (2022) described these threshold concepts as "Value Engineering/ Value Analysis (VE/VE), Just-in-time, Jidoka, Heijunka, Standardized Work, Kaizen, TPM, 5S, and Problem-solving." The troublesome problems associ-

Table 3.1   Threshold concepts and troublesome knowledge

Threshold concepts	Lean condition / troublesome knowledge	Examples of tools
VA/VE	How do we satisfy every customer completely?	Lean product development tools
Pull/flow – Just-in-time	How do we create the flexibility to make every part, every product when we need it to reduce lead-time to a minimum?	Kanban/ one-piece flow
Jidoka – don't make, don't pass defect	How do we build in quality to not make and not pass defects?	Andon. Poka-Yoke
Heijunka – load leveling	How do we utilize the capacity of our resources in a balanced way without overburdening them?	Yamazumi, SMED
Standardized work	How do we create the conditions for every worker to achieve mastery of know-how?	Takt-time, job breakdown sheet
Kaizen	How do we always increase our mastery of every process?	QC-circles, 8-step method
5S – ownership of workspace	How do we create the conditions for autonomous teams that own their process and equipment?	5S tools
Problem-solving	How do we achieve individual autonomy where every person takes responsibility for their own work?	5 why, problem-solving sheet
TPM	How do we create the conditions for all our support systems to always work?	TPM tools

ated with them align with the ideal lean conditions: "Customer Satisfaction, Lead-time, Built-in-quality, Capacity utilization, mastery of know-how, always increasing know-how, autonomous teams, individual autonomy and support systems that work (machines, IT and so forth)" (see Figure 3.1 and Table 3.1). These models have since been slightly adapted.

Moving down the TPS allows us to both identify weak points in our understanding of concepts by comparing them to ideal conditions and to find problems that can help us learn and eventually master the threshold concepts. However, as the lean conditions we strive for give us direction, and the threshold concepts help us surface troublesome knowledge, we still need a classroom and a guide to help us climb the learning curve, one problem, one sequence, one job at a time.

The classroom and the teacher: Gemba and the sensei

Before Toyota opened production in Georgetown, their first fully owned trans-plant in the United States, they took great care in training the new managers destined for the site. Some of these were seasoned managers who had worked in the automotive industry their entire careers, but Toyota did not just put them to work. They first put them through a rigorous training program to see if they were up to the task of being a manager in a Toyota plant. Leuchel (2020) describes the rigorous mentoring they went through. In one telling story, the American manager reminisced how the Japanese trainer, his sensei, would take him to a spot in the factory and tell him to "stand, look." Puzzled, the American wondered out loud what he was looking for, to which the Japanese trainer's answer was: "Yes, looking." The trainer disappeared for about two hours and upon his return asked: "What did you see?" Realizing that the job was to observe what was happening in that area of the factory, the American proceeded with informing the trainer what he had seen. To which the trainer answered: "Good, now look more."

Another example of this approach can be found in Spear (2004) where we follow a young and talented American manager's learning journey as he is trained for the role of plant manager. In the first three months of his journey, he is not even at the plant he is supposed to take over. Instead, he was first brought to a nearby engine plant and then to a Toyota plant in Japan to learn how to observe and improve both manual labor jobs and machines. He con-cluded the training by presenting his improvements to a group of managers from different levels in the plant. Spear summarized the experience in four lessons: (1) there is no substitute for direct observation, (2) proposed changes should always be structured as experiments, (3) workers and managers should experiment as often as possible, and (4) managers should coach, not fix problems.

These stories give us a good insight into how and where teaching and learning should happen. In problem-based learning, the student is presented with a real-world problem, and there is nothing more real than the Gemba. Be it the customer Gemba, the production floor, or the suppliers' Gemba. In *The Lean Sensei* (Ballé et al., 2019), the authors delve deeper into the role of the sensei who, unlike a consultant, is not there to implement anything, and not there to help people find their inner strength like a coach. A sensei doesn't necessarily teach much (besides showing or sketching out lean tools). The role of the sensei is to act as a guide in the discovery process. She does so by creating awareness and thoughtfulness and not accepting what she is told but rather encouraging people to look deeper into the issues at hand to discover the real problems they are facing. As such, and especially when working with senior managers, the sensei is more akin to a strategic advisor in the sense that she uses TPS to find and face the key, typical problems that any company operating in the same industry is facing. The sensei doesn't create the strategy but assists in first finding problems, then facing the knowledge gap – the troublesome knowledge that the organization is not dealing with – then the sensei leaves it to the company themselves to frame the strategic challenges so that everyone can contribute to forming the new path (Ballé et al., 2017). However, if an organization is too preoccupied with delivery, and doesn't set aside time for discovery, there will be no time to learn.

Finding the gold: battling with typical problems leads to innovative countermeasures

What the lean education system does is create conditions in which everyone in the organization can, if they want to, develop their technical skills, knowledge, and teamwork skills. However, the real breakthrough happens when companies find unique countermeasures to typical industry problems. If we go back to Toyota again, they made two breakthroughs that had big implications for the auto industry. First, they built quality into the product rather than fixing it at the end, and second, they went beyond the flexibility vs efficiency trade-off in the early 1980s (and quite possibly earlier), which gave them a considerable cost advantage compared to their competitors (Adler et al., 1999). Other manufacturing industries do share some similarities with the automotive industry, and therefore some of Toyota's countermeasures or solutions to their typical problems will have an effect. However, as one moves further away from lean's point of inception it becomes increasingly more silly to think that Toyota's countermeasures will magically solve the typical problems of other industries. Hence, "it doesn't work here, we are not Toyota / we are not in the auto-industry / we are not a manufacturing company."

Again, we are starting with the wrong set of questions or assumptions. Instead of looking for which "best practice" to copy and implement, practitioners should be encouraged to apply the TPS threshold concepts to discover the typical problems of their industry and come up with countermeasures to these problems with whatever technology is available. Researchers could then study how well and where the concepts, rather than the tools, transfer to other settings. Such an approach would help organizations clear the window of things that clutter up their view of typical problems. The gold lies in finding innovative countermeasures to these typical problems using the lean education system to discover and learn about these problems.

Conclusion and future research

The argument presented here is that the strategic potential of lean which former CEO of Wiremold Art Byrne described as "halve the bad, double the good" (Ballé et al., 2017) is best achieved when companies and people set out to replicate the learning curves of Toyota on customer value, quality, flexibility, lead-time, logistics, and so forth. It implies that engineering and production practices are a result of people's cognitive abilities that can be developed systematically. The shift in perspective is to move from a view of learning in lean as learning lean tools to interpreting the lean tools as devices for discovering what we need to learn to develop people and in effect the company. This is akin to the adage of looking at the finger pointing at the moon. The finger is the tool, and the moon represents what we need to learn to succeed. This does not mean that tools are not important, they are, but the intent with which one uses the tools shifts.

This chapter argues that lean production will never magically transfer from one company to another, from one industry to another through a process of best practice implementations. Such a view agrees wholeheartedly with the operations management point that lean production viewed as the implementation of tools and processes to create efficient processes will not be a good fit everywhere. It might not fit anywhere. However, in opposition to the view of lean presented by Hopp and Spearman (2021), the chapter suggests that research should continue to explore lean production in the context of "first we make people, then we make products." Arguably, one of Toyota's key insights was that industrial engineers are no match for the local knowledge of people doing the actual value-creating work on the product. Giving front line operators the ownership of their work and the opportunity to improve it leads to far better results that are stickier compared to an approach where the design of work processes and the execution of the design are separated.

A learning and discovery interpretation of lean allows anyone to apply the TPS education system in their organization to better understand how and where they are not satisfying customers, not creating the right quality first time, and delivering their work as the work is needed. It allows people to explore how their organization's capacity is utilized, where there are overburdens, and where the load is not level. It allows people to explore where they are struggling with teaching the established know-how and how they are developing that know-how further. It allows people to see where teams and individuals are autonomous and have ownership in their work, where they are not, and where support systems are not working as they should.

Exploring this view on lean production, an approach to developing people and processes in parallel through technical problem-solving guided by the threshold concepts and troublesome knowledge of the TPS should be of interest to researchers in both the general management field and the operations management field. Areas of collaboration and further research could be to examine the effect of this approach on adult learning and development and how the lean education system can support lifelong learning inside organizations. Another area of further research could be to investigate the effects of digitalization on hindering or enhancing learning in the context of the lean education system. Researchers could investigate the potential barriers to a learning and development approach to lean, as well as the sustainable results of such an approach on people, the planet, and profit. Any of these suggestions for further research opens up for extensive collaboration with researchers from outside the operations management field of research such as psychology, learning theory, general management theory, and sustainability.

References

Adler, P. S., Goldoftas, B., and Levine, D. I. (1999). Flexibility versus efficiency? A case study of model changeovers in the Toyota production system. *Organizational Science*, 10(1), 43–68.

Anderson, K. and Yoshino, I. (2020). *Learning to Lead, Leading to Learn*. California: Integrand Press.

Arbesman, S. (2013). *The Half-Life of Facts: Why Everything We Know Has an Expiration Date*. New York: Penguin.

Ballé, M., Chaize, J., Fiancette, F., and Prévot, E. (2010). The lean leap: Lean as a learning accelerator. *Reflections*, 10(3), 1–17.

Ballé, M., Chartier, N., Coignet, P., Olivencia, S., Powell, D., and Reke, E. (2019). *The Lean Sensei: Go See Challenge*. Boston: Lean Enterprise Institute Inc.

Ballé, M., Jones, D., Chaize, J., Fiume, O., and Ehrenfeld, T. (2017). *The Lean Strategy: Using Lean to Create Competitive Advantage, Unleash Innovation, and Deliver Sustainable Growth*. New York: McGraw-Hill Higher Education.

Ballé, M., Morgan, J., and Sobek, D. K. (2016). Why learning is central to sustained innovation. *Sloan Management Review*, 57(3), 63–71.

Cousin, G. (2006). An introduction to threshold concepts. *Planet*, 17(1), 4–5.

Cusumano, M. A., Holweg, M., Howell, J., Netland, T., Shah, R., Shook, J., Ward, P., and Womack, J. (2021). Commentaries on "The Lenses of Lean". *Journal of Operations Management*, 67, 627–639.

Fujimoto, T. (1999). *Evolution of Manufacturing Systems at Toyota*. New York: Oxford University Press.

Furuta, K. (2022). *Welcome Problems, Find Success*. Boca Raton, FL: CRC Press.

Hayashi, N. (2018). Toyota production system and the roots of lean. Goldratt Consulting. https://vimeo.com/300443389.

Hines, P., Holweg, M., and Rich, N. (2004). Learning to evolve. *International Journal of Operations & Production Management*, 24(10), 994–1011.

Hopp, W. J. and Spearman, M. S. (2021). The lenses of lean: Visioning the science and practice of efficiency. *Journal of Operations Management*, 67(5), 610–626.

Hung, W., Jonassen, D. H., and Liu, R. (2008). Problem-based learning. In J. M. Spector, M. D. Merrill, H. van Merriënboer, and M. P. Driscoll (eds.), *Handbook of Research on Educational Communications and Technology*. New York: Lawrence Erlbaum, pp. 485–506.

Leuchel, S. R. (2020). *Sensei Secrets: Mentoring at Toyota Georgetown. A Qualitative Study of the Sensei-Protégé Relationship at Toyota*. Align Kaizen Publishing.

Meyer, J. H. F. and Land, R. (2003). Threshold concepts and troublesome knowledge: Linkages to ways of thinking and practising within the disciplines. In C. Rust (ed.), *ISL10 Improving Student Learning: Theory and Practice Ten Years On*. Oxford: Oxford Brookes University, pp. 412–424.

Meyer, J. H. F. and Land, R. (2005). Threshold concepts and troublesome knowledge (2): Epistemological considerations and a conceptual framework for teaching and learning. *Higher Education*, 49(3), 373–388.

Morgan, J. M. and Liker, J. K. (2019). *Designing the Future*. New York: McGraw-Hill.

Netland, T. H. and Powell, D. (eds.) (2017). *The Routledge Companion to Lean Management*. New York: Routledge.

Netland, T. H., Powell, D. J., and Hines, P. (2019). Demystifying lean leadership. *International Journal of Lean Six Sigma*, 11(13), 12–19.

Netland, T. H., Schloetzer, J. D., and Ferdows, K. (2021). Learning lean: Rhythm of production and the pace of lean implementation. *International Journal of Operations and Production Management*, 41(2), 131–156.

Powell, D. and Coughlan, P. (2020). Rethinking lean supplier development as a learning system. *International Journal of Operations and Production Management*, 40(7/8), 921–943.

Powell, D. and Reke, E. (2019). No lean without learning: Rethinking lean production as a learning system. In F. Ameri, K. E. Stecke, G. von Cieminski, and D. Kiritsis (eds.), *Advances in Production Management Systems: Production Management for the Factory of the Future. APMS 2019*. Cham: Springer, pp. 62–68.

Reke, E., Powell, D., and Mogos, M. F. (2022). Applying the fundamentals of TPS to realize a resilient and responsive manufacturing system. *Procedia CIRP*, 107, 1221–1225.

Reke, E., Powell, D., Olivencia, S., Coignet, P., Chartier, N., and Ballé, M. (2020). Recapturing the spirit of lean: The role of the sensei in developing lean leaders. In M. Rossi, M. Rossini, and S. Terzi (eds.), *Proceedings of the 6th European Lean Educator Conference*. Cham: Springer, pp. 117–125.

Senge, P. M. (2006). *The Fifth Discipline: The Art & Practice of the Learning Organization*, 2nd edition. London: Random House.

Shah, R. and Ward, P. T. (2003). Lean manufacturing: Context, practice bundles and performance. *Journal of Operations Management*, 21(3), 129–149.

Shah, R. and Ward, P. T. (2007). Defining and developing measures of lean production. *Journal of Operations Management*, 25(2), 785–805.

Shimokawa, K. and Fujimoto, T. (2009). *Birth of Lean*. Cambridge, MA: Lean Enterprise Institute Inc.

Spear, S. J. (2004). Learning to lead at Toyota. *Harvard Business Review*, 82(5), 78–86, 151.

Sugimori, Y., Kusunoki, K., Cho, F., and Uchikawa, S. (1977). Toyota production system and kanban system materialization of just-in-time and respect-for-human system. *International Journal of Production Research*, 15(6), 553–564.

Womack, J. P., Jones, D. T., and Roos, D. (1990). *The Machine That Changed the World: The Story of Lean Production, Toyota's Secret Weapon in the Global Car Wars That Is Now Revolutionizing World Industry*. New York: Simon & Schuster.

4 Building lean capabilities through action learning

Henrik Saabye

Introduction

Lean capabilities involve three key elements: flow, pull, and continuous improvement. Flow refers to the smooth and efficient movement of products, services, and information through the value stream. Pull refers to the ability to produce only what the customer needs when they need it. Finally, continuous improvement refers to the ongoing effort to identify and eliminate waste and improve processes (Womack and Jones, 2003). Moreover, lean capabilities encompass an organization's ability to continuously improve its processes, systems, and people through a systematic approach that involves learning from past experiences, experimentation, and reflection. In this context, lean capabilities are not just a set of skills or tools but a mindset that encourages a culture of continuous learning, adaptation, and innovation (Ballé et al., 2017). *But how do organizations build lean capabilities?* In the early extant lean literature emerging from investigating the Toyota Production System (TPS), this question was examined through an industrial engineering lens with a focus on best practice application of tools and methods within a manufacturing context (Bicheno, 1994; Harrison, 1992; Hines, 2022; Ishiwata and Katō, 1991). However, this early research on lean was criticized for omitting the human dimension of lean adoption (Hines, 2022) or what, according to the Toyota Way, is understood as *hitozukuri*, which can be translated to "making people" (Saito et al., 2013). The *hitozukuri* dimension, or "respect for people" (Ljungblom and Lennerfors, 2021; Saito et al., 2013; Sugimori et al., 1977), is the art and passion of educating people through lifelong learning. As a result, employees are provided with the opportunity to contribute and gain self-realization while maximizing their effectiveness by being developed in their areas of expertise and ability to work together across functional boundaries (Ljungblom and Lennerfors, 2021).

Hitozukuri is understood as the enabling dimension to another and the more technical dimension of TPS, which is *monozukuri*, translated as "making value-adding things" and which is Toyota's "all-encompassing passion for innovating and doing things well" (Liker and Convis, 2011, p. 229). Complementing the *hitozukuri* dimension (making people) to enable *monozukuri* (making things) is the dimension of *kotozukuri*, which refers to the passion for "making things happen" (Ljungblom and Lennerfors, 2021). Two fundamental elements are at the heart of *kotozukuri*. Firstly, the presence of strong ambition or visions (e.g. a new product or production concept) communicated through a story that engages people and makes them come together, and secondly, the manager's ability to foster continuous learning originating from problem-solving and making improvements.

Research into the *hitozukuri* (making people) and *kotozukuri* (making things happen) dimensions of lean has increased significantly within the last decade (Hines, 2022; Magnani et al., 2019). However, according to Magnani et al. (2019, p. 139), there is still "an overall scarcity of research on the human dimension of lean". Therefore, they propose a further investigation into the human resource development (HRD) practices associated with lean capability building of (1) shaping employees' perceptions and behaviours, (2) impacting employees' development through continuous learning and group activities, and (3) establishing developmental (learning) systems and interactions between managers and employees.

Throughout the history of HRD as a research stream and practice, learning and action have been central components (Cho and Egan, 2023). Action-oriented approaches in the workplace are rooted in practices, theories, and literature that predate the definition and formation of the HRD field. One of these approaches is that of action learning (AL). In its earliest form, AL was developed by Reg Revans during the 1930s and 1940s to develop the organization members' skills in finding, facing, framing, and solving real-world problems in a group at the workplace (Cho and Bong, 2013). An underlying assumption of AL is that developing the organization's members' ability to solve problems requires critical reflection (Høyrup, 2004) and scrutinizing their own and the organization's underlying assumptions. Moreover, a foundational mental model of AL is that for organizations to cope with the increasing velocity of change, they must learn at a rate equal to or faster than the changes within the external environment (Revans, 1982). Today AL is regarded as an effective HRD methodology for developing collective leadership within an organization (Raelin, 2021) by expanding its members to solve challenges in the workplace as problem-based (Scott, 2017) and experiential learning (Yeo and Marquardt, 2015).

Emerging from a nascent research stream on lean and AL complementarity (Kristensen et al., 2022; Pedler and Abbott, 2008; Powell and Coughlan, 2020;

Saabye, 2023; Saabye and Powell, 2022; Saabye et al., 2022, 2023), it is suggested that AL as a theory and practice provides a lens to understand and develop the *hitozukuri* (making people) and *kotozukuri* (making things happen) dimensions when building lean capabilities that foster *monozukuri* (making things).

Therefore, this chapter aims to outline and provide insights into how AL as an action-oriented HRD theory and practice fosters *hitozukuri* (making people) and *kotozukuri* (making things happen) towards building and institutionalizing sustainable lean capabilities. The remainder of this chapter is organized as follows. Firstly, the theoretical foundation for connecting lean and AL is presented. Secondly, the complementarity of lean and AL is presented as an integrated theory and practice underlying *hitozukuri* (making people) and *kotozukuri* (making things happen). Thirdly, from presenting three cases of building lean capabilities through AL, implications for practitioners are extrapolated through a lean-AL lens. Finally, this chapter concludes and discusses future research directions on lean-AL research by adopting Coghlan and Coughlan's (2010, 2015) four quality criteria for research on action learning: engagement with problems, collaboration with organizational members and stakeholders, reflection on the iterative cycles of an action learning process, and actionable outcomes.

Literature review

Lean as a learning system founded on a learning-to-learn capability

The critique for omitting the human dimension of lean adoption (Hines, 2022) has nurtured the *learning* stream within lean research, which argues for redefining lean away from the *efficacy* understanding of lean as applying a set of tools to reduce waste towards a lifelong learning journey of instituting a lean learning or education system (Ballé et al., 2017, 2019; Powell and Coughlan, 2020; Powell and Reke, 2019).

The literature on lean emphasizes that it is a dynamic capability, which refers to a meta-routine that enables organizations to change and improve their operational routines (Peng et al., 2008). Organizational learning is also viewed as a dynamic capability that can enhance efficiency if the appropriate infrastructure is in place, such as standardized improvement methods, participation structures, training, and organizational direction (Anand et al., 2009; Galeazzo et al., 2017). Furlan and Vinelli (2018) advocate a perspective of manufacturing plants in terms of capabilities that rest on routine-changing routines or meta-routines, which transform knowledge into production processes. They suggest that improvement and innovation are dynamic capabilities that consist of bundles of interrelated routine-changing routines or meta-routines. They argue that effective process management does not require trading off innovation for improvement but rather facilitates firms in fostering creative thinking, establishing a learning base, and ultimately triggering innovation.

In addition, Ballé et al. (2019, p. 3) present lean as a learning system in the following way:

> Lean is a system to continuously develop people and create a culture of problem-solving; a strategy to face challenges by engaging and involving all problem-solvers into exploring issues and forming unknown solutions by learning experientially from practical countermeasures. Lean tools are techniques to create the conditions for such experiential learning, and the lean approach turns management upside down by turning the chain of command into a chain of help: challenge and support, rather than command and control.

According to the *learning* research stream, lean is built on a fundamental cognitive capability and readiness of learning-to-learn (Ballé et al., 2019; Powell and Coughlan, 2020; Saabye et al., 2022). Without a fundamental learning-to-learn capability comprising systematic problem-solving abilities (Mohaghegh and Furlan, 2020), leaders serving as learning facilitators (Maalouf and Gammelgaard, 2016; Saabye, 2023) and the presence of a supportive learning environment (Edmondson, 1999; Marsick and Watkins, 2003), organizations will have difficulty overcoming several challenges related to building and institutionalizing lean capabilities.

Since learning is at the core of a lean learning system, the role of leaders becomes one of being a learning facilitator (Kristensen et al., 2022; Maalouf and Gammelgaard, 2016; Saabye, 2023). Moreover, according to Mann (2009), only 20 per cent of the effort in building lean capabilities is adopting new methods and practices; the rest concerns changing leadership thinking and behaviours. Leaders are often unconsciously incompetent in facilitating learning. They believe that learning equals sponsoring people obtaining new knowledge from attending courses, online self-studies, or taking formal education, e.g. applying lean methods. In other instances, leaders hire consultants to, for example, build lean capabilities and facilitate learning and change. But as soon as the engagement with these consultants is ended, the initiated learning and change process slows significantly or stops (Holmemo et al., 2018).

Developing lean capabilities through the lens of action learning

Fundamental to action learning is the distinction between puzzles and problems (Revans, 2011). A *puzzle* is an issue that an expert or specialist can resolve because it has one specific and correct solution. In contrast, Revans (2011) notes that *problems* do not have one single solution but multiple ones influenced by the many perspectives of an organization, reflected by the current situation, various value systems, and the external environment. Problems are amenable to action learning.

In addition to Revans' (2011) distinction between problems and puzzles, action learning can be defined with a learning equation which states that L (learning) = P (programmed knowledge) + Q (questioning insights). Programmed knowledge (P) is understood as knowledge gained or provided by experts or acquired through the syllabuses of teaching institutions. Still, when facing problems where we cannot know what exactly will happen next, managers and employees must initiate asking insightful questions (Q). Consequently, adopting lean becomes a matter of both acquiring knowledge (P) about methods and practices associated with *monozukuri* (making things) and, equally as important, asking many questions (Q) to facilitate and foster *hitozukuri* (making people) and *kotozukuri* (making things happen) through problem-solving.

Underlying the L = P + Q learning equation, Revans (1971) also defines action learning as a science of praxeology consisting of the three cyclical and intertwined systems of alpha, beta, and gamma.

- System alpha concerns finding, facing, and framing challenging organizational problems to ensure the organization's ongoing success. Problem owners must analyze the external environment to identify challenges and opportunities (for example, related to improving operational performance or developing new products or services) and the status of the available internal resources exploiting these aspects (Pedler and Abbott, 2013). Moreover, when framing more complex problems, the problem owner must also consider the history, cultures, power, and politics embedded in the organization and the differences in opinions concerning the best course of action among different groups (Revans, 1971).
- System beta encompasses the scientific method of solving problems in an ongoing cycle of planning, action, reflection, and learning. The system beta model, for example, involves Revans' (2011, p. 13) five-stage cycle of the scientific method: (1) Observation or survey, (2) Theory or hypothesis, (3) Test or experiment, (4) Audit or evaluation, and (5) Review or control. Within lean, Deming's more familiar learning cycle of Plan, Do, Check,

Act (PDCA) is another manifestation of the scientific method (Sobek and Smalley, 2008). Simultaneously with solving concrete problems using the scientific method, an underlying institutional learning process also occurs (Revans, 1971, p. 129), resembling *hitozukuri* (making people) and *kotozukuri* (making things happen). As part of the problem-solving process, stakeholders, such as sponsors, clients, partners, and colleagues, are engaged in negotiating common meanings and understanding of the problem, as learning from engaging stakeholders and conducting experiments may uncover new options and opportunities for resolving a problem (Pedler and Abbott, 2013).

•   System gamma is the personal learning and reflective process emerging from engaging in system alpha and beta activities and can be understood as critical reflection (Boshyk and Dilworth, 2010). Critical reflection is a process of addressing underlying basic assumptions and mental models (Høyrup, 2004). Mental models refer to deep-held beliefs or basic assumptions regarding how the surrounding environment works; these beliefs help individuals understand, interpret, and predict events (Senge, 1990). Unfortunately, leaders often become caught in an uncritical acceptance of distorted perspectives because their frame of reference, derived from their mental models, can be wrong (Høyrup, 2004).

In the lean literature, critical reflection or deep reflection is referred to as *hansei*. It is the practice of self-development and entails the conscious process of looking back at yourself, reflecting on what went well and what did not, and adapting these insights for future actions (Liker and Convis, 2011, p. 70).

In the context of developing lean capabilities, system alpha, beta, and gamma are foundational for the learning process of enabling *monozukuri* (making things) through *hitozukuri* (making people) and *kotozukuri* (making things happen). When building lean capabilities, an organization must first engage in an explorative process of defining specific and strategic problems (system alpha). Afterwards, it must follow the scientific method (system beta) to sense and seize the proper methods and practices to analyze the problem at hand and, through experimentation, creativity and reflections, conceive effective countermeasures to be subsequently implemented. This process requires multiple cycles of asking insightful questions (Q) to scrutinize the assumptions underpinning our beliefs and mental models when framing the problem and countermeasures. These system gamma activities foster changing one's behaviour in response to the knowledge learned from the system alpha and beta activities.

Because action learning focuses on solving problems in praxis (Coghlan and Rigg, 2021), it has been further operationalized, for example, by Marquardt et al.'s (2018, p. 28) six interactive components of action learning. These components, presented in the following list, become central (learning) design criteria when designing an intervention to develop and build lean capabilities:

1. A problem or opportunity of complex organizational issues that concern different parts of the organization and are not amenable to expert solutions is selected and addressed.
2. A group of people who work together as a set of peers and members act as critical friends to challenge and support one another's learning.
3. A commitment to taking action in which implementation, rather than recommendations to others, is central.
4. The commitment to learning goes beyond merely solving immediate problems. The ultimate outcomes are increased knowledge and the capacity to adapt to change more effectively.
5. The participants engage in a questioning and reflective process. Learning occurs through asking questions, investigating, experimenting, and reflecting rather than relying on external expertise.
6. A learning coach or facilitator facilitates the action-learning process as a peer challenge or critical friend who helps the group establish ground rules and develop questioning, reflective, and inclusive team practices.

Marquardt et al. (2018, p. 29) propose that these six components, combined with two ground rules, encompass the core elements of developing people and create a foundation for solving problems innovatively, similar to *hitozukuri* (making people) and *kotozukuri* (making things happen). The two ground rules are the following:

1. Statements should only be made in response to questions.
2. The action-learning coach has the power to intervene when they see an opportunity to improve the performance and learning of the group.

Figure 4.1 presents a combined action-learning model devised from Revans (1971, 2011) and Marquardt et al. (2018).

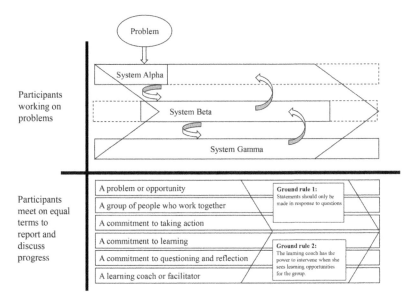

Source: Adapted from Coghlan and Coughlan (2010, p. 200).

Figure 4.1   Model of action learning

Integration of lean and action learning

From investigating the complementarity of lean and AL (see Figure 4.2), Saabye et al. (2023) propose that integrating the existing AL and lean research streams provides an opportunity to progress towards an integrative intervention design for building lean capabilities. Furthermore, they suggest that this integration will lead to more sustainable lean capability building and add new depth to the theoretical explanation of the success and failures when building lean capabilities (Saabye et al., 2023).

Outlining six lean and AL complementing similarities

The concepts of lean and AL have been extensively studied in recent years. Saabye et al. (2023) have identified six complementing similarities between lean and AL, which are depicted in Figure 4.2. This illustration is inspired by the Toyota Production System (TPS) house, which is widely regarded as the birthplace of lean manufacturing (Liker, 2021).

The six complementing similarities between lean and AL are oriented in a manner that reflects the underlying learning process that defines both lean and AL. (1) At the foundation of this process is the scientific method, which is used to solve problems. This involves gathering data, analysing it, and drawing conclusions based on the evidence. The two pillars of (2) individual learning and (3) group learning support the scientific method by providing the necessary knowledge and skills. Individual learning involves the acquisition of knowledge and skills by an individual, while group learning involves the sharing of knowledge and skills within a team. Both pillars are essential to the learning process, as they enable individuals and teams to acquire and apply new knowledge and skills. The core of the learning process is (4) asking insightful questions over statements of knowledge. This involves challenging assumptions and seeking to understand the underlying causes of problems. By asking insightful questions, individuals and teams can identify the root causes of problems and develop effective solutions. Improving the whole (5) system is another complementing similarity between lean and AL. This involves looking beyond individual problems and seeking to improve the entire system. By improving the whole system, individuals and teams can create a more efficient and effective organization. Finally, demonstrating (6) respect for employees, customers, and partners as well as serving and improving society is another important complementing similarity of lean and AL. By treating people with respect and working to improve society, organizations can create a positive work environment that fosters creativity and innovation.

In conclusion, Figure 4.2 illustrates the six complementing similarities between lean and AL developed by Saabye et al. (2023), which are all oriented towards a learning process that emphasizes problem-solving, individual and group learning, insightful questioning, improving the whole system, and demonstrating respect for people and society.

Problem-solving by scientific method

Ballé et al. (2017) suggest that the core of lean is centred around identifying and addressing the right problems while also developing the organization's members to solve them. Similarly, action learning involves enabling individuals to solve unfamiliar, real, urgent, and significant problems in a complementary manner (Boshyk and Dilworth, 2010). Therefore, if there are no problems to solve, the foundation for action learning is absent (Marquardt et al., 2018; Pedler and Abbott, 2013).

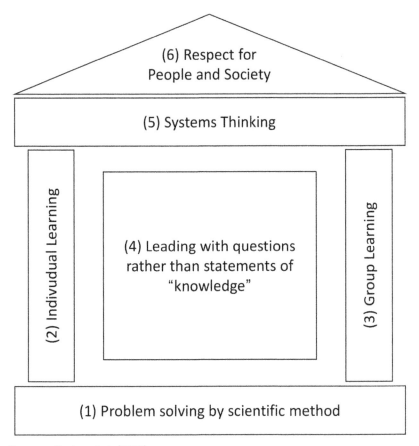

Source: Saabye et al. (2023).

Figure 4.2   The lean-action learning theoretical lens

Individual learning

Lean and action learning share a common foundation that involves solving relevant problems, generating insights, fostering learning, and improving the organization's ability to solve future problems more effectively, ultimately leading to strategic success (Ballé et al., 2017; Liker, 2021; Marquardt et al., 2018).

Group learning

A group or team frequently conducts problem-solving according to the liter-ature on lean methodologies (Franken et al., 2021; Liker, 2021; Rother, 2010). Similarly, action learning emphasizes the group or set as the central entity responsible for reframing problems, evaluating various actions, setting goals, defining actions, and executing those actions (Marquardt et al., 2018, p. 53).

Leading with questions rather than statements of "knowledge"

The lean and action learning domains share a similarity in their emphasis on leading change through questioning and self-reflection (Liker and Convis, 2011; Marquardt et al., 2018). In the lean approach, leaders play a critical role in developing themselves and others in problem-solving through coaching and asking questions (Liker and Convis, 2011). Similarly, in action learning, asking insightful questions is foundational for enabling groups to understand and explore problems and actions (Marquardt et al., 2018). Critical reflection is also a dominant element in both domains, with lean referring to it as *hansei* and action learning emphasizing the importance of upstream and downstream learning (Liker and Convis, 2011; Marquardt et al., 2018).

Systems thinking

Systems thinking involves recognizing patterns and understanding that what affects one part of an organization also affects other parts in planned and unplanned ways (Senge, 1990). Lean thinkers perceive organizations as dynamic and unpredictable living systems and invest in continuous adjust-ments instead of expecting simple cause-and-effect relationships (Ballé et al., 2017; Liker, 2021). A systems viewpoint is applied when solving problems, as solving a problem in one part of an organization can impose a new problem in another part. Action learning is developed on the proposition that achieving effective problem-solving requires systems thinking (Marquardt et al., 2018). The roots of systems thinking can be traced back to early leaders at Toyota (Liker, 2021), and accounts suggest that Revans applied a systems approach to healthcare as far back as 1938 (Boshyk and Dilworth, 2010).

Respect for people and society

Both lean and action learning emphasize the importance of respecting people and society over profit, which is a fundamental element of both domains (Ballé et al., 2017; Boshyk and Dilworth, 2010; Liker, 2021). In the lean domain, respecting people involves caring deeply about every employee, customer satisfaction, partners' successes, and the well-being of the surrounding communities (Ballé et al., 2017; Liker, 2021). Similarly, within action learning, Revans promotes ethical values and principles such as honesty and social responsibility while promoting behaviour based on humility and respect for others (Boshyk and Dilworth, 2010, p. 53). Both domains believe that respecting people is not only the right thing to do but also a requirement for long-term profitability.

Implications for practice

In this section, three cases of deliberately building lean capabilities through an integrative AL-lean intervention design are presented and analyzed through the lean-action learning theoretical lens (Figure 4.2). All three cases demonstrate a significant correlation between building lean capabilities by adopting AL for enabling *monozukuri* (making things) through *hitozukuri* (making people) and *kotozukuri* (making things happen).

Kongsberg Maritime, Norway (Powell and Coughlan, 2020)

The first lean-AL case took place at the Subsea Division of Kongsberg Maritime in Norway and six of its strategic suppliers and resulted in improved on-time delivery performance and quality. The purpose of this initiative was to address the problem of addressing the pressure from low-cost competitors and improve supply chain collaboration by developing a shared understanding and practices of lean through network-action-learning (NAL). According to Coughlan and Coghlan (2011), the advancement of strategic improvement through collaboration necessitates the development of a learning capacity within and across networks. This capacity should extend beyond individuals and be particularly focused on enhancing learning within and between organizations. This lean-AL initiative consisted of six interventions: (1) Co-learning at a lean lab, (2) Best practice study visits to exemplary lean enterprises, (3) Individual company lean self-assessments, (4) Lean coaching and individual company consultations, (5) Extended value stream mapping, and (6) Rapid lean assessments. These interventions were designed as NAL cycles of facilitating, monitoring, and reflecting on the interventions from individuals, groups, organizations, and inter-organizational perspectives. Powell and Coughlan (2020) emphasize the distinction between learning about and implementing lean capabilities and adopting a learning-to-learn perspective to build lean capabilities consistent with lean thinking and practice. Hence developing a learning-to-learn capability is a core and critical success factor and AL process for developing sustainable lean capabilities.

LEGO, Denmark (Kristensen et al., 2022)

The second AL-lean case took place at a product-development support department at LEGO. This AL-lean initiative aimed to address the problem of coping with double-digit growth without an explosion in cost stemming from the expansion of the product assortment, a demand for reduced time to market, and the digitalization of products, sales channels, and marketing materials. The AL-lean initiative was conceived on the cyclical and intertwined systems of alpha, beta, and gamma to (1) develop senior leaders and leaders as sponsors, to build required lean problem-solving and learning capabilities among employees, (2) develop leaders as learning facilitators to facilitating AL-groups among employees to face, frame, and solve concrete problems, and (3) establish a new learning and performance management system. Kristensen et al. (2022) found that as a result of an AL-lean initiative for building lean capabilities in a non-manufacturing context that focuses on problem-solving, along with leaders who serve as learning facilitators, the dimensions of learning organizations were significantly improved, as well as quality and efficiency. A positive relationship exists between AL-lean interventions and quality performance, while AL-lean interventions directly affect efficiency.

VELUX, Denmark (Saabye et al., 2022)

The third example of an AL-lean case took place at the Danish roof-top manufacturer, VELUX, intending to build learning-to-learn capabilities based on lean thinking and practices to adopt and utilize data generated by Industrial Internet-of-Things (IIoT) technology within one of their production sites to cope with agendas of growth, digitalization, and sustainability. The purpose of the VELUX AL-lean initiative was (1) to develop leaders to become proficient in framing and solving problems and facilitating learning to enable and empower their subordinates to solve concrete problems by practising asking insightful questions, and (2) empower and develop the shop-floor workers to face, frame, and solve problems systematically using digital data. Saabye et al. (2022) found that this learning process requires leaders and employees to accept the notion of going slow – to go fast and to focus on asking insightful questions (Q) instead of seeking the correct answers. Many experienced this learning process as counterintuitive and painful. However, committing to (action) learning and instituting a higher-order learning-to-learn capability consisting of Revans' system alpha, beta, and gamma, this learning process can result in a personal leap of development for many leaders and employees. This is both an end in itself, and a means for companies to build lean capabilities enabled to adopt and utilize IIoT technology.

Lean-AL theoretical lens case analysis

From a lean-action learning theoretical lens (Figure 4.2) perspective, the three cases share common characteristics of (1) being initiated and aimed at solving problems to ensure the organization's ongoing success following the scientific method while (2) developing systematic problem-solving abilities among the organization's members, (3) fostering a supportive learning environment where the participants work together in (AL) groups to find, face, frame, and solve concrete problems, (4) facilitated by leaders as learning facilitators, who lead with questions rather than statements of "knowledge". (5) The AL-lean initiatives also promoted a system thinking lens to solving problems and understanding lean as a learning system. (6) Lastly, all three cases also encompass "respect for people and society". All the case organizations have a set of values that involves and cares deeply about every employee, and part- ners' successes, customer satisfaction, and the well-being of the surrounding communities.

Conclusion and future research

As an integrative intervention design for building lean capabilities, this chapter has presented the theoretical and practical similarities and complementarity of lean and AL and how they can lead to more sustainable lean capability build- ing. This integrative intervention design encompasses the capacity to explain the success and failures of building lean capabilities through the lean-AL the- oretical lens (Figure 4.2). Furthermore, the lean-AL theoretical lens provides a (theoretical) approach, applied in practice (demonstrated by the three cases) of fostering the *hitozukuri* dimension (making people) and *kotozukuri* (making things happen) to enable *monozukuri* (making things).

Another common epistemological characteristic of the three presented cases is the application of mode 2 knowledge production (Gibbons, 1994), support- ing an endeavour to answer the question of *how* to develop lean capabilities based on action-orientated methodologies. Mode 2 knowledge creation, in contrast to the prevalent mode 1 lean knowledge production (Gibbons, 1994), concerns producing particular knowledge of problems within a specific context, in which the researchers are immersed and engage in reflections with the actors of the research setting (Coghlan and Coughlan, 2010). A strength of the action-oriented mode 2 research approach is that its contribution to both theory and practice is integrated and both are equally as important. Therefore, leading operations management journals encourage researchers to submit mode 2 research and find this form of research underrepresented. Action learning supports and enables various mode 2 research methodologies like action research, design science, and action science, which prioritize collaboration, problem-solving, and the application of research findings to practical problems. However, there are some differences between these three methodologies.

Action research is a methodology that involves a cyclical process of planning, acting, observing, and reflecting on solving practical problems (Coughlan and Coghlan, 2002). The focus is on working collaboratively with stakeholders to identify problems, develop solutions, and evaluate the effectiveness of those solutions. Action research emphasizes the active involvement of stakeholders in the research process, and the results are intended to have practical applications.

Design science, on the other hand, is a methodology that involves creating new solutions to problems through a process of designing, building, and testing artefacts. The focus is on creating new knowledge by designing and developing innovative artefacts, such as new technologies or systems (Hevner et al., 2004). Design science emphasizes the creation of new artefacts that can be applied to solve practical problems.

Action science is a methodology that examines and improves how people work together to solve problems. The focus is on understanding the social and organizational factors that contribute to problems and developing strategies for improving organizational communication, collaboration, and problem-solving (Argyris and Schön, 1974). Action science emphasizes the importance of reflective practice, learning from experience, and ongoing improvement.

A potential avenue for future research on building lean capabilities through action learning is, therefore, to encourage the lean research community to be informed by Coghlan and Coughlan's (2010, 2015) four quality criteria for research on action learning by applying a mode 2 knowledge creation methodology when researching lean capability building:

1. **Framing research questions based on real-world organizational challenges:** When framing research questions, it is essential to consider problems stemming from real-world organizational challenges, such as coping with climate change and adapting to changing business environments. This is in contrast to framing puzzles, which are self-contained and often disconnected from the realities of organizational challenges. By focusing

on real-world challenges, research can generate insights that are more relevant and applicable to practitioners, leading to more significant impact and positive change.

2. **Engaging and utilizing the insights and practices of organizational members and stakeholders:** As researchers, we must become better at engaging and utilizing the insights and practices of organizational members and stakeholders. By involving these individuals in the research process, we can gain a deeper understanding of the challenges they face and the solutions they have developed. This approach ensures that research is grounded in the experiences and perspectives of those affected by organizational challenges, and it increases the likelihood that the resulting knowledge and outcomes will be actionable and impactful.

3. **Collaboration and reflecting on the iterative cycles of an action learning process:** Collaboration is essential to effective research that generates actionable knowledge and outcomes. Through collaboration, researchers can draw on the expertise and experiences of others, enriching their understanding of the research problem and potential solutions. An action learning process, which involves iterative cycles of problem-solving and reflection, can be particularly effective in this regard. By working collaboratively and reflecting on the outcomes of each cycle, researchers can continually refine their understanding and approach, leading to more impactful outcomes.

4. **Producing actionable knowledge and outcomes:** Ultimately, the goal of research is to produce actionable knowledge and outcomes that can drive positive change in real-world organizational settings. By framing research questions around real-world challenges, engaging with organizational members and stakeholders, collaborating effectively, and reflecting on an action learning process, researchers can generate insights that are relevant, actionable, and impactful. By doing so, research can play a critical role in addressing some of the most significant challenges facing organizations today, from climate change to changing business environments.

References

Anand, G., Ward, P. T., Tatikonda, M. V., and Schilling, D. A. (2009). Dynamic capabilities through continuous improvement infrastructure. *Journal of Operations Management*, 27(6), 444–461.

Argyris, C. and Schön, D. A. (1974). *Theory in Practice: Increasing Professional Effectiveness*. San Francisco: Jossey-Bass.

Ballé, M., Chaize, J., and Jones, D. (2019). Lean as a learning system: What do organisations need to do to get the transformational benefits from Toyota's method? *Development and Learning in Organisations: An International Journal*, 33(3), 1–4.

Ballé, M., Jones, D., Chaize, J., Fiume, O., and Ehrenfeld, T. (2017). *The Lean Strategy: Using Lean to Create Competitive Advantage, Unleash Innovation, and Deliver Sustainable Growth*. New York: McGraw-Hill Higher Education.

Bicheno, J. (1994). *The Quality 50: A Guide to 8 Gurus, 7 Tools, 7 Wastes, 6 New Tools, 20 Techniques, 2 Systems*. Victoria: Nestadt Consulting.

Boshyk, Y. and Dilworth, R. L. (Eds.) (2010). *Action Learning*. Basingstoke: Palgrave Macmillan.

Cho, Y. and Bong, H. (2013). *Trends and Issues in Action Learning Practice: Lessons from South Korea*. New York: Routledge.

Cho, Y. and Egan, T. (2023). The changing landscape of action learning research and practice. *Human Resource Development International*, 26(4), 378–404.

Coghlan, D. and Coughlan, P. (2010). Notes toward a philosophy of action learning research. *Action Learning: Research and Practice*, 7(2), 193–203.

Coghlan, D. and Coughlan, P. (2015). Effecting change and learning in networks through network action learning. *The Journal of Applied Behavioral Science*, 51(3), 375–400.

Coghlan, D. and Rigg, C. (2021). Writing an account of practice as a process of theorising in action learning. *Action Learning: Research and Practice*, 18(3), 250–256.

Coughlan, P. and Coghlan, D. (2002). Action research for operations management. *International Journal of Operations & Production Management*, 22(2), 220–240.

Coughlan, P. and Coghlan, D. (2011). *Collaborative Strategic Improvement through Network Action Learning: The Path to Sustainability*. Cheltenham, UK and Northampton, MA, USA: Edward Elgar Publishing.

Edmondson, A. (1999). Psychological safety and learning behavior in work teams. *Administrative Science Quarterly*, 44(2), 350–383.

Franken, J. C. M., van Dun, D. H., and Wilderom, C. P. M. (2021). Kaizen event process quality: Towards a phase-based understanding of high-quality group problem-solving. *International Journal of Operations & Production Management*, 41(6), 962–990.

Furlan, A. and Vinelli, A. (2018). Unpacking the coexistence between improvement and innovation in world-class manufacturing: A dynamic capability approach. *Technological Forecasting and Social Change*, 133, 168–178.

Galeazzo, A., Furlan, A., and Vinelli, A. (2017). The organisational infrastructure of continuous improvement: An empirical analysis. *Operations Management Research*, 10(1), 33–46.

Gibbons, M. (Ed.) (1994). *The New Production of Knowledge: The Dynamics of Science and Research in Contemporary Societies*. London: Sage Publications.

Harrison, A. (1992). *Just-in-Time Manufacturing in Perspective*. Englewood Cliffs, NJ: Prentice Hall.

Hevner, A. R., March, S. T., Park, J., and Ram, S. (2004). Design science in information systems research. *MIS Quarterly*, 28(1), 75–105.

Hines, P. (2022). Human centred lean: Introducing the people value stream. *International Journal of Lean Six Sigma*, 13(5), 961–988.

Holmemo, M. D.-Q., Rolfsen, M., and Ingvaldsen, J. A. (2018). Lean thinking: Outside-in, bottom-up? The paradox of contemporary soft lean and consultant-driven lean implementation. *Total Quality Management & Business Excellence*, 29(1–2), 148–160.

Høyrup, S. (2004). Reflection as a core process in organisational learning. *Journal of Workplace Learning*, 16(8), 442–454.

Ishiwata, J. and Katō, K. (1991). *IE for the Shop Floor*. Cambridge, MA: Productivity Press.

Kristensen, T. B., Saabye, H., and Edmondson, A. (2022). Becoming a learning organisation while enhancing performance: The case of LEGO. *International Journal of Operations & Production Management*, 42(13), 438–481.

Liker, J. K. (2021). *The Toyota Way: 14 Management Principles from the World's Greatest Manufacturer*, 2nd edition. New York: McGraw-Hill Education.

Liker, J. K. and Convis, G. L. (2011). *The Toyota Way to Lean Leadership: Achieving and Sustaining Excellence through Leadership Development*. New York: McGraw-Hill.

Ljungblom, M. and Lennerfors, T. T. (2021). The lean principle respect for people as respect for craftsmanship. *International Journal of Lean Six Sigma*, 12(6), 1209–1230.

Maalouf, M. and Gammelgaard, B. (2016). Managing paradoxical tensions during the implementation of lean capabilities for improvement. *International Journal of Operations & Production Management*, 36(6), 687–709.

Magnani, F., Carbone, V., and Moatti, V. (2019). The human dimension of lean: A literature review. *Supply Chain Forum: An International Journal*, 20(2), 132–144.

Mann, D. (2009). The missing link: Lean leadership. *Frontiers of Health Services Management*, 26(1), 15–26.

Marquardt, M. J., Banks, S., Cauweliwe, P., and Seng Ng, C. (2018). *Optimizing the Power of Action Learning: Real-Time Strategies for Developing Leaders, Building Teams and Transforming Organizations*, 3rd edition. Boston: Nicholas Brealey.

Marsick, V. J. and Watkins, K. E. (2003). Demonstrating the value of an organization's learning culture: The dimensions of the learning organization questionnaire. *Advances in Developing Human Resources*, 5(2), 132–151.

Mohaghegh, M. and Furlan, A. (2020). Systematic problem-solving and its antecedents: A synthesis of the literature. *Management Research Review*, 43(9), 1033–1062.

Pedler, M. and Abbott, C. (2008). Lean and learning: Action learning for service improvement. *Leadership in Health Services*, 21(2), 87–98.

Pedler, M. and Abbott, C. (2013). *Facilitating Action Learning: A Practitioner's Guide*. Maidenhead: Open University Press.

Peng, D. X., Schroeder, R. G., and Shah, R. (2008). Linking routines to operations capabilities: A new perspective. *Journal of Operations Management*, 26(6), 730–748.

Powell, D. and Coughlan, P. (2020). Rethinking lean supplier development as a learning system. *International Journal of Operations & Production Management*, 40(7–8), 921–943.

Powell, D. and Reke, E. (2019). No lean without learning: Rethinking lean production as a learning system. In F. Ameri, K. E. Stecke, G. von Cieminski, and D. Kiritsis (Eds.), *Advances in Production Management Systems: Production Management for the Factory of the Future*. Cham: Springer International Publishing, pp. 62–68.

Raelin, J. (2021). Action learning as a human resource development resource to realise collective leadership. *Human Resource Development Review*, 20(3), 282–288.

Revans, R. W (1971). *Developing Effective Managers: A New Approach to Business Education*. London: Longman.

Revans, R. W. (1982). *The Origins and Growths of Action Learning*. Bromley: Chartwell-Bratt.

Revans, R. W. (2011). *ABC of Action Learning*. London: Routledge.

Rother, M. (2010). *Toyota Kata: Managing People for Improvement, Adaptiveness, and Superior Results*. New York: McGraw-Hill.

Saabye, H. (2023). Advancements on action learning and lean complementarity: a case of developing leaders as lean learning facilitators. *Action Learning: Research and Practice*, 20(1), 38–56.

Saabye, H. and Powell, D. J. (2022). Fostering insights and improvements from IIoT systems at the shop floor: A case of industry 4.0 and lean complementarity enabled by action learning. *International Journal of Lean Six Sigma*. https://doi.org/10.1108/IJLSS-01-2022-0017.

Saabye, H., Kristensen, T. B., and Wæhrens, B. V. (2022). Developing a learning-to-learn capability: Insights on conditions for Industry 4.0 adoption. *International Journal of Operations & Production Management*, 42(13), 25–53.

Saabye, H., Powell, D. J., & Coughlan, P. (2023). Lean and action learning: towards an integrated theory?. *International Journal of Operations & Production Management*, 43(13), 128–151.

Saito, K., Salazar, A. J., Kreafle, K., and Grulke, E. (2013). Hitozukuri and monozukuri in relation to research and development in surface coating. In K. Toda, A. Salazar, and K. Saito, (Eds.), *Automotive Painting Technology*. Dordrecht: Springer, pp. 169–184.

Scott, K. S. (2017). An integrative framework for problem-based learning and action learning: Promoting evidence-based design and evaluation in leadership development. *Human Resource Development Review*, 16(1), 3–34.

Senge, P. M. (1990). *The Fifth Discipline: The Art and Practice of the Learning Organization*. New York: Doubleday/Currency.

Sobek, D. K. and Smalley, A. (2008). *Understanding A3 Thinking: A Critical Component of Toyota's PDCA Management System*. Boca Raton, FL: CRC Press.

Sugimori, Y., Kusunoki, K., Cho, F., and Uchikawa, S. (1977). Toyota production system and kanban system materialization of just-in-time and respect-for-human system. *International Journal of Production Research*, 15(6), 553–564.

Womack, J. P. and Jones, D. T. (2003). *Lean Thinking: Banish Waste and Create Wealth in Your Corporation*. New York: Simon & Schuster.

Yeo, R. K. and Marquardt, M. J. (2015). (Re)interpreting action, learning, and experience: Integrating action learning and experiential learning for HRD. *Human Resource Development Quarterly*, 26(1), 81–107.

PART III

Lean and sustainability: people, planet, profit

5   Lean and the planet

Rose Heathcote

Introduction

Sustainability is fast becoming a company's licence to operate. The chapter sketches a sobering outlook for humanity and business survival, challenging enterprises to rethink their position and capitalize on unleveraged competitive capabilities. The return on effort is financially rewarding, and fusing the natural fit of sustainability and lean is underpinned by a solid business case. Conversely, the return on no-effort is a financially precarious pathway with a high cost of doing nothing. The obligation to change is charged by influential forces such as investor interests, financial reporting initiatives, supplier selection and contracts, evolving regulatory frameworks, attractive cost benefits and an amplifying undercurrent from the talent pool. Additionally, a benign climate and stable business environment is a powerful motivator for change. The chapter petitions enterprises to intimately understand their value chains, establishing connections between business activities and effects, stepping up company-wide efforts to radically reduce planetary impact. Integrating sustainability into lean efforts breaks new ground for many organizations, but sustainability thinking is inherent in lean thinking, tracing back to a core focus of the Toyota Production System (Toyota Motor Corporation, 1998). Respect for people – a tenet of lean thinking – cannot be claimed without respect for humanity and, therefore, respect for the planet.

Planetary tipping points are business tipping points

Planet health depends on flourishing natural systems and wise stewardship of natural resources. Although the challenge transcends borders requiring global coordination, solutions include multidisciplinary, local-level efforts too. Companies are urged to think global and act local, by holistically exploring the interrelationships between their activities, the environment and human well-being (Sajjad, 2019), spurring change to reduce impact and improve planet health. Business survival is inextricably linked to planet health and every organization relies on the planet providing clean air and water, food, soil, a benign climate, and productive seas, free of charge (World Wildlife Fund, n.d.). As such, planetary tipping points should be viewed as tipping points for business, which left uncared for, elevate to extreme conditions to contend with. As Sun Tzu suggests, we should plan for what is difficult while it is still easy to do (Tzu, 1988) – a sobering reminder to voluntarily address issues affecting planetary boundaries before laws and conditions force the hands of the companies within an overwhelming timeframe.

The current state

Looking back 10,000 years, humanity has thrived in a relatively uneventful period of stability on earth, even with major environmental changes along the way. Geologists refer to the period as the *Holocene*, a stable interglacial state of the planet where temperatures were regular, freshwater was abundant and biogeochemical flows stayed within a narrow range (Rockström et al., 2009). Since the industrial revolution, a fossil-fuel driven world economy triggered the great acceleration – an acceleration in the concentration of greenhouse gases, destruction of forests, reduction in soil health, marine fish capture, ocean acidification and population growth to name a few. The planet has subsequently been steered towards a new geological epoch, called the *Anthropocene*, identifying humans as the largest driver of change on earth whereby continued activities could push us out of the comfort zone of the Holocene. Although some effects may only realize in centuries to come, humanity is witnessing the first signs of a planet pushed beyond its tipping points, calling for mitigation and adaption (Thunberg, 2022).

To remain in the Holocene state, Rockström et al. propose a framework based on nine planetary boundaries to protect and conserve a safe operating space for humanity. In 2015 their research suggested we could soon approach the limits for global freshwater use, change in land-use, ocean acidification and interference with the global phosphorus cycle and that climate change, biodiversity loss and interference with the nitrogen cycle had transgressed their limits. Updated in 2023, research now indicates that six of the nine planetary boundaries are being crossed, while simultaneously pressure in all boundary processes is increasing, suggesting Earth is now well beyond safe operating limits for humanity (Richardson et al., 2023). The boundaries are connected, indicating that one boundary influences another and that one cannot be isolated, ignoring others. For example, degrading marine ecosystems reduces the capacity to absorb carbon dioxide which affects the climate boundary (Rockström et al., 2009).

Our greatest challenge is to avoid crossing planetary tipping points by understanding how we impact the fragile limits and leverage ways to reduce pressure with urgency – by becoming a sustainable enterprise.

More than environment

Environmental issues continue to monopolise the list of global severe risks reported by the World Economic Forum, whereby the health of the planet dominates concerns for environmental risk featuring extreme weather events, critical change to Earth systems, biodiversity loss and eco-system collapse, and natural resource shortages at the top of the severe list (World Economic Forum, 2024). But there is more to the story than environmental damage. Other global risks threaten to undermine planetary stability that organisations benefit from as they go about their business. Such risks include economical, societal and technological tensions. A Global Risk Perception study affirms societal-level uneasiness for livelihood crisis and mental health deterioration. Risks such as digital inequality and cybersecurity failure emerge as strong contenders. Economic tensions following on from the pandemic include rising inflation, increased debt and concerns for economic recovery (World Economic Forum, 2022). As such, it is important to appreciate the myriad of influencers on business, which is why moving beyond environmental focus to one of sustainability is necessary. Although there is a call for an updated version of the definition and a shift towards regenerative thinking, the 1987 United Nations Brundtland Commission defines sustainability as meeting the needs of the present without compromising the ability of future generations to meet their own needs (United Nations, n.d.).

Faced with the urgent responsibility to hand on to future generations fewer problems, both environmentally charged and social issues are clearly important under the banner of sustainability. Economist Kate Raworth builds on the work of Rockström and his colleagues, proposing a target space where humanity can survive and thrive – a sweet spot where we do not overshoot ecological tipping points or fall short on social foundations. In this safe but also just operating space, organizations should look holistically to their impact on planetary boundaries and social foundations as they identify areas of impact and influence (Raworth, 2022). This aligns well with the Sustainable Development Goals (United Nations, n.d.b) and the Paris Climate Change

Agreement (United Nations Climate Change, n.d.) providing us with a new frame through which to scrutinize value chain consequences on planetary boundaries and essentials for life.

Sustainable enterprises harmonize competitiveness, resilience and responsibility for planetary boundaries and social foundations, enjoying both profit and prosperity. Lean thinkers have a critical role to play and are obligated to build flourishing companies that simultaneously decouple growth from impact, doing well while doing good. The goal is leading lean transformations that advance competitiveness while reducing impact – because respect for humanity relies on it.

A positive outlook

With bad news laid bare, the situation may present as *doomism* (to be avoided) or strike a *denialism* nerve (to be overcome). The science published on the most severe global risks affirms there is still time to make a difference and that the problem is undeniable (Intergovernmental Panel on Climate Change, 2022). Humans are wonderfully innovative and will find ways to adapt to new living and working conditions. Our homes, organizations, cities, mobility and supply chains will reform, and this transition stimulates a number of benefits including: accelerated innovation; new angles for competitiveness; job creation; enriched values-driven careers; better ways to spend our days; and a compelling reason to treat fellow inhabitants and neighbours (people and nature) with respect and equality (Godin, 2022). Lean thinking is a noble response to shape a better world by helping companies see their way through the challenges, from incremental, to breakthrough to innovative changes shaping enterprises that outstrip the competition while treading lightly and morally on the planet. This commitment is rewarded with a solid business case for change that goes beyond economic measures.

The business case for a healthier planet

Humans are more dependent on the planet than the planet is on humans. Regardless of floods, drought, sea level rise, temperature rise and destabilized ecological and social systems, the planet carries on with or without us. It is humanity and the other inhabitants of the earth that are under threat. A palpable case for humanity to do better is in plain sight, but what is the business case for a healthier planet and how can thinking lean help? The rewards extend beyond economic benefit (Heathcote, 2023).

Basic stability

In a general sense *basic stability* refers to consistency and predictability with respect to people, machines, materials, supply and methods engaged in producing products or servicing customers. Such fundamentals lay a foundation for improved flow to customer buying rates. Basic stability also implies stable employment and access to the essentials for life. Viable, sustainable enterprises provide the means for employees and their families to buy food, shelter and education – satisfying some of humanity's basic needs. Organizations also hold the power to provide physical and psychological safety in the workplace. In the absence of job security, living standards and safety, employees cannot perform at their best and may disengage and productivity levels could suffer, thus affecting competitiveness.

Research indicates that highly engaged business units could realize as much as an 81 per cent difference in absenteeism; 14 per cent difference in productivity; 10 per cent difference in customer ratings; 18 per cent difference in sales; 23 per cent difference in profitability; and 43 per cent difference in employee turnover (Harter and Mann, 2017). Companies focused on profit-first may not have employees' best interests at heart, offering a poor value proposition to their people and surrounding communities, resulting in apathetic, disengaged employees.

Attract and retain customers

A sustainable enterprise is more innovative and entrepreneurial than the competition, pre-empting issues ahead of others. Customer interest in sustainably sourced, designed, produced and delivered goods that also meet quality, price and speed requirements is growing. Customers increasingly migrate from companies that do not meet their values, are unwilling to change or no longer solve their problems and it could cost between five and twenty-five times more to acquire a new customer than to retain an existing customer (Gallo, 2014). For example, Bain & Company indicate that a 5 per cent increase in customer retention in the financial services sector produces more than 25 per cent in profit (Reichheld, n.d.). The sustainable enterprise devises offerings customers are prepared to pay for, and customers reward companies with their loyalty and cash.

Attract and retain talent

Companies expect committed people, but people want companies they can also commit to – companies that care for the well-being and futures of employees and their families. Employees invest their time and skills and are fast becoming another investor to please (Esty and Winston, 2006) and with a six-month breakeven on hiring new employees, they are certainly worth holding on to (Mueller, 2022). With a shift in what employees need from their employers, organizations need to assess how attractive they are. Sustainable enterprises prioritizing sustainability and people development in the business model and strategy excel as employers of choice securing a healthy talent pool.

Lower cost of capital and tax breaks

Sustainable enterprises attract investor funds. Savvy investors and financial institutions are starting to favour organizations with sustainable business models giving preference to applicants that pollute less and deliver positive impact. Companies that do not prepare will see their businesses and valuations suffer and it will become difficult to attract investment (Fink, 2022). Sustainable enterprises are also recognized and rewarded through tax regimes, for instance, receiving tax breaks for investment in renewable energy (United Nations Environment Programme, 2012).

Risks revealed saves costs and reputation

Unmitigated risk left untended could ruin a business, reputation and career. It pays to identify risks the organization is exposed to. Assessing risk is a fiduciary duty and failing to address risks erodes reputation, attracts hefty fines and could result in jail time. Regulations and laws managing risk are also dynamic with amendments requiring companies to continuously improve. For instance: companies now forced to take responsibility for their historical pollution by paying for clear-ups years after the offence; market mechanisms neutralizing any competitive advantage that polluting brings by charging companies for their contribution to pollution; companies like electronics manufacturers forced to take responsibility for their products from cradle to grave prompting new designs and reverse logistics solutions; spikes in resource costs that alter cost structure thus eroding margins (Esty and Winston, 2006). These are very good reasons to keep a finger on the pulse of risk and to respond pro-actively.

Reduced operating costs

Sustainable enterprises benefit from spin-off cost benefits when everyone, every day solves problems that matter. Cutting wasted resources, shortening lead times, conserving energy, utilizing capacity efficiently and avoiding unnecessary investment, conserving materials, improving product yield and avoiding fines, all point to lower operating costs and improved bottom line performance. Developing problem solvers to take on these challenges and address challenges already on the horizon (such as ensuing greenhouse gas emission charges or carbon taxes) is a pathway to resilience in turbulent, uncertain times. Thinking lean and sustainably is a pro-active, risk mitigating, untapped goldmine awaiting exploration.

A licence to operate and grow

Stakeholders can deny a licence to operate. Customers, regulators, the media and society compel companies to take better care of people and nature, boycotting offenders that continue along the unsustainable path. For instance, a company may require permits for expansion but if business activities compromise biodiversity and land-use, they may encounter barriers, halting expansion. Companies that embrace stakeholder value are rewarded with leeway and cooperation (Esty and Winston, 2006). It is important for organizations to show willing by actively and visibly decoupling growth from impact, demonstrating their understanding of the organization's impact on planetary health and how well they take care of stakeholders while taking care of business.

To transform and extract benefits while supporting a healthier planet requires a sustainable enterprise business model – a well-balanced and financially viable model that is both nature-centric and human-centric (Heathcote, 2023). This is a model that protects natural capital through regenerative leadership and by learning from nature through examples of biomimicry (Losey, 2022). This is also a model that commits to people-first resting on a foundation of respect for people and continuous improvement (Toyota Global, 2020). Lean and sustainability thinking are a mutual symbiosis.

Delivering sustainable value through lean

Grounded by a sustainable enterprise business model, organizations move to rethink value in a more holistic sense, going beyond the boundaries of the organization and into the world of stakeholders. But, delivering on this value requires employees to be oriented towards a reasonable, yet challenging, summit. To accomplish reasonableness, leaders visit and connect closely with their operations – where the actual work is taking place – to understand the reality of the situation and to visibly offer their help. In this way, employees are supported to improve in the general direction of the challenge which has been conditioned by Gemba insights.

An evolving meaning of value

In 1996 Womack and Jones presented principles of lean to guide lean think-ing, starting with a focus on customer value (Womack and Jones, 1996). Understanding what the end customer truly values and is prepared to pay for is crucial so that value streams can be improved, allowing value-adding work to flow into the hands of internal and external customers, as they require it, without disruptions or avoidable problems. The principle is still relevant today but expanding on this thinking, organizations can reshape how value is defined by exploring the value to the customer, the organization (Jones, 2012), to humanity and the employee. What problem will be solved for the customer (good product, right price, right time, produced and delivered responsibly)? What results will bring value to the organization (delivering on values, purpose and profit)? What value will the organization bring humanity (protecting plan-etary boundaries and building social foundations)? What value proposition will the employee benefit from (aligning with employee values and purpose, yield job security and safety)? The customer's meaning of value is changing as they require new offerings to solve new problems – for instance, respon-sible offerings that still meet other performance requirements. Revisiting the meaning of value will help employees look to their value chains and value streams through a more holistic lens as they navigate learning opportunities.

Benefiting from an array of teachers

Learning hails from various sources in the quest to become a sustainable enterprise. The *sensei* will help you to look beyond what you currently know to solve problems differently and discover a deeper meaning (Ballé et al., 2019). The *Gemba*, a Japanese word meaning the workplace where the action happens (Ohno, 2013), is a source of learning for problems to be solved and a place to gather evidence informing better decision making. The *employee* holds a wealth of experience of the Gemba and its challenges, and its impact on people and customers. *Nature* teaches how systems work in harmony for the common good, for instance, nature's perfect circular economy where everything is reused or repurposed (World Economic Forum, 2020a) and waste becomes food for another. Nature also inspires new designs as we learn from biomimicry. Limiting learning to what *you* know limits the problems you find and the ideas you experiment with, and opening up to an array of teachers will access new horizons (Heathcote, 2023).

Hoshin and cycles of learning

Perhaps one of the greatest challenges for enterprises is to connect vision with strategy to what everyone is doing, every day. Learning from the real challenges at the Gemba, experienced by the real people and the real facts surrounding the situation, is important intelligence to feed into the strategy before deploying it. Ignoring the reality from the ground situation invariably produces an unreasonable strategic plan. For instance, if the vision is to cut emissions in half by 2030 and the challenge is to cut emissions by 20 per cent within three years, then walking the Gemba and gathering facts at the operation, supplier or the customer offers a realistic perspective of the situation. At the Gemba, we use our senses to see, smell, hear and feel – this could reveal poor lagging on steam pipes, fugitive emissions, lost heat, poor designs and pollution for example. Asking good questions and showing genuine curiosity for how things work uncovers truths, and the strategic task becomes more credible (Heathcote, 2023). A Gemba-informed strategy is then ready to share through the ranks providing a sense of direction to kaizen activities, providing employees with something realistic to aim for. Through nested cycles of learning (Plan Do Check Act) employees work through each opportunity or problem to be solved, following a scientific mindset and aligning each cycle to the business reason for change. The learning cycle is then shared and challenged through an A3 report.

Making planetary health connections

With a clear challenge in hand, it is possible to traipse the value chain in search of opportunities, examined through a sustainability lens. Depending on the business environment, looking up and down the value chain may reveal planetary impact areas and possible mitigation opportunities, for instance (Heathcote, 2023):

1. *Climate change*: Target greenhouse gas emissions, biodiversity loss and unnecessary consumption.
2. *Biodiversity loss and land conversion*: Improve use of existing capacity and regenerate fauna, flora, organisms.
3. *Energy*: Consume less, design products for lower energy use and switch to planet-friendly alternatives.

4. *Landfill*: Keep products and material in circulation, regenerate, dispose unavoidable responsibly.
5. *Air pollution*: Improve energy sources, reduce pollution at source and capture unavoidable pollution.
6. *Chemical pollution*: Eliminate toxins from product and process design and regenerate contaminated land.
7. *Ocean degradation*: Target greenhouse gas emission and eliminate ocean pollution.
8. *Freshwater withdrawals and contamination*: Consume less, harvest more and clean inhouse.
9. *Ozone layer depletion*: Deal with residual chlorofluorocarbons and improve alternatives for less impact.
10. *Deforestation*: Use less, keep materials in circulation and regenerate.
11. *Nitrogen and phosphorous loading*: Protect soil and waterways from excess fertilizers and human waste, and regenerate.

Coupled with a view to raise competitiveness, evaluate the value chain for areas to operate sustainably, regenerate and improve performance to customer needs. This requires a new model of thinking and operating.

A systems view of the value chain

Systems are all around: global systems, social systems, learning systems, healthcare systems and ecological systems to name a few. A system is a set of things working together as a complex whole to achieve something (Meadows, 2009). But, to appreciate systems we have to understand their interconnected parts, not only the independent parts (Brant, 2010). The product of their interactions is where it gets interesting. To appreciate some of the parts making up the whole and their interactions, we look closer to how we source, design, produce, deliver, return, digitally enable and support, some of which are explored below (Heathcote, 2023).

Sourcing

Companies are the company they keep. This includes sourcing from responsible partners that not only provide what is needed for a solution package (quality, cost, reliability, etc.), but also care about developing their own sustainability-conscious supply chains. Buyers can set up sourcing criteria to ensure fair labour practices, greenhouse gas emissions transparency and reduction, recyclability rates and water consumption per ton of product for instance on the supplier scorecards. The focus should be on collaboration and support rather than coercion. Guided by sustainable product design, sourcing also refers to finding sustainable alternatives and substitute inputs.

Design for sustainability

The earlier companies get the design right, the more cost-effective and lower the impact, since these characteristics are locked in early. Typically, 75 per cent of the cost of a product is committed by the end of the conceptual design phase (Sousa, 2008) and multiples of energy can be saved by designing products that use less energy – for example a kilowatt of energy saved at the consumption-end saves as much as ten times the energy needed at the production end (Lovins, 2013). Good products are designed for purpose, longevity, production, maintenance, low impact and regeneration. Tools such as Life Cycle Analysis and Quality Function Deployment are invaluable companions in the quest for sustainable designs.

Producing

Doing more with less means extracting the maximum output from the least effort and use of resources. Doing more with more is the antithesis of lean and leads to using natural resources unnecessarily and releasing emissions into the atmosphere. Value streams saddled with wastes spawn from inherent system flaws and poor assumptions and lead to a rise in carbon emissions and other environmental impacts. For example:

1. *Overproduction*: Making more product than is required by the customer, consuming resources, energy and capacity.
    i.   In its worst form, the unwanted product is sent to landfill.
2. *Inventory*: Holding excessive inventories requires housing and managing the inventory, requiring additional space and transport, loss of biodiversity and increased emissions.
3. *Defect*: Producing poor quality products consumes additional resources to repair or replace them, requiring additional energy, materials and resulting in increased emissions. Accomplishing better yields from inputs used results in less use of materials and energy.
4. *Waiting*: Machine downtime means excess capacity may be required to complete the work. Catching up on lost capacity by adding capacity uses more energy and potentially space.
    i.   New facilities may be built to compensate for inefficient use of existing capacity, increasing environmental impact. Waiting may continue to use energy while machines and equipment are idle.

5. *Transport*: Layouts, locations, loading and routes drive transport waste, unnecessary fuel usage and wear and tear. Optimizing reduces transport energy and associated emissions.
6. *Overprocessing*: Complexity in tasks or doing more work than is required consumes additional capacity and draws more energy.

Waste builds up even in sustainably designed products and processes, problems constantly emerge and performance regresses. As such, the continuous development of people to see waste, solve problems and satisfy customers while reducing impact is key, nurturing a kaizen spirit in people, who always look for better ways of delivering a new kind of value.

Delivering

Approximately 73 per cent of greenhouse gas emissions stems from energy with 16 per cent from transport (Ritchie, 2020), making how we deliver and using which modes, wrapped in which kind of packaging and at what environmental impact, significant areas of interest. Road transport contributes the most to greenhouse gas emissions followed by aviation, shipping then rail. Packaging choices also have a far-reaching impact on deforestation and the paper and pulp industry. Consciously building a system of delivery that performs beyond current state becomes a competitive advantage for the sustainable enterprise, for example:

1. Use reusable, returnable packaging designed to suit the package size.
2. Decarbonize road transport.
3. Select low impact shipping providers.
4. Select low impact air shipping for unavoidable shipments.
5. Optimize routes and use of carrying capacity.
6. Reduce distances between storage and delivery locations.
7. Share transport with partners or empty vehicle spaces en route.
8. Compare the use of alternative vehicles (electric) and fuels such as biofuels and hydrogen fuels.
9. Improve efficiencies such as tyre friction, aerodynamics, light-weight bodies and engine efficiency. (Chapman, 2022)

'Last mile' delivery is also emerging as a way to achieve more sustainable delivery. The last mile accounts for 53 per cent of the total cost of shipping and its 41 per cent contribution to total supply chain cost, and carbon emissions from urban delivery is set to jump by 32 per cent from a 36 per cent rise in delivery vehicles by 2030. This confirms the demand for lower-footprint urban delivery as urgent (World Economic Forum, 2020b).

Seeing the whole is important to taking a systems view, but even on a smaller scale this is useful. For example, a company is located in a water-stressed area and a very good suggestion materializes. The team sketch a closed-loop water system that recycles and cleans the water consumed, eliminating the need for freshwater withdrawals and saving money. The team implements the improvement, and upon studying the results, the change generates immediate benefits, but the energy costs to power the system climb. The team realize the unintended impact and design a renewable source with lower consumption, improving the overall system in both key metrics (energy and water consumption). Looking further than the individual parts, the net effect of the change is better understood, leading to a more holistic solution. Thinking in systems enables teams to see the net effect of their ideas.

Improvement for the better at every level

Looking up and down the value chain to identify possible impact areas is a good, system-level place to begin. But, showing people how to look closer at the granular, daily work to find ways to capitalize on those opportunities, is just as important. This requires sensitizing employees with an adequate dose of technical information, at all levels, on the topics of biodiversity, emissions, energy, water, materials, waste, land-use and transport – asking them to challenge the status quo and look for alternative ways to define, understand and improve upon the current state. As employees learn to see the opportunities through a sustainability lens so they will need support and encouragement to discern abnormal from normal, go to source and use their skills to grasp the situation, get to the heart of the problem and derive possible countermeasures (Heathcote, 2023). Toyota benefited from more than 100 million creative ideas implemented through employee suggestion schemes (Smalley, 2018); granted they were not all environmentally driven ideas, but green thinking certainly features in Toyota's kaizen. Imagine the impact of everyone, every day, solving problems that matter, at every level – a remarkable competitive advantage.

Looking ahead

Supported by government and the Council for Scientific and Industrial Research, the author was a privileged member of the pioneering team to introduce lean thinking to South African automotive supplier networks, more than two decades ago. In retrospect, more stories of accomplishments than academic theories were needed at the time, garnering practical insights for practical people to learn from and try. The concept of sustainability is not new, and companies such as Toyota have engaged in responsible operations for decades, but it is new to many. It is pioneering work to merge lean and sustainable thinking forces in a significant way, demonstrating clear results from a refocused learning scaffold.

Translating ideals for zero emissions and sustainable supply chains can be overwhelming and difficult to distil into what to do at an everyday level. Moving away from buzzwords and high-level pipe dreams, to practical, digestible things people can learn and do is crucial to building confidence in companies to take the next step. As such, future research should be action-learning oriented, capturing successful cases (and not-so-successful), identifying system interrelationships relevant to business, and confirming connections between sustainable strategies and everyday action. There is also an opportunity to showcase sustainable enterprise business models that demonstrate a viable, human-centric and nature-centric business model, which raises competitiveness by engaging everyone to help. Such companies exist or are in the making, and sharing their stories illustrates what is possible and offers hope.

References

Ballé, M., Chartier, N., Coignet, P., Olivencia, S., Powell, D., and Reke, E. (2019). *The Lean Sensei: Go See Challenge*. Boston: Lean Enterprise Institute.

Brant, S. (2010). *If Russ Ackoff had given a TED Talk* (online video). https:// www .youtube.com/watch?v=OqEeIG8aPPk (accessed 28 December 2022).

Chapman, K. (2022). *Racing Green: How Motorsport Science Can Save The World*. London: Bloomsbury Publishing.

Esty, D. C. and Winston, W. S. (2006). *Green to Gold: How Smart Companies Use Environmental Strategy to Innovate, Create Value, and Build Competitive Advantage*. Hoboken, NJ: John Wiley & Sons.

Fink, L. (2022). *The Power of Capitalism*. Blackrock. https:// www .blackrock .com/ corporate/investor-relations/larry-fink-ceo-letter (accessed 27 December 2022).

Gallo, A. (2014). The value of keeping the right customers. *Harvard Business Review*, 29 October. https:// hbr .org/ 2014/ 10/ the -value -of -keeping -the -right -customers (accessed 29 December 2022).

Godin, S. (2022). *The Carbon Almanac: It's Not Too Late*. Dublin: Penguin Random House.

Harter, H. and Mann, A. (2017). *The Right Culture: Not Just About Employee Satisfaction*. https:// www .gallup .com/ workplace/ 236366/ right -culture -not -employee-satisfaction.aspx (accessed 28 December 2022).

Heathcote, R. (2023) Becoming a sustainable enterprise: how thinking lean improves competitiveness, resilience and the world. Buckingham. H&A.

Intergovernmental Panel on Climate Change (2022). The evidence is clear: The time for action is now. We can halve emissions by 2030. IPCC. https://www.ipcc.ch/2022/04/04/ipcc-ar6-wgiii-pressrelease/ (accessed 28 December 2022).

Jones, D. T. (2012). Keynote Address: Lean in 10 slides. Lean Summit France, 27 March, Lyon. Lean Enterprise Academy. https://www.youtube.com/watch?v=NLeQdRDf5D8 (accessed 27 December 2022).

Losey, K. (2022). *6 Innovations Shaped by the Most Powerful Force on Earth*. Biomimicry Institute. https://biomimicry.org/6-innovations-shaped-by-the-most-powerful-force-on-earth/ (accessed 27 December 2022).

Lovins, A. B. (2013). *Reinventing Fire: Bold Business Solutions for the New Energy Era*. White River Junction, VT: Chelsea Green Publishing.

Meadows, D. H. (2009). *Thinking in Systems: A Primer*. White River Junction, VT: Chelsea Green Publishing.

Mueller, A. (2022). The cost of hiring a new employee. *Investopedia*. https://www.investopedia.com/financial-edge/0711/the-cost-of-hiring-a-new-employee.aspx (accessed 19 December 2022).

Ohno, T. (2013). *Taiichi Ohno's Workplace Management, Special 100th Birthday Edition*. New York: McGraw-Hill.

Raworth, K. (2022). *Doughnut Economics: Seven Ways to Thinking Like a 21st-Century Economist*. Dublin: Penguin Random House.

Reichheld, F. (n.d.). *Prescription for Cutting Costs*. Bain & Company. https://media.bain.com/Images/BB_Prescription_cutting_costs.pdf (accessed 29 December 2022).

Richardson, K. et al. (2023) Earth beyond six of nine planetary boundaries, *Science Advances*, 9(37). Available at: https://www.science.org/doi/10.1126/sciadv.adh2458 (accessed 25 January 2024).

Ritchie, H. (2020). Sector by sector: Where do global greenhouse gas emissions come from? *Our World in Data*. https://ourworldindata.org/ghg-emissions-by-sector (accessed 28 December 2022).

Rockström, J. et al. (2009). A safe operating space for humanity. *Nature*, 461. https://www.nature.com/articles/461472a.pdf (accessed 27 December 2022).

Sajjad, P. (2019). *Grounding Corporate Strategy in Planet Health*. School of Anthropology & Museum Ethnography, University of Oxford. https://www.planetaryhealth.ox.ac.uk/wp-content/uploads/sites/7/2019/10/Corporate-Strategy-and-Planetary-Health-for-web-1.pdf (accessed 29 December 2022).

Smalley, A. (2018). *Four Types of Problems: From Reactive Troubleshooting to Creative Innovation*. Cambridge, MA: Lean Enterprise Institute.

Sousa, I. (2008). Part 1: The genesis of sustainable minds: The conception of 'learning surrogate LCA'. *Sustainable Minds*. http://www.sustainableminds.com/industry-blog/part-1-genesis-sustainable-minds-conception-learning-surrogate-lca (accessed 28 December 2022).

Thunberg, G. (2022). *The Climate Book*. Dublin: Penguin Random House.

Toyota Global (2020). *Toyota Way 2020*. https://global.toyota/en/company/vision-and-philosophy/toyotaway_code-of-conduct/?padid=ag478_from_header_menu (accessed 27 December 2022).

Toyota Motor Corporation (1998). *The Toyota Production System*. Public Affairs Division and Operations Management Consulting Division.

Tzu, S. (1988). *The Art of War*. Boston: Shambhala Publications.

United Nations (n.d.a). *Sustainability*. https://www.un.org/en/academic-impact/sustainability (accessed 26 December 2022).

United Nations (n.d.b). *The 17 Goals*. https://sdgs.un.org/goals (accessed 27 December 2022).

United Nations Climate Change (n.d.). *The Paris Agreement: What is the Paris Agreement?* https://unfccc.int/process-and-meetings/the-paris-agreement/the-paris-agreement (accessed 29 December 2022).

United Nations Environment Programme (2012). *The Business Case for the Green Economy: Sustainable Return on Investment*. https://wedocs.unep.org (accessed 19 December 2022).

Womack, J. P. and Jones, D. T. (1996). *Lean Thinking: Banish Waste and Create Wealth in Your Corporation*. New York: Simon & Schuster.

World Economic Forum (2020a). *4 Lessons from Nature to Build a Circular Economy*. https://www.weforum.org/agenda/2020/11/4-lessons-from-nature-to-build-a-circular-economy/ (accessed 28 December 2022).

World Economic Forum (2020b). *The Future of the Last-Mile Ecosystem*. https://www3.weforum.org/docs/WEF_Future_of_the_last_mile_ecosystem.pdf (accessed 28 December 2022).

World Economic Forum (2022). *Global Risks Report 2022*. https://www3.weforum.org/docs/WEF_The_Global_Risks_Report_2022.pdf (accessed 26 December 2022).

World Economic Forum (2024) Global Risks Report 2024. WEF. Available at: https://www3.weforum.org/docs/WEF_The_Global_Risks_Report_2024.pdf (accessed 25 January 2024).

World Wildlife Fund (n.d.). *Our Planet: Our Business*. https://www.wwf.org.uk/our-planet-our-business (accessed 27 December 2022).

6 The people value stream: an extension to lean

Peter Hines and Florian Magnani[1]

Introduction

Lean, the managerial system exemplified by the Toyota Production System (TPS), has spread across organisations since the 1980s. Compared to mass production systems, lean systems ultimately transform the work design, the way employees behave within their work environment and the interactions between employees and managers. Despite significant improvements in lean research, most attempts to adopt lean underestimate the human dimension, as companies focus on implementing the technical elements, without having a clear idea of the potential gains from a human perspective (Netland, 2013).

While lean and TPS have been studied by researchers as innovative operations and organisation management concepts, the second part of Toyota's motto – "We do not just build *cars, we build people*" – has not been fully taken into consideration (Koenigsaecker, 2012). The human dimension of lean has received surprisingly limited attention until recently (Fenner et al., 2023; Koemtzi et al., 2023). The explanation comes from Toyota itself: the most important challenge of lean adoption is the apprehension of the sociotechnical system. Lean calls for changes in human resource management (Olivella et al., 2008) that affect the role of employees (de Treville and Antonakis, 2006), the development of their competencies (MacDuffie, 1995), their relationship to work (de Menezes et al., 2010), and their ability to solve problems and to challenge existing practices (Saito et al., 2011). Research, mainly in the last decade, shows that lean can have a significant impact on working conditions with human resource practices regarding employee development playing a key role in moderating the outcomes of lean adoption (Magnani et al., 2019).

---

[1] This chapter is based on three of our previous papers: Magnani et al. (2019), Hines (2022) and Hines et al. (2022). We would like to acknowledge the contribution in these of Valentina Carbone, Valérie Moatti, Chris Butterworth, Caroline Greenlee, Cheryl Jekiel and Darrin Taylor.

Fujio Cho, then president of Toyota, introduced "The Toyota Way", the first attempt to make the human dimension of TPS explicit as a new set of values that guide behaviours regarding employee competencies' development. "Making things" (Monozukuri) was the nature of the industry, but the Toyota Way added the "educating people" dimension (Hitozukuri), promoting the ongoing development of skills and abilities in an environment of mutual trust (Saito et al., 2011; Ballé et al., 2019a, 2019b). The Hitozukuri dimension, also known as "Respect for People" (Sugimori et al., 1977), is reflected in human mechanisms and benefits the organisation by providing employees with the opportunity to contribute and achieve self-realisation while maximising their performance (Emiliani and Stec, 2005). The "Respect for People" dimension presented in the Toyota Way demonstrates one of the prevalent convictions that Toyota cultivates: TPS was first and foremost a human-based system in which people were engaged in the continuous improvement of organisational processes and in which people's needs were both understood and respected (Dahlgaard and Dahlgaard-Park, 2006).

Hitozukuri is engrained in the process of educating and raising the competence of every employee (Saito et al., 2011), but also in the social mechanisms that give employees the opportunity to develop competencies through solving problems in an atmosphere of mutual trust (Ballé et al., 2019a, 2019b). Thus methods like quality control circles at Toyota are primarily aimed at developing people with their improvement results of secondary importance. By empowering employees, they naturally deepen their practice and learn on their own to perform them more effectively. Indeed, Cho, in the early drafting of the Toyota Way presented "respect for people" as a foundation to "continuous improvement" rather than presenting it in parallel (Jeff Liker, personal comms, 2022). Hence, Toyota demonstrated that the just-in-time system and quality management system (Basu and Miroshnik, 1999) were built upon and deeply rooted in "respect for people" (Liker and Hoseus, 2010). Even though the human dimension described in the Toyota Way appears to be explicitly related to its technical dimension, a comprehensive characterisation of the human dimension of TPS remains absent from the literature.

In the last decade researchers have highlighted that lean primarily focuses on employees, at least in the TPS (Jayamaha et al., 2014). Specifically, these new studies consider the human dimension as undoubtedly one of the most influential parameters in the successful adoption of lean by an organisation (Bortolotti et al., 2015). Other recent studies have reinforced the understanding of lean as a sociotechnical system (Soliman et al., 2018), which consequently opened the door to discussions about the human (soft) dimension (Preece and Jones, 2010; Taylor et al., 2013) and its interactions with the technical (hard) dimension.

As a result, there has been a shift from seeing lean as purely a process-oriented strategy to lean as a people-oriented strategy (Jayamaha et al., 2014; Marodin and Saurin, 2013).

However, a number of key issues remain, including: the debate around whether lean is positive for employees (Bouville and Alis, 2014; Koemtzi et al., 2023), theoretical considerations associated with the human dimension (Magnani et al., 2019; Taylor et al., 2013) and the fact that the human dimension of lean has rarely been put into practice by managers (Emiliani, 2003; Jekiel, 2020). In this chapter, we will seek to contribute to these areas.

In the following section, we will first show how human resources are depicted in the lean research literature. The next section will present the People Value Stream as a continuous improvement process to better understand the employee experience in a lean organisation, and we will discuss how it triggers self-development in employees. We will conclude by offering research perspectives to continue improving the understanding of the human dimension's role in a lean organisation.

Human resources in lean management literature

Some researchers have attempted to characterise the elements of human resource (HR) management specific to lean. Sugimori et al. (1977) were the first to highlight the importance of the human dimension of TPS. Focusing above all on the individual level, they show the impact of the system on employees' role in identifying and reducing non-value-added, calling on their abilities. Dankbaar (1997) adds that this system relies on specific competencies held by the employees involved in continuous improvement activities, which has the effect of transforming their problem-solving behaviours. A work transformation also seems to be taking place with employees who see their responsibility increase (Seppälä and Klemola, 2004).

Human resources department role

In support of this work transformation, managerial and human resource practices (Shah and Ward, 2003) evolve into a management system that involves all members of the organisation and encourages a culture of accepting problems as learning opportunities (Emiliani, 2003). Shah and Ward (2003) have specified HR practices that are put in place during adoption, such as job rotation, job design and extension, cross-training programmes, and problem-solving groups. They also include the creation of flexible, cross-functional teams and the autonomous organisation of these teams. Shah and Ward (2007) end up summarising all of these HR practices as the mechanism for engaging employees impacted by adoption.

On the other hand, Moyano-Fuentes and Sacristán-Díaz (2012) clarified the specific aspects of work organisation and its evolution during the lean adoption: the degree of accountability of HR, the influence on the work organisation, and the effects on human resources management. Previous studies have suggested that appropriate HR practices moderate the possible negative outcomes of lean adoption (Martínez-Jurado et al., 2013) while maintaining a cooperative and committed workforce (Bonavia and Marin-Garcia, 2011). Researchers add that when HR professionals do not participate in the adoption, employees and managers are more reluctant to adopt fully lean practices (Thirkell and Ashman, 2014). The HR department frames the learning mechanisms of all these actors (Ballé et al., 2019a, 2019b) to bring forth creative thinking that enables the organisation to respond to contemporary issues.

Management role

Recently, an interest has emerged in research on these human variables and their influence on the process of creating this learning system, initially considering the impacts on the individual, then expanding to incentive HR practices and the supporting HR architecture (Koemtzi et al., 2023). Researchers observed a significant increase in lean adoption levels when HR practices supported the lean implementation initiative through the managerial role (Camuffo et al., 2017). A change in the interactions between employees and managers is regularly mentioned, particularly around the role of managers who ensure that an environment conducive to employee development is in place. Direct managers empower employees and provide them with developmental activities and new forms of recognition (Marin-Garcia and Bonavia, 2015). This is illustrated through mentoring/coaching activities at the individual level, interpersonal communication, and group activities at the team level, as well as structured strategical problem-solving guidelines (Hoshin Kanri) at the organisational level (Tortorella et al., 2015). These interactions also moderate employee outcomes and facilitate the alignment of individual and organisational lean adoption.

To summarise, the human resources presented in the lean literature can be summed up as follows: (1) the HR department, throughout HR practices, has an important role to create a protective atmosphere and mutual trust culture in the organisation; (2) this mutual trust is exemplified by the managers' role and will increase employees buying-in the lean initiative. Thus, a lean environment reinforced by HR practices and managerial support can assist employees in harnessing their intellect and becoming creative system thinkers.

The people value stream

Lean is characterised by a system fostering individual and collective learning that is the result of organisational directives, including those from human resources and managers (Ballé and Régnier, 2007). This observation highlights different employees' roles in lean adoption and therefore the need to create a new employee experience. This experience gives rise to the People Value Stream, which, through employee development, serves as a moderating element in lean adoption, reinforcing appropriate working conditions and creating new interactions. This development requires a change in the role of both human resources management and management.

In this section, we will outline the conceptual framework of the People Value Stream (Hines, 2022). Based on our observation over the last 30 years of how people are managed, we develop a Current State Value Stream Map (Hines and Rich, 1997; Rother and Shook, 1998) of how the lean thinker might view the employee journey (Figure 6.1). What we can see are a number of typical features. There is little connection between HR (the equivalent of production control) and the customer (the internal line manager here). Hence, the people lifecycle is determined to a large degree by the optimisation of the classic HR sub-functions such as recruitment, compensation, and training and development (Liker and Hoseus, 2010).

The result of this is that the journey of the employee is far from optimised as they are often recruited on a different basis from how they are inducted, with each of the other elements of the HR team doing their best within their particular silo (Sparrow and Otaye-Ebede, 2014). However, from the point of view of the employees, they feel that they are being continually pushed around without anyone looking after their journey.

Consequently, the employee journey is far from optimised and invariably leads to insecurity and frustration in the employee, the HR team and the line managers (Camuffo et al., 2017). This frustration is built upon the fact that there is huge wasted human potential (the so-called "eighth lean waste" as per Bicheno and Holweg, 2009), lower than potential employee value-added ratios, and high staff turnover rates. In this current state caricature (Figure 6.1), we show an employee value-adding ratio of 45 per cent with a staff retention span of 4 years. This 45 per cent (or 1.8 years over 4 years) accords with the typical personal value-adding ratio found in research carried out by Hines et al. (2002). This previous research suggests that the other 40 per cent of employees' time is necessary non-value-adding with the remaining 15 per cent waste. Such a low value-adding ratio and staff high turnover further inhibits employee development and productivity by shortening the learning curve effects. It also places substantial financial burdens on the organisation with the cost of employing a new person often being well over one year's salary as the full cost of recruitment is usually hugely underestimated by most organisations (James, 2018). Taken all together, this is a far from satisfactory position all-round.

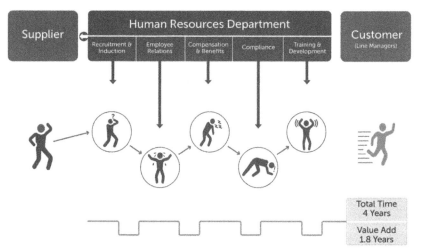

Source: Hines (2022).

Figure 6.1   The current state: how the lean thinker might see the employee lifecycle

In Figure 6.2, we illustrate a future state caricature of the People Value Stream. Here the changes are analogous to the changes in the future state of the traditional (Product) Value Stream Map (Rother and Shook, 1998). There is a direct pull from the line manager in terms of their needs for appropriate competencies, behaviours, engagement, people numbers and employee wellness. The role of HR is transformed into a set of cross-intra-functional processes such as setting behavioural norms and coaching of line managers in the new competencies they require. The figure also illustrates seven personal flows that the individual will focus on during their career including their learning and the development flow, and the mental and physical well-being flow. The degree to which each of these flows is important and how fast the employee needs to develop in each will vary from employee to employee based on their individual aspirations and needs for growth and development. As in the traditional (Product) Value Stream, these flows are achieved in a more focused, faster and efficient way. Hence, the employees develop faster, are more engaged and hence stay longer and have higher value-adding ratios. In the case of the People Value Stream, the primary focus is on the growth and development of the employee (Kaur Paposa et al., 2023).

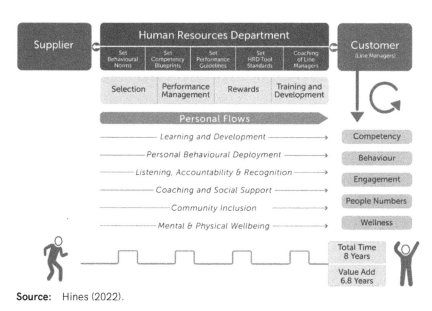

Source: Hines (2022).

Figure 6.2   The future state: the people value stream

Employee experience

The idea of the employee experience is at the heart of the People Value Stream concept. Here we are seeking to make life better for the employee so that they can be more motivated and engaged and consequently contribute more including their discretionary effort. The first to give insights about the People Value Stream of lean and its inherent employee experience were Liker and Hoseus (2008). They illustrated the employee experience to go from a capable employee to a committed employee. Even if this first attempt was pictured as a sequential stream, we argue that in some organisations, it can be more complex and simultaneous. We found that selection, performance management, rewards and training and development need to be addressed in a concurrent manner to improve the engagement rate.

When looking further into the employees' view of what engages them, Qualtrics (2020) found that it was more useful to link engagement with what the employee wants rather than what the organisation wants. A summary of these findings is shown in Figure 6.3. These factors revolve around learning, manager support, linking with people's work and company objectives, trust and belief in managers, and career development. All of these are very personal to the individual concerned and their subjective experience of work.

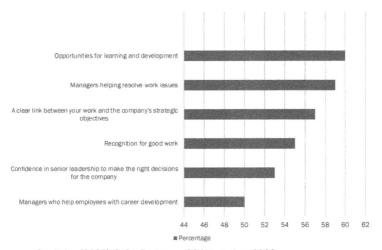

Source: Qualtrics (2020) © SA Partners, 28 November 2023.

Figure 6.3   What drives employee engagement according to employees

As a result, in the People Value Stream Organisation, we believe there should be a major focus on the employee experience and the psychology driving it. This of course is personal, governed by expectations, and viewed through their perception of the workplace. We might liken this to an attempt to move from a parent–child relationship to an adult–adult relationship (Berne, 1957). The ensuing problem is that both the manager and employee need to move to an adult ego from the parent and child egos respectively. This is hard. For the manager, this requires a move from judgemental or critical words, impatient body-language and expressions, finger-pointing, and patronising language and gestures to leading by asking questions and being attentive and non-threatening (Eyre, 2021). In essence it means a move to an upside-down organisation with autonomy lying at the individuals' level with support provided by leaders (Figure 6.4).

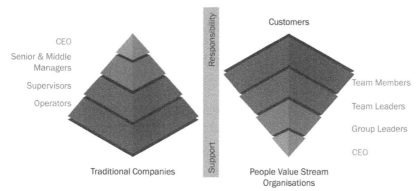

Source: Modified from Hines and Butterworth (2019) © SA Partners, 28 November 2023.

Figure 6.4   Turning lean upside down

Perhaps even more problematic is that the employee needs to shift to an adult ego and move away from rolling eyes, shrugging shoulders, exaggerated language, and responses such as "whatever … worst day of my life" and an overly "I" focus (Davidson and Mountain, 2021). This requires self-reliance, confidence, belief, and a clear purpose. Although this might be the case from time to time, rarely have organisations fully created the environment for this to flourish in transformational leadership. More problematic still is that we need the change to occur in *both* the manager and the employee.

This desired adult–adult relationship is only likely to occur under an even more enlightened style of leadership such as true Servant Leadership or Agile Leadership (Dank and Hellström, 2021). Servant leadership was first articulated by Robert Greenleaf in 1977 (Greenleaf, 2002). He asserted that a leader's primary passion, motivation, and role is to serve and meet the needs of others. Servant leadership is viewed as benefiting the employee as well as the organisation. For the employee, it improves well-being, satisfaction and work engagement. It also benefits the organisation by enhancing employee task performance, their organisational citizenship and their innovative work behaviour (Solaimani et al., 2019).

Self-development and growth

The essence of the People Value Stream approach is the self-development and growth of the individual with the support of leadership and the people and culture team (Kaur Paposa et al., 2023). This journey is personal, and needs to be defined by the individual so that they can flow along their own career journey. Hence, there needs to be a plan for every person. This self-development is achieved through the personal flows presented in Figure 6.2. For each of the personal flows, the starting point for this is creating a people version of the established PDCA (Plan-Do-Check-Act) thinking-based process improvement cycle termed the "self-development & growth cycle" (Hines et al., 2022). This is a type of self-reliant management system.

There are four elements of the feeling-based cycle: Meaning (~Plan), Flow (~Do), Reflect (~Check), and Act (Figure 6.5). This second cycle is necessary as humans are both thinking and feeling beings. Our brains are organised into a hierarchy wherein we process through the most primitive parts of our brain first, before getting to the smarter parts. Hence, we process in the limbic part of our brain that governs our feelings and emotions before we process in the cortex or thinking part of our brain (Perry and Winfrey, 2021). So in fact we might argue that the self-development & growth cycle should precede the PDCA cycle because if we do not successfully pass through the limbic part of the brain, our logical thinking ability will be severely limited and our functioning IQ reduced by around 20 per cent (Perry and Winfrey, 2021).

This self-development & growth cycle is based on the feelings of the individual and can be undertaken at a series of timescales from daily right up to a whole career. It equates closely to Saito's view of hitozukuri: "a continuous process that is more than just following education. It is a lifelong process that shows the ingredients of a personal maturation and the maturation of ones [sic] craftsmanship" (Saito, 2020).

Meaning

The first element is meaning, which is in effect the equivalent of the behavioural and strategy deployment within a lean organisation, but here taken to the individual level (Hines and Butterworth, 2019) with influences both from within themselves as well as the wider team they work within (Carraro et al., 2022). Creating meaning for the work performed by employees is the first step in increasing their self-reliance, ensuring an improved employee experience and achieving greater happiness (Rosso et al., 2010). It serves

Source: © SA Partners, 28 November 2023.

Figure 6.5   The self-development and growth cycle

two psychological needs: competence and connection (May et al., 2004). As a result, employees take more interest in their job, thus positively impacting their engagement. We suggest that meaning for the individual is based on two parts: aligning the purpose of the organisation with that of the employees, and taking into account individual beliefs and aligning them with the values of the organisation. Here we take individual purpose to be what the individual wishes to achieve both in the short term and over their lifetime. This is the set of aspirations that motivates our activities (Ivtzan et al., 2016). We take personal beliefs to be what people hold dear such as a religious or environmental belief and link this with things that they think are possible to achieve for themselves. There is a need to overcome the quite widespread imposter syndrome whereby individuals feel that they are not worthy or were only lucky in the past and are not up to a particular role (Hunt, 2020).

The meaningfulness of work was first widely discussed by Hackman and Oldham (1976) in their Job Characteristics Model where jobs designed for employees were likely to be meaningful (and hence contribute to internal motivation) if they had high skill variety, task identity, and task significance. However, here we are more concerned with jobs designed by employees or those that they have a significant input in shaping (Thoren, 2020). We also see meaning as forward looking, changeable, and dynamic (Wrzesniewski and Dutton, 2001), and that the individual needs to have confidence that their individual purpose is possible to be achieved.

Flow

Within flow, we are trying to achieve high levels of competence and connection to the organisation that will lead to increased motivation. The concept of flow is well-established within the lean community and has been widely advocated and applied within the flow of product and services (Rother and Harris, 2001). Indeed, to take Taiichi Ohno's words somewhat out of context, we will "let the flow manage the processes, and not let management manage the flow" (Miller, 2017). However, we have taken the principle of flow more widely aligned with developments in positive psychology by Csikszentmihalyi (1990). According to Csikszentmihalyi, flow is a state of mind in which a person becomes fully immersed in an activity and is using their skills to the maximum. In essence, we are looking to create a position where all employees can attain all levels of Maslow's Hierarchy, including physiological needs, safety, love and belonging, esteem, and self-actualisation (Maslow, 1954).

Within the context of our conceptual framework, we will now use the term "flow" in extending its traditional lean view which is "the progressive achievement of tasks along the value stream so that a product proceeds from design to launch, order to delivery, and raw material into the hands of the customer with no stoppages, scrap, or backflows" (Womack and Jones, 1996, p. 306). In our sense, we are applying this thinking to people's careers and hence we modify the definition of flow to "the progressive achievement of challenges throughout their career so that every individual person proceeds from recruitment to post-retirement by maximising their potential and creating value to their team and the organisation they work within". We are therefore seeking to create the type of continuous flow (Rother and Harris, 2001) and flow efficiency (Modig and Åhlström, 2012) that is called for in the Product Value Stream, but here applying it to the People Value Stream.

In common with the traditional lean concept of value stream(ing), we identify a series of value stream flows that the individual will need to progress along during their career (Hines, 2022). These are learning and development, personal behavioural deployment, listening, accountability and recognition, coaching and social support, community inclusion, mental and physical well-being. As Ryan (1995, pp. 411–412) states: "domains and situations in which individuals find their basic psychological needs supported will be those in which integrated processes will be most evident, and in which persons will tend to experience the greatest well-being and satisfaction". The individual will require considerable support from team peers, their team leader, and senior leaders. Their role and behaviours will need to be developed considerably from the classic lean organisation. This will require changes to the language used, for instance, terms like "people and culture" rather than "human resource management". The People and Culture team will also have an important and quite different role to play.

To do this requires a "plan for every person" so as to maximise the employee experience throughout the flow. However, in contrast to traditional organisations, this plan is, as much as possible, developed by the individual themselves. Of course, complete autonomy is very rare, and the level of autonomy will depend on the role and the organisational setting. An important approach in this area is the concept of job crafting which moves on from the historical job design by management (Hackman and Oldham, 1976) to job design (largely) by the individual (Wrzesniewski and Dutton, 2001). Job crafting "involves redefining your job to incorporate your motives, strengths, and passions. The exercise prompts you to visualise the job, map its elements, and recognise them to better suit you" (Wrzesniewski et al., 2010, p. 1). However, it is our belief that it is necessary to do more than just craft the job itself, which is a key part of our first flow, but also the other flows that we illustrate above (Figure 6.2) in order to achieve the greatest possible motivation. We might consider that, apart from the first flow, the others are primarily outside the job and so these might be termed "extra job crafting" or perhaps "flow crafting". Hence, leaders should pay attention to the needs of employees both within their working hours but critically also in the time at work before work starts, during breaks and after-work time. It is in these, often short but valuable and informal times that many employees gain the most satisfaction and connection and hence motivation.

Reflect

As we noted above, humans have the equivalent of two minds: one that thinks and the other that feels (Goleman, 1997). The first of these is often the only one considered in a lean environment, which, at least in the Western world, is often dominated by male, middle-aged white men who often have an engineering or operations management background. The Deming Cycle is often very appealing here as it is simple, logical, and effective. However, for the other feeling mind, this type of classic lean approach makes little sense as it is hard, impersonal, stressful, and often uncaring. According to Goleman, the second, feeling mind contributes 80 per cent of success in life through our emotional intelligence (EI). He identifies five key areas of EI: self-awareness, managing emotions, self-motivation, empathy, and handling relationships. The emotional mind is impulsive and powerful, and the two usually work in parallel; however, when under stress, the emotional mind can dominate the rational mind.

He considers that skills like self-awareness and self-motivation are instilled (or destroyed) in childhood, a point further developed by Marc Brackett (2019). In our context, we could also apply this to the workplace. In order to become good at feeling, Brackett proposes that we should work on recognising, understanding, labelling, and expressing emotions, which will then help in regulating emotions and developing ourselves.

We therefore propose that individuals reflect and internalise within the self-development and growth cycle in order to feel what they have done during the flow by reflecting on their experience. This is because there are great opportunities for growth, with growing evidence that the brain is "livewired" and not like a computer but more like an electric, living fabric that is constantly reweaving itself (Eagleman, 2021). This reflection is done in as positive a way as possible, and likely shared with other employees and leaders, although we suggest only if the employee wishes to do so.

As Goleman (1997) states, optimism is an emotional attitude that boosts performance in the business world. Hence here, we follow the 4-to-1 principle of Ogden Lindsley where, for every corrective reflection (negative psychology), there should be four optimistic achievement reflections (positive psychology). This is based on his educational research that found when teachers praised children more than they criticised them, the children achieved far greater performance. The exact optimum he found was 3.57:1 (Lindsley, 1990). For us, this is about self-appreciation: "even seek 4-to-1 when talking to yourself! High performers have positive thoughts about themselves and do not indulge in negative self-talk or self-pity" (Miller, 2011, p. 184).

We are therefore suggesting that the reflection should primarily be on what has been achieved. However, like Lindsley, we see a small amount of corrective (or opportunity) focus is necessary for the development and growth of the individual. This refection might take a number of forms. The first might be done daily with the self-identification of the equivalent of improvement suggestions and secondly it might be done weekly or monthly against major self-developed growth targets, the equivalent of A3 reviews. These "Tier Zero" reviews are the core of this reflection activity (Hines et al., 2022).

Act

The last of our four elements, as in the Deming Cycle, is act. For us there are two parts to this. The first is an update of what we might do as an individual, or a reset of our meaning or flows based on our reflection. This update could, for instance, include trying more of an activity where we have achieved something, or doing less or stopping if that has led to a negative experience and calls for a correction, or, more positively, an opportunity (Collins, 2001). This might mean that we need to undertake some job crafting, or extra job crafting, within our flows, or simply internalise what we have done well or what we need to let go of (Dweck, 2017).

What it is likely to require, certainly for any major opportunity, is support from others, whether they be peers, team leaders, senior management, and/or people and culture professionals. Hence, we are suggesting, as in the Product Value Stream, that we generate a pull within the People Value Stream (Roth and DiBella, 2015). Hence, the starting point for annual reviews and periodic check-ins, and even discussions during Gemba walks is as much about the needs of the individual as it is the needs of the organisation. Consequently, the support and coaching provided to the employee are significantly pulled by the employee needs. In general, we are looking for some stretch in this revision (Csikszentmihalyi, 1990) by applying the eustress principle wherein the target is just out of reach but with support can be achieved without overwhelming the individual (Frink and Ferris, 1998). As a result, the individual is supported and encouraged to stretch to achieve their potential.

This will allow the individual to stay in control (autonomy) and pull from someone they trust (connection) and feel will be able to help (belief). This type of pull, or Voice of the Employee (VOE), is, of course, at the heart of what servant leadership should really be about and should set the agenda for much of the Leader Standard Work (LSW). As Nancy Kline (2015) contends, the quality of everything we do depends on the quality of the thinking we do first, here based on the VOE. As a result, this is an extension from the advanced lean concept of each team developing the agenda for the LSW of the above team (Mann, 2009). This will then further increase the meaning and openness of individuals to the work of their leaders in such areas as Gemba walks and kata coaching.

Conclusions and future research

This chapter demonstrates that the human dimension of lean, i.e. "respect for the person", is the result of organisational injunctions, including those coming from human resources management and the sum of the actors' understanding and their behaviours. This human dimension encompasses three interdependent elements: interactions between actors through mutual trust, the development of individual and collective skills, and behaviours that generate organisational learning. The human dimension integrates and balances the interests of each stakeholder in order to moderate the relationships between actors during adoption. We postulate that the technical system is no longer sufficient to explain the adoption process. Based on the aspirational situations generated by the inclusion of the human dimension, we postulate that the positive evolution of the human dimension would allow us to understand the changes in positive behaviours towards adoption. These elements of the human dimension represent the interpretive variables of adoption. The inclusion of the elements of the human dimension also leads to the protection of the sociotechnical system from potential drifts that could lead to its degeneration.

We have outlined above a major rethinking of lean and how organisations might move to a People Value Stream approach, and starting with individual employees developing an understanding of meaning for themselves as well as how they might contribute to the organisation. This can be then used for them to choose how they flow along their career. They will regularly reflect on how they are progressing, with an emphasis more on the positive psychology feel of what has gone well and with a focus on how they can continue to grow, develop, stretch, and challenge themselves. During this journey, they will also need to update their plan to keep it current and to pull support from the wider organisation, in particular their team leaders and people and culture team.

The People Value Stream might be a logical extension of the lean approach and bring to bear a way to truly "respect every individual". It is likely to overcome some of the negative aspects sometimes associated with lean such as low job satisfaction and health risks, particularly around stress (Koemtzi et al., 2023). The approach described here is not, however, without its problems. Chief among these is the weight of inertia that affects most organisations. We therefore envisage that there will have to be some significant change in the mindset, structure, and actions of most organisations. The individual-centred approach will impact other parts of the People Value Stream model. This will include a rethinking and crafting of employee roles where individuals are provided with the opportunity for greater self-reliance, development, and growth requiring significant support on this motivating journey.

We suggest that there is a rethinking of the role of the human resources department towards one concerned with People and Culture. This will include a move from the traditional language of human resource management, such as "engagement" and "management", to that of People and Culture with terms such as "employee experience" and senior roles such as Chief Joy Officer (Sheridan, 2018). It will also mean there might be a move from the management of sub-functions like recruitment and reward and recognition to end-to-end processes that support employee career paths. The People and Culture team should lead or inspire a movement to remove, or dramatically reduce, the hygiene factors in the organisation so that employees can focus on their growth needs.

We also suggest that there should be a review of who is recruited based on their self-reliance potential and past behaviours; a move from performance management to individual-led development and growth with input from the team; a move from imposed job descriptions to how to support bottom-up job crafting with co-created job descriptions; a move to a new approach to rewards and recognition based more on contribution rather than a job title, with a greater reward for specialist knowledge and competence without necessarily a managerial role; a move from HR event- and push-based training to experiential lifelong learning where the pull is based on the individual and team/organisational need and a complete review of promotion and succession planning and how this can be driven as much as possible by the individuals and peer groups concerned (the boss we want) rather than top-down planned.

We believe there should be a rethinking of the role of senior managers towards true servant leaders that respond to, support, and coach individuals across the business. This should include the advent of a caring infrastructure that focuses on the needs of individuals, especially those requiring major support; as well as a focus on ways of capturing the VOE such as running lunch-and-listen sessions (where senior managers mostly listen) and creating an employee council. A further role for such leaders is in the development of a psychologically safe organisation for people to work within (Edmondson, 2019) where leaders drive out fear (Deming, 1982) and support employees. For example, Gemba walks might have the aim of not telling people what they should do or blaming them if things go wrong, but developing one idea to implement to support the people seen, as at Thermo Fisher Scientific in Vilnius (Hines and Butterworth, 2019). This will help create an environment of high trust (Brown, 2018) and let go of the last remnants of the command-and-control culture and move to high levels of delegation (Blanchard, 2020).

There will also be changes required for front-line team leaders including a rethinking of their role, from the deployer of organisation strategy to one of emotionally intelligent coaching of individuals in the team. This will mean that more time is spent on coaching, training, and emotionally supporting, with a much greater focus on listening and acting on bottom-up input. This will in turn create an environment where employees have the skills and emotional safety to raise and solve their own problems. Supporting these moves should be a move to team measures that centre on the development and growth of individuals in the team and their ability to contribute to the team.

We would also like to suggest that there are implications for the role of unions as they continue to evolve from protecting worker rights to perhaps being the instigator or champion of the People Value Stream approach and the development and growth of their members.

As we have sought to turn lean on its head, we have perhaps raised more questions than we have answered and thus we see a significant need for future research in some of these areas and a focus on the empirical testing of the application of the People Value Stream, the further development of the roles and activities of individuals, senior management, leaders, and the people and culture team, as well as how the different flows we discuss operate.

References

Ballé, M. and Régnier, A. (2007). Lean as a learning system in a hospital ward. *Leadership in Health Services*, 20(1), 33–41.

Ballé, M., Chartier, N., Coignet, P., Olivencia, S., Powell, D., and Reke, E. (2019a). *The Lean Sensei: Go See Challenge*. Boston: Lean Enterprise Institute.

Ballé, M., Powell, D., and Yokozawa, K. (2019b). *Monozukuri, Hitozukuri, Kotozukuri*. https:// planet -lean .com/ monozukuri -hitozukuri -kotozukuri/ (accessed 20 December 2022).

Basu, D. and Miroshnik, V. (1999). Strategic human resource management of Japanese multinationals: A case study of Japanese multinational companies in the UK. *Journal of Management Development*, 18(9), 714–732.

Berne, E. (1957). Ego states in psychotherapy. *American Journal of Psychotherapy*, 12(2), 293–309.

Bicheno, J. and Holweg, M. (2009). *The Lean Toolbox*, 4th edition. Buckingham: Picsie Books.

Blanchard, K. (2020). *Leading at a Higher Level: Blanchard on Leadership and Creating High Performance Organizations*. London: Financial Times/Prentice Hall.

Bonavia, T. and Marin-Garcia, J. A. (2011). Integrating human resource management into lean production and their impact on organizational performance. *International Journal of Manpower*, 32(8), 923–938.

Bortolotti, T., Boscari, S., and Danese, P. (2015). Successful lean implementation: Organizational culture and soft lean practices. *International Journal of Production Economics*, 160, 182–201.

Bouville, G. and Alis, D. (2014). The effects of lean organisational practices on employees' attitudes and workers' health: Evidence from France. *The International Journal of Human Resource Management*, 25(21), 3016–3037.

Brackett, M. (2019). *Permission to Feel: Unlock the Power of Emotions to Help Yourself and Your Child Thrive*. London: Quercus.

Brown, B. (2018). *Dare to Lead*. London: Vermilion.

Camuffo, A., De Stefano, F., and Paolino, C. (2017). Safety reloaded: Lean operations and high involvement work practices for sustainable workplaces. *Journal of Business Ethics*, 143(2), 245–259.

Carraro, M., Furlan, A., and Netland, T. (2022). Are we proactive? Supporting proactivity in the shop floor by developing a shared mental model. *Academy of Management Annual Meeting Proceedings*. https://doi.org/10.5465/AMBPP.2022.11143abstract.

Collins, J. (2001). *Good to Great*. London: Random House.

Csikszentmihalyi, M. (1990). *Flow: The Psychology of Optimal Experience*. New York: Harper & Row.

Dahlgaard, J. and Dahlgaard-Park, S. (2006). Lean production, Six Sigma quality, TQM and company culture. *TQM Magazine*, 18(3), 263–281.

Dank, N. and Hellström, R. (2021). *Agile HR*. London: Kogan Page.

Dankbaar, B. (1997). Lean production: Denial, confirmation or extension of sociotechnical systems design? *Human Relations*, 50(5), 567–584.

Davidson, C. and Mountain, A. (2021). Transactional analysis – Eric Berne. https://www.businessballs.com/building-relationships/transactional-analysis-eric-berne/ (accessed 19 December 2022).

de Menezes, L. M., Wood, S., and Gelade, G. (2010). The integration of human resource and operation management practices and its link with performance: A longitudinal latent class study. *Journal of Operations Management*, 28(6), 455–471.

de Treville, S. and Antonakis, J. (2006). Could lean production job design be intrinsically motivating? Contextual, configurational, and levels-of-analysis issues. *Journal of Operations Management*, 24(2), 99–123.

Deming, W. E. (1982). *Out of the Crisis*. Cambridge, MA: MIT Center for Advanced Engineering Study.

Dweck, C. (2017). *Mindset: Changing the Way You Think to Fulfil Your Potential*. London: Robinson.

Eagleman, D. (2021). *Livewired: The Inside Story of the Ever-Changing Brain*. Edinburgh: Canongate Books.

Edmondson, A. (2019). *The Fearless Organisation: Creating Psychological Safety in the Workplace for Learning, Innovation, and Growth*. Hoboken, NJ: Wiley & Sons.

Emiliani, M. (2003). Linking leaders' beliefs to their behaviors and competencies. *Management Decision*, 41, 893–910.

Emiliani, M. and Stec, D. (2005). Leaders lost in transformation. *Leadership & Organization Development Journal*, 26(5), 370–387.

Eyre, K. (2021). *9 Voices – Own Your Conversation*. Bristol: Soundwave.

Fenner, S., Arellano, M., von Dzengelevski, O., and Netland, T. (2023). Effect of lean implementation on team psychological safety and learning. *International Journal of Operations & Production Management*, 43(2), 308–331.

Frink, D. and Ferris, G. (1998). Accountability, impression management, and goal setting in the performance evaluation process. *Human Relations*, 51(10), 1259–1283.

Goleman, D. (1997). *Emotional Intelligence*. New York: Bantam.

Greenleaf, R. K. (2002). *Servant Leadership: A Journey into the Nature of Legitimate Power and Greatness*. Mahwah, NJ: Paulist Press.

Hackman, J. R. and Oldham, G. R. (1976). Motivation through the design of work: Test of a theory. *Organizational Behavior and Human Performance*, 16(2), 250–279.

Hines, P. (2022). Human centred lean: Introducing the people value stream. *International Journal of Lean Six Sigma*, 13(5), 961–988.

Hines, P. and Butterworth, C. (2019). *The Essence of Excellence: Creating a Culture of Continuous Improvement*. Caerphilly: S A Partners.

Hines, P. and Rich, N. (1997). The seven value stream mapping tools. *International Journal of Operations & Production Management*, 17(1), 46–64.

Hines, P., Butterworth, C., Greenlee, C., Jekiel, C., and Taylor, D. (2022). Turning the lean world upside down. *International Journal of Lean Six Sigma*, 13(5), 989–1024.

Hines, P., Silvi, R., and Bartolini, M. (2002). *Lean Profit Potential*. Cardiff: Lean Enterprise Research Centre.

Hunt, J. (2020). *Unlocking Your Authentic Self: Overcoming Imposter Syndrome, Enhancing Self-Confidence, and Banishing Self-Doubt*. Little Rock, AR: Author. Kindle Edition.

Ivtzan, I., Lomas, T., Hefferon, K., and Worth, P. (2016). *Second Wave Positive Psychology: Embracing the Dark Side of Life*. Abingdon: Routledge.

James, L. (2018). The true cost of recruitment. https://www.quarsh.com/blog/the-true -cost-of-recruitment/ (accessed 19 December 2022).

Jayamaha, N. P., Wagner, J. P., Grigg, N. P., Campbell-Allen, N. M., and Harvie, W. (2014). Testing a theoretical model underlying the "Toyota Way": An empirical study involving a large global sample of Toyota facilities. *International Journal of Production Research*, 52(14), 4332–4350.

Jekiel, C. (2020). *Lean Human Resources: Redesigning HR Processes for a Culture of Continuous Improvement*. New York: Routledge.

Kaur Paposa, K., Thakur, P., Antony, J., McDermott, O., and Garza-Reyes, J. A. (2023). The integration of lean and human resource management practices as an enabler for lean deployment: A systematic literature review. *The TQM Journal*. https://doi.org/ 10.1108/TQM-12-2022-0355.

Kline, N. (2015). *More Time to Think: The Power of Independent Thinking*. London: Cassell.

Koemtzi, M., Psomas, E., Antony, J., and Tortorella, G. (2023). Lean manufacturing and human resources: A systematic literature review on future research suggestions. *Total Quality Management & Business Excellence*, 34, 468–495.

Koenigsaecker, G. (2012). *Leading the Lean Enterprise Transformation*. New York: Productivity Press.

Liker, J. and Hoseus, M. (2008). *Toyota Culture: The Heart and Soul of the Toyota Way*. New York: McGraw-Hill.

Liker, J. and Hoseus, M. (2010). Human resource development in Toyota culture. *International Journal of Human Resources Development & Management*, 10(1), 34–50.

Lindsley, O. R. (1990). Precision teaching: By teachers for children. *Teaching Exceptional Children*, 22(3), 10–15.

MacDuffie, J. P. (1995). Human resource bundles and manufacturing performance: Organizational logic and flexible production systems in the world auto industry. *Industrial & Labor Relations Review*, 48(2), 197–221.

Magnani, F., Carbone, V., and Moatti, V. (2019). The human side of lean: A literature review. *Supply Chain Forum: An International Journal*, 20(2), 132–144.

Mann, D. (2009). *Creating a Lean Culture: Tools to Sustain Lean Conversions*. New York: Productivity Press.

Marin-Garcia, J. A. and Bonavia, T. (2015). Relationship between employee involvement and lean manufacturing and its effect on performance in a rigid continuous process industry. *International Journal of Production Research*, 53(11), 3260–3275.

Marodin, G. and Saurin, T. (2013). Implementing lean production systems: Research areas and opportunities for future studies. *International Journal of Production Research*, 51(22), 6663–6680.

Martínez-Jurado, P. J., Moyano-Fuentes, J., and Gómez, P. J. (2013). HR management during lean production adoption. *Management Decision*, 51(4), 742–760.

Maslow, A. (1954). *Motivation and Personality*. New York: Harper & Row.

May, D. R., Gilson, R. L., and Harter, L. M. (2004). The psychological conditions of meaningfulness, safety and availability and the engagement of the human spirit at work. *Journal of Occupational and Organizational Psychology*, 77(1), 11–37.

Miller, J. (2017). Masaaki Imai remembers Taiichi Ohno. https://blog.gembaacademy .com/2012/03/04/masaaki_imai_remembers_taiichi_ohno/ (accessed 19 December 2022).

Miller, L. M. (2011). *Lean Culture: The Leader's Guide*. Annapolis, MD: LM Miller Publishing.

Modig, N. and Åhlström, P. (2012). *This is Lean*. Stockholm: Rheologica Publishing.

Moyano-Fuentes, J. and Sacristán-Díaz, M. (2012). Learning on lean: A review of thinking and research. *International Journal of Operations & Production Management*, 32(5), 551–582.

Netland, T. (2013). Exploring the phenomenon of company-specific production systems: One-best-way or own-best-way? *International Journal of Production Research*, 51(4), 1084–1097.

Olivella, J., Cuatrecasas, L., and Gavilan, N. (2008). Work organisation practices for lean production. *Journal of Manufacturing Technology Management*, 19(7), 798–811.

Perry, B. D. and Winfrey, O. (2021). *What Happened to You? Conversations on Trauma, Resilience, and Healing*. Denver, CO: Bluebird.

Preece, D. and Jones, R. (2010). Introduction: Human resource development/management in lean production. *International Journal of Human Resources Development & Management*, 10(1), 1–13.

Qualtrics (2020). 2020 global employee experience trends. http://www.qualtrics.com/ ebooks -guides/ 2020 -global -employee -experience -trends -report/ (accessed 19 December 2022).

Rosso, B. D., Dekas, K. H., and Wrzesniewski, A. (2010). On the meaning of work: A theoretical integration and review. *Research in Organizational Behavior*, 30, 91–127.

Roth, G. L. and DiBella, A. J. (2015). *Systemic Change Management: The Five Capabilities for Improving Enterprises*. New York: Palgrave Macmillan.

Rother, M. and Harris, R. (2001). *Creating Continuous Flow*. Cambridge, MA: The Lean Enterprise Institute.

Rother, M. and Shook, J. (1998). *Learning to See*. Cambridge, MA: The Lean Enterprise Institute.

Ryan, R. (1995). Psychological needs and the facilitation of integrative processes. *Journal of Personality*, 63(3), 397–427.

Saito, K. (2020). Hitozukuri. http:// www .makigami .info/ hitozukuri/ (accessed 30 August 2021).

Saito, K., Salazar, A. J., Kreafle, K. G., and Grulke, E. A. (2011). Hitozukuri and Monozukuri: Centuries' old Eastern philosophy to seek harmony with nature. *Interdisciplinary Information Sciences*, 17(1), 1–9.

Seppälä, P. and Klemola, S. (2004). How do employees perceive their organization and job when companies adopt principles of lean production? *Human Factors and Ergonomics in Manufacturing*, 14(2), 157–180.

Shah, R. and Ward, P. T. (2003). Lean manufacturing: Context, practice bundles, and performance. *Journal of Operations Management*, 21(2), 129–149.

Shah, R. and Ward, P. T. (2007). Defining and developing measures of lean production. *Journal of Operations Management*, 25(4), 785–805.

Sheridan, R. (2018). *Chief Joy Officer*. New York: Portfolio/Penguin.

Solaimani, S., Haghighi Talab, A., and van der Rhee, B. (2019). An integrative view on lean innovation management. *Journal of Business Research*, 105, 109–120.

Soliman, M., Saurin, T., and Anzanello, M. (2018). The impacts of lean production on the complexity of socio-technical systems. *International Journal of Production Economics*, 197(C), 342–357.

Sparrow, P. and Otaye-Ebede, L. (2014). Lean management and HR function capability: The role of HR architecture and the location of intellectual capital. *International Journal of Human Resource Management*, 25(21), 2892–2910.

Sugimori, Y., Kusunoki, K., Cho, F., and Uchikawa, S. (1977). Toyota production system and Kanban system materialization of just-in-time and respect-for-human system. *International Journal of Production Research*, 15(6), 553–564.

Taylor, A., Taylor, M., and Sweeney, A. (2013). Towards greater understanding of success and survival of lean systems. *International Journal of Production Research*, 51(22), 6607–6630.

Thirkell, E. and Ashman, I. (2014). Lean towards learning: Connecting lean thinking and human resource management in UK higher education. *International Journal of Human Resource Management*, 25(21), 2957–2977.

Thoren, P.-M. (2020). *Agile People: A Radical Approach for HR & Managers*. Muskego, WI: Lioncrest Publishing.

Tortorella, G. L., Marodin, G. A., Fogliatto, F. S., and Miorando, R. (2015). Learning organisation and human resources management practices: An exploratory research in medium-sized enterprises undergoing a lean implementation. *International Journal of Production Research*, 53(13), 3989–4000.

Womack, J. and Jones, D. (1996). *Lean Thinking: Banish Waste and Create Wealth in Your Corporation*. London: Simon & Schuster.

Wrzesniewski, A. and Dutton, J. E. (2001). Crafting a job: Revisioning employees as active crafters of their work. *The Academy of Management Review*, 26(2), 179–201.

Wrzesniewski, A., Berg, J. M., and Dutton, J. E. (2010). Managing yourself: Turn the job you have into the job you want. *Harvard Business Review*, June. https://hbr.org/2010/06/managing-yourself-turn-the-job-you-have-into-the-job-you-want (accessed 19 December 2022).

7 Lean as a compensatory tool for neurodiverse employees

Matteo Zanchi, Paolo Gaiardelli, Giuditta Pezzotta and Daryl Powell

Introduction

The word "neurodiversity", originally coined by Australian sociologist Judy Singer in 1998, refers to a different way cognitive processes of human beings take place. The meaning has changed throughout time, and today, rather than referring to a condition, syndrome, or illness, the term "neurodiversity" defines atypical neurological development as a natural variation of the human brain.

These days, the discussion of neurodiversity is mainly found in educational settings, where neurodiverse individuals are supported and tutored through specific educational programmes. However, scientific literature on the topic demonstrates that these same concerns receive far less attention when it comes to the working world and, in particular, to the manufacturing context. Over the last few years, the question of whether the current working environments are inclusive in respect of neurodiverse people has come up due to the growing awareness regarding the relative prevalence of neurodiverse conditions among the population.

A more accommodating environment may actually help neurodiverse people perform a variety of jobs with less tension and anxiety, feelings which are frequently brought on by tasks originally not supposed to be carried out by subjects of this kind. As a result, neurodiverse people are mostly shut out of the labour force because of the lack of adequate facilities that typically mean that neurodiverse workers are not accommodated in the working place. Only in the United States, for example, employed working-age adults affected by neurodiverse conditions amount to 37 per cent of the population, as opposed to 79 per cent of neurotypical people (Krzeminska et al., 2019).

Therefore, there is a societal need to make working realities more accessible and inclusive in the world of neurodiversity. In this regard, lean management practices can represent a viable way to respond to this need (Mascarenhas et al., 2019) as they emphasise the human element and increases its efficacy by relying on people involvement (a principle known in the lean lexicon as "Hitozukuri", i.e. "the art of doing people well").

Given this foundation, the lean methodology's characteristic inclusion for neurodiverse persons has not yet been demonstrated, particularly in terms of the capacity of each lean practice to contribute to the construction of a more accommodating workplace.

The particular traits of the three statistically most prevalent neurodiversity conditions in the population – autism, dyslexia, and attention deficit hyperactivity disorder (ADHD) – will be thoroughly explored in this chapter, and a description will then be given of which lean management practices and tools might serve as a compensatory mechanism for such people, highlighting the potential impact that they might have on neurodiverse employees' work lives based on multiple human factors, defined as "all physical, psychological, and social characteristics of the humans, which influence the action in sociotechnical systems" (Stern and Becker, 2019).

Lean management practices and tools

Lean management is a recognised approach for improving a company's overall operational performance. Successful implementation of lean practices depends on several factors, including the complexity inherent in implementing such techniques, the presence of contingency factors that limit their positive impact, and human resource management (Bortolotti et al., 2015).

In particular, lean management practices and tools can be classified into hard and soft. The former refers to technical and analytical tools, while the latter concern people and relationships, which are necessary to achieve superior and long-lasting performance. A lean strategy must be applied while considering both factors for it to be entirely successful (Rodríguez et al., 2016). This way, the effects of each will be amplified by the other.

Based on Bortolotti's model, a subdivision of the different lean techniques and principles into macro-families was made, taking into account their distinctive characteristics and linking them by affinity.

Hard practices and tools

These refer to technical and analytical practices and tools concerned with maximising machine efficiency and optimising maintenance, as well as eliminating inefficiencies along the value stream and, finally, pursuing defect-free production and continuous improvement:

- Set-up time reduction. The Single Minute Exchange of Die (SMED) technique has been assigned to the macro-family related to set-up time reduction practices. SMED is one of the main approaches to reducing waste in a production process. It is a tool that stems from the need to minimise the machine set-up time, i.e. the time interval between the manufacture of the last good part of one series and the achievement of the first good part of the next series, at a nominal rate. Reducing retooling time brings many benefits to companies, especially in terms of stock reduction and WIP (work in process), i.e. the total volume of semi-finished products in the production system, which leads to improved quality and production flexibility.
- Just-in-time (JIT) delivery by suppliers. Including JIT delivery practices and synchronisation of supply systems to which techniques such as Kanban, Junjo Sequence & Just-in-Sequence have been assigned. This macro-family includes the strong involvement of suppliers in production, who are often required to know how to interact with tools such as kanban, so as to be able to respond to customer orders on time.
- Equipment layout for continuous flow. Layout (re)configuration logics for flow management include the practices of VSM (Value Stream Mapping), Spaghetti chart, 5S, Yamazumi chart, Cell-Design, and Chaku-Chaku.
- Kanban. The set of material management tools, including the adoption of Kanban systems, Heijunka, Kanban & Milk Run, Water spider & Mizusumashi.
- Statistical process control. Quality control is crucial for understanding, monitoring, and improving performance and processes over time. Contained within this macro-family are techniques such as Jidoka, Ishikawa, Andon, Kamishibai, and Poka-Yoke.
- Autonomous maintenance. Mostly consisting of the TPM (Total Productive Maintenance) technique, autonomous maintenance encompasses a set of tools to define a routine maintenance logic on all equipment (e.g. cleaning, lubrication, and minor repairs) following a standardised procedure. Operators are more involved as they are directly responsible for the equipment at their stations. TPM refers to productive maintenance carried out by all employees through activities organised in small groups, through a series of methods aimed at ensuring that production processes never stop. Thus, the operator becomes primarily responsible for the care of the

machine, flanked by the maintenance technician in charge of the overhaul, inspection, and management of high safety risk activities.

Soft practices and tools

Important for sustaining change through the involvement of people in the long term, soft practices and tools include factors, such as continuous learning, education, training, and involvement, which enable employees to effectively handle lean management tools (Bonekamp and Sure, 2015).

- Small group problem solving. Problem solving, i.e. the organisation of employees into teams to solve problems, is also a macro-family of soft practices. Within this macro-category one can find techniques such as Brain Storming, 5 Whys, Genchi Genbutsu, and A3 sheets.
- Training employees. That is, the implementation of a job rotation policy so that workers are trained on different tasks, duties, and responsibilities related to a specific job activity. Included within this macro-family are the techniques of job enlargement, job enrichment, Coaching Kata, and OPL (One Point Lesson).
- Top management leadership and supplier partnership. Top management leadership constitutes a further descriptive macro-family of factors according to which managers can act as role models for the assumption of lean methodology-compliant behaviour, taking initiatives, defining and communicating goals. The techniques and principles within this macro-family are: Hoshin Kanri, Walk the floor (Genchi Genbutsu), Challenge, Teamwork (Scrum meeting), Respect, and Kaizen mind.
- Customer involvement. Macro-family practices helpful in involving people in value definition, including techniques such as Gemba walking, Stand-up meetings, Obeya room, and Catchball approach.
- Continuous improvement. Including techniques such as PDCA/SDCA, Hansei ("make it ugly"), Kintsugi, and Shu-Ha-Ri.

Human factors

To accomplish a successful conversion that follows a lean logic, enterprises must do more than simply use lean practices and tools; they must also take into account how people contribute to customer value delivery (Liker, 2004). As a result, emphasising human factors participation and motivation is practically required (Gaiardelli et al., 2019).

Human factors are described in existing literature as "all physical, psychological, and social characteristics of the humans, which influence the action in sociotechnical systems" (Stern and Becker, 2019). From this definition, it becomes clear that human capabilities can serve both social and business objectives. Human factors can be divided into:

- Physical human factors – anatomical, anthropometric, physiological, and biomechanical aspects of humans that can be related to the physical activities performed by operators (Cimini et al., 2021). The nine physical human factors considered are: Working postures, Materials handling, Repetitive movements, Workplace layout, Risk of accident, Fitness for duty, Reactivity, Perception and Available time / Rapidity / Time pressure.
- Human cognitive factors – the mental processes that entail, for example, reasoning and memory, but also the expertise needed to perform an activity. Cognition also includes the process of information seeking and processing to find solutions and make decisions (Longo et al., 2019). The seven human cognitive factors taken into account are: Memory, Decision-making, Complexity (reasoning and parallel tasks), Skilled performance / Experience, Human error probability, Work stress, and Training.
- Organisational human factors – social and process variables (such as, for example, climate, communication, and development), that is to say, those capabilities that influence the work of human beings in sociotechnical systems (Cimini et al., 2021). The organisational area includes seven human factors: Policies, Processes formalisation, Communication, Crew resource management / Leadership, Teamwork, Proactivity, Self-management.

Neurodiversity

The definition we now have of neurodiversity results from years of development. Since Judy Singer first used the term "neurodiversity" in 1998, it has mainly been used to describe the wide range of circumstances that underlie people's various cognitive abilities, including conditions such as autism, dyslexia, dyspraxia, dyscalculia, Tourette's syndrome, and attention deficit hyperactivity disorder (ADHD). Even though the word "neurodiversity" has frequently been linked to a medical condition, it now refers to an unusual neurological development that is simply a normal variation of the human brain without any genuine neurological deficit (meaning, in our case, an Intelligent Quotient higher than 70 points) (Doyle, 2020). Cognitive scores related to verbal skills (capacity for verbal communication), working memory (capacity-limited structure that retains and processes information for a fixed period of time), visual skills (attention to details), and processing speed (ability to understand ambiguous idiomatic expressions and unpredictable expressions) in neurotypical subjects fall within tolerance of one and two standard deviations from the average IQ (Intelligent Quotient) value, delineating a relatively flat cognitive profile; in neuro-diverse individuals, scores vary significantly beyond this threshold, delineating peaks and troughs in correspondence of the respective strengths and weaknesses (Figure 7.1). While neurotypical people's abilities tend to hover around an average IQ of 100, neurodiverse people have more pronounced abilities in some cognitive areas where IQ values are significantly higher than the average. However, they have serious deficits in other cognitive areas where IQ values are significantly lower than the average.

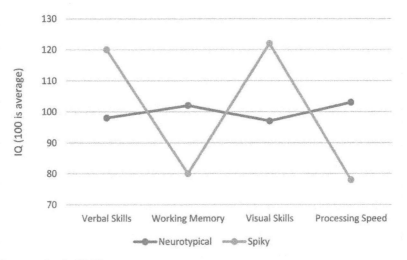

Source: Doyle (2020).

Figure 7.1   Example of IQ scores comparison between neurotypical and neurodiverse people across different cognitive dimensions

Three relationship maps were produced using data from the body of literature, as well as the extensive knowledge of the lean management (LM) topic that the three scholars involved in the study hold. Each map was created with specific neurodiversity in mind, with particular regard to the set of strengths and weaknesses characteristic of each condition, to properly illustrate how LM practices affect the physical, cognitive, and organisational aspects of neurodiverse employees.

On the basis of the distinguishing characteristics of neurodiverse individuals, the relevant human factors were then identified. Tables 7.1, 7.2, and 7.3 depict human factors that best describe a specific facet of the neurodiversity condition analysed, consistently with the strengths and/or weaknesses that characterise it.

Thereafter, the effects of every single "LM Tool" were considered among the full range of human factors throughout the assessment process. A score of +1 was given when the LM tool had a favourable impact on the human factor under consideration, a score of −1 in all cases where negative effects were present, and a score of 0 if the use of the thought-out approach had both benefits and drawbacks. No score was provided for any of the other scenarios in which no relevant impacts were evident.

Tables 7.4, 7.5, and 7.6 show, for each relationship, the number of possible interactions resulting from the influence of each specific "LM Practice" group on the considered HF (human factor) category. For example, in consideration of the strengths and weaknesses of people affected by ASD (autistic spectrum disorder), the number of interactions, whether positive or negative, resulting from the applications of the two "Just-in-time delivery by suppliers" practices and tools on the 7 different human factors of the "Cognitive" area results in 5 interactions out of a maximum of 14.

In addition to the number of possible interactions between LM practices and HFs, the tables also provide an overall assessment in terms of feedback, whether positive or negative, resulting from the adoption of lean tools on the working context from the perspective of a neurodiverse worker. The mentioned piece of information is reported in brackets throughout all of the tables (ratio between the sum of scores and the number of interactions: "=" for neutral feedback → 0%; "+ /−" for slight positive or negative feedback → 1% ~ 49%; "+ + / − −" for mild positive or negative feedback → 50% ~ 99%; "+ + + / − − −" for strong positive or negative feedback → 100%; "/" for no interaction). In the previously mentioned example, "Just-in-time delivery by suppliers" practices would be expected to provide, considering "Kanban" and "Junjo Sequence & Just-in-Sequence" tools altogether, benefits over 4 different "Cognitive" HFs and disadvantages over only 1 aspect (in this case, "Work Stress"), thus showing an overall mild positive effect (+60% → + +) over the considered class of HFs.

Table 7.1 Relationships between strengths/weaknesses and human factors for autism

AUTISM

Strengths	Physical HF	Cognitive HF	Organisational HF
High concentration on topics of high interest	Reactivity	Human error probability	Proactivity
Attention to detail	Risk of accident	Complexity Human error probability	
Respect for routines	Workplace layout	Training	
Skills in STEM disciplines		Complexity	
Memory capacity on repetitive tasks		Memory	
Predilection towards visual-spatial processes	Workplace layout	Complexity	
Weaknesses			
Difficulty concentrating on subjects of little interest	Risk of accident	Human error probability Work stress	Proactivity
Patterns of behaviour	Repetitive movements		
Restricted and repetitive interests or activities		Work stress	Proactivity
Social interaction difficulties and behavioural problems		Work stress	Communication Teamwork
Difficulties in executive functions		Decision-making Human error probability	Teamwork
Episodic memory deficiency		Memory	
Difficulties in imagination	Risk of accident		
Little preference for temporal processes	Available time / Rapidity / Time pressure	Complexity	
Sensory hypersensitivity to environmental conditions	Workplace layout Perception	Work stress	

Table 7.2   Relationships between strengths/weaknesses and human factors for ADHD

ADHD			
Strengths	*Physical HF*	*Cognitive HF*	*Organisational HF*
Verbal communication			Communication
Strong creative skills			
Logical skills		Complexity	
Outstanding sensitivity and empathy			Teamwork Communication
Strong decision-making skills		Decision-making	Teamwork
Weaknesses			
Written communication			Communication
Concentration	Risk of accident Reactivity	Human error probability	
Lack of order	Workplace layout Risk of accident	Human error probability	
Difficulties in (self)control	Repetitive movements Risk of accident Available time / Rapidity / Time pressure	Work stress	Proactivity
Inhibition of inappropriate behaviour	Repetitive movements		Teamwork
Severe agitation	Repetitive movements Available time / Rapidity / Time pressure	Work stress	
Oppositional behaviour		Work stress	Teamwork
Hyperactivity, inattention, impulsiveness	Repetitive movements Reactivity		Proactivity
Sensory hypersensitivity to undesirable conditions	Workplace layout Perception	Work stress	

Table 7.3   Relationships between strengths/weaknesses and human
factors for dyslexia

DYSLEXIA

Strengths	Physical HF	Cognitive HF	Organisational HF
Learning from experience		Training Skilled performance / Experience	
Strong creativity			
High memory capacity		Memory	
Oral communication			Communication Teamwork
Practical skills		Complexity	
Visual-spatial skills	Workplace layout	Complexity	
Narrative skills			Teamwork Communication
Weaknesses			
Alphabetisation (low propensity to read and write)		Training	Communication
Written communication			Communication
Reading comprehension difficulties	Risk of accident Reactivity		
Stress management	Available time / Rapidity / Time pressure	Human error probability Work stress	
Cognitive functioning and social self-esteem		Work stress	Teamwork

Autism

With a prevalence of 1.6 per cent globally, autism spectrum disorder is a neu-
rodevelopmental condition characterised by difficulties in social and communication interaction, sensory apathy (i.e. disconnection to stimuli from the
surrounding environment), as well as the presence of restricted and repetitive
interests in individuals with this condition. Autistic individuals show uneven
development of certain skills. Autism is a neurological psychiatric condition,

with infantile onset within the first three years, and lasting throughout life, resulting in differences in perception, learning style and thinking, behaviour, traits and mannerisms (Volk et al., 2011). On the other hand, autistic people have abilities including excellent memory (Meilleur et al., 2015), creative thinking, and keen observation (Armstrong, 2011).

Regarding autistic subjects, little information is available after completing compulsory schooling with regard to: occupation, love life, and quality of life in general. Moreover, many individuals only discover they are autistic in adulthood, especially for women who manage to "camouflage" and disguise certain personality traits to adapt to specific environmental needs (Ferrara et al., 2021). Unfortunately, there are no guidelines for the diagnosis and management of autism in adulthood. Indeed, young people and adults with autism receive less help than other categories, despite the importance of adequate support for these individuals from an early age being scientifically recognised. It is also well known that in adulthood, the behaviour of individuals with autism tends to stabilise, especially in women: they are less likely to develop externalising behaviour such as hyperactivity, impulsivity, and conduct problems, but at the same time are more likely to develop internalising problems such as anxiety, depression, and eating disorders, and have a lower propensity towards repetitive and stereotyped behaviour. Research on the interventions needed to improve the living conditions of autistic adults further highlights the limitations inherent in "health barriers", as current health services, also in terms of funding and training of physicians, are not yet calibrated for this part of the population.

In relation to autism, cognitive HFs are the most impacted by LM Practices (a total of 44 interactions), although this only results in a little overall effect. In reality, physical HFs are the ones who gain the most from an LM implementation programme. Speaking of "LM Practices", however, "Statistical Process Control" tools generally exhibit the most significant influence, both in terms of the numerosity of relations discovered and effectiveness; in contrast, "Supplier Partnership", "Set-up Time Reduction", and "Customer Involvement" exhibit the lowest efficacy, both in terms of the relations discovered and the detrimental effects (Zanchi et al., 2023).

ADHD

With a prevalence of around 5 per cent among the worldwide population, attention deficit and hyperactivity disorder (ADHD) is one of the most common neuro-behavioural disorders. It manifests itself in early childhood with a pronounced level of inattention and a series of behaviours that empha-

Table 7.4   Effect of LM tools on human factors for autism condition

LM Categories (number of associated practices and tools)	Physical HF (9)	Cognitive HF (7)	Organisational HF (7)
Set-up time reduction (1)	2 (- - -)	/	/
Just-in-time delivery by suppliers (2)	2 (- - -)	5 (+ +)	2 (+ + +)
Equipment layout for continuous flow (6)	8 (+ + +)	8 (+ +)	1 (=)
Kanban (4)	/	3 (+ + +)	2 (+ + +)
Statistical process control (5)	12 (+ + +)	7 (+ + +)	4 (+ + +)
Autonomous maintenance (1)	2 (+ + +)	/	/
Small group problem solving (4)	1 (- - -)	5 (- - -)	3 (- - -)
Training employees (4)	2 (- - -)	5 (+)	/
Top management leadership (6)	1 (- - -)	3 (- - -)	1 (- - -)
Supplier partnership (3)	/	/	/
Customer involvement (4)	1 (- - -)	5 (- - -)	3 (- - -)
Continuous improvement (4)	/	3 (+)	/

sise hyperactivity and impulsivity. This disorder presents relevant symptoms and associated problems that affect various functional aspects of everyday life. Symptoms inherent to inattention are mainly found in children who, compared to their peers, have obvious difficulties concentrating or working on the same task for a prolonged period of time. The manifestations of hyperactivity and impulsivity seem to be attributable to difficulty in inhibiting inappropriate behaviour.

In the past, this was thought to be a disorder that only affected children. Over time, however, research in the field has led to the conclusion that this disorder also persists into adulthood, impairing the social and working life of individuals. Scientific evidence shows that it tends to persist throughout life in up to 85 per cent of cases (Kessler et al., 2006), causing significant difficulties. The symptoms found in children with ADHD change over time, and as they grow up, only 1/3 of children are diagnosed with ADHD. There are two different types of adult ADHD patients. The first is characterised by the predominance of inattention symptoms and organisational difficulties due to cognitive and pragmatic performance difficulties. It is frequently combined with depression and anxiety. The second type, on the other hand, is characterised by marked impulsivity and hyperactivity, in addition to a wide overlap with the bipolar

Table 7.5   Effect of LM tools on human factors for ADHD condition

LM Categories (number of associated practices and tools)	Physical HF (9)	Cognitive HF (7)	Organisational HF (7)
Set-up time reduction (1)	2 (- - -)	/	/
Just-in-time delivery by suppliers (2)	2 (- - -)	5 (+)	2 (=)
Equipment layout for continuous flow (6)	8 (=)	8 (- -)	1 (+ + +)
Kanban (4)	/	3 (+ + +)	2 (=)
Statistical process control (5)	12 (+ +)	7 (+ + +)	3 (+ + +)
Autonomous maintenance (1)	2 (- - -)	/	/
Small group problem solving (4)	1 (+ + +)	5 (+ + +)	3 (+ + +)
Training employees (4)	2 (+ + +)	5 (+)	/
Top management leadership (6)	1 (+ + +)	3 (+ + +)	1 (+ + +)
Supplier partnership (3)	/	/	/
Customer involvement (4)	1 (+ + +)	5 (+ + +)	3 (+ + +)
Continuous improvement (4)	/	3 (-)	/

spectrum and personality disorders. Compared to children, adults have a 50 per cent decrease in hyperactivity, 40 per cent decrease in impulsivity and 20 per cent decrease in inattention. Thus, adult ADHD and adolescent ADHD present fewer problems in terms of motor agitation and impulsivity, which are still prevalent but adapted to age and social contexts. Attention problems persist, in an important way, negatively affecting student and working life.

Despite these cognitive disorders, people with ADHD have higher levels of creativity (6) and visual-spatial reasoning (Grant, 2009). Regarding ADHD, cognitive HFs still have the most interactions (44), but this time, organisational HFs are generally more positively modified by such instruments. Although the most helpful LM tools are under the "Small group problem solving" and "Customer involvement" categories, "Statistical Process Control" tools still have a more substantial impact on employees who have neurodiversity (22); this is because they are used in lean practices. The HFs of subjects with ADHD are unaffected by "Supplier partnership" practices, instead these people suffer the most from the adoption of "Set-up time reduction" and "Autonomous maintenance" practices (Zanchi et al., 2023).

Dyslexia

With an incidence of up to 10 per cent of the global population, dyslexia is a specific reading impairment that causes difficulties decoding texts. Falling under the umbrella of Specific Learning Disorders (SLD), dyslexia impairs an individual's reading ability, which manifests in difficulties decoding text. Dyslexia presents characteristic symptoms, recognisable as early as school age, common among people who present this neurodiversity. In particular, the most significant difficulties concern memorising the letters of the alphabet, inaccuracy, slow reading, and difficulties understanding a text. Other signs that can be recognised before school age are: language delay, difficulty in learning new words and expanding one's vocabulary, and poor coordination in movements. Dyslexia is a chronic disorder that persists throughout life, although it takes on different aspects depending on the severity, cognitive characteristics of the subject and educational or relational opportunities. The assessment of dyslexia in adults must include the analysis of both the areas specifically involved in the disorder and the complementary areas that allow the diagnosis to be directed towards other areas (anxiety, depression, executive functions, intellectual functions).

Nevertheless, people with dyslexia possess average levels of IQs (Kirby, 2018), a strong sense of creativity and cognitive control (Leather et al., 2011), as well as visual thinking abilities (Von Karolyi et al., 2003). Similar to what has been observed for ADHD and even for dyslexia, cognitive HFs have the most interactions (35), while organisational HFs are often the ones that are most positively affected by such tools. Dyslexic people are unaffected by "Autonomous maintenance" strategies, particularly in the form of Total Productive Maintenance (TPM), whereas "Set-up time reduction" techniques have the most negative effects. However, "Statistical Process Control" is the most effective instrument (15) and is also the most influential (Zanchi et al., 2023).

Discussion

Based on this analysis, knowing on the one hand the relationship between the characteristics of each condition and human factors, and on the other hand the effects of the latter exerted by the adoption of LM practices and tools, it is possible to identify techniques that could provide greater support for the neurodiversity studied.

Table 7.6 Effect of LM tools on human factors for dyslexia condition

LM Categories (number of associated practices and tools)	Physical HF (9)	Cognitive HF (7)	Organisational HF (7)
Set-up time reduction (1)	2 (- - -)	/	/
Just-in-time delivery by suppliers (2)	2 (- - -)	5 (+)	2 (=)
Equipment layout for continuous flow (6)	/	2 (+ + +)	1 (+ + +)
Kanban (4)	/	3 (+ + +)	2 (=)
Statistical process control (5)	5 (+ + +)	6 (+ + +)	4 (+ + +)
Autonomous maintenance (1)	/	/	/
Small group problem solving (4)	1 (- - -)	5 (- - -)	3 (+ + +)
Training employees (4)	/	3 (+ + +)	/
Top management leadership (6)	1 (- - -)	3 (- - -)	1 (+ + +)
Supplier partnership (3)	/	/	/
Customer involvement (4)	1 (- - -)	5 (- - -)	3 (+ + +)
Continuous improvement (4)	/	3 (+ + +)	/

In general, the techniques that were most widely used in this study are, as far as hard practices are concerned, those associated with the macro-family of "Just-in-time delivery by suppliers" and "Kanban" such as Kanban and Just in Sequence & Junjo Sequence. Or, for "Equipment layout for continuous flow" macro-family, techniques such as VSM, Spaghetti chart, Cell-design, and Chaku-Chaku. Techniques belonging to the "Statistical process control" macro-family such as Jidoka, Ishikawa diagram, Andon, Kamishibai, and Poka-Yoke were also widely applied within the analysis. On the other hand, concerning soft practices, the techniques that have found greater use are those belonging to the macro-family of "Customer involvement" such as the Gemba walk, or those belonging to the macro-family of "Small group problem solving" such as Brainstorming, 5 Whys, and Genchi Genbutsu. The techniques, in general, have proven to be advantageous or disadvantageous depending on the neurodiversity considered, as well as human and environmental factors. A technique such as the Gemba Walk, for example, might prove useful and advantageous for individuals with ADHD or dyslexia, as it leverages their ability to establish a highly collaborative relationship with people, especially from a communicative and empathic point of view, while, on the contrary, it might be a hindrance for autistic operators, as it is a technique that requires teamwork and a certain ability in terms of social interaction (recognised factors of weakness for this category of people) to solve a problem. Instead, a technique such as Poka-Yoke could be supportive for all three forms of neurodiversity as, in general, it aims to reduce the possibility of human error (Zanchi et al., 2023).

Conclusions

This chapter has defined the influence of lean management techniques on the working life of neurodiverse individuals, in light of the different human factors analysed. According to the study, certain techniques taken into consideration could have a positive impact on the working environment of neurodiverse workers, while others could have a negative impact.

Similarly, certain lean management tools appear to have the potential to be used as support tools for neurodiverse persons, the effectiveness of which also depends on the human factor considered and the respective strengths and weaknesses of the operators involved.

Possible future studies could include interviews with neurodiversity experts in order to substantiate whether such techniques can offer real and meaningful support to neurodiverse persons. It could also be interesting, as a final validation, to go and study directly in the field how neurodiverse workers react to the implementation of such practices, verifying whether these actually manage to provide them with physical and psychological support. The results of the analysis conducted, possibly deepened with further studies, could prove to be a valuable aid not only for neurodiverse subjects, but for all operators involved in factory work, who would know how to better interact and relate with these people.

References

Armstrong, T. (2011). *The Power of Neurodiversity: Unleashing the Advantages of Your Differently Wired Brain* (published in *Hardcover as Neurodiversity*). Boston: Da Capo Lifelong Books.
Bonekamp, L. & Sure, M. (2015). Consequences of Industry 4.0 on human labour and work organisation. *Journal of Business and Media Psychology*, 6(1), 33–40.
Bortolotti, T., Boscari, S., & Danese, P. (2015). Successful lean implementation: Organizational culture and soft lean practices. *International Journal of Production Economics*, 160, 182–201.

Cimini, C., Lagorio, A., Pirola, F., & Pinto, R. (2021). How human factors affect operators' task evolution in Logistics 4.0. *Human Factors and Ergonomics in Manufacturing & Service Industries*, 31(1), 98–117.

Doyle, N. (2020). Neurodiversity at work: A biopsychosocial model and the impact on working adults. *British Medical Bulletin*, 135(1), 108.

Ferrara, R., Iovino, L., Ricci, P., Ricci, L., Latina, R., Carbone, G., & Ricci, S. (2021). Autismo in età adulta: Uomini e donne autistici tra criticità e risorse. *Phenomena Journal-Giornale Internazionale di Psicopatologia, Neuroscienze e Psicoterapia*, 3(2), 131–139.

Gaiardelli, P., Resta, B., & Dotti, S. (2019). Exploring the role of human factors in lean management. *International Journal of Lean Six Sigma*, 10(1), 339–366.

Grant, D. (2009). The psychological assessment of neurodiversity. In D. Pollak (ed.), *Neurodiversity in Higher Education: Positive Responses to Specific Learning Differences*. Hoboken, NJ: John Wiley & Sons, pp. 33–62.

Kessler, R. C., Adler, L., Barkley, R., Biederman, J., Conners, C. K., Demler, O., … Zaslavsky, A. M. (2006). The prevalence and correlates of adult ADHD in the United States: Results from the National Comorbidity Survey replication. *American Journal of Psychiatry*, 163(4), 716–723.

Kirby, P. (2018). A brief history of dyslexia. *Psychologist*, 31(3).

Krzeminska, A., Austin, R. D., Bruyère, S. M., & Hedley, D. (2019). The advantages and challenges of neurodiversity employment in organizations. *Journal of Management & Organization*, 25(4), 453–463.

Leather, C., Hogh, H., Seiss, E., & Everatt, J. (2011). Cognitive functioning and work success in adults with dyslexia. *Dyslexia*, 17(4), 327–338.

Liker, J. K. (2004). *Toyota Way: 14 Management Principles from the World's Greatest Manufacturer*. New York: McGraw-Hill Education.

Longo, F., Nicoletti, L., & Padovano, A. (2019). Modeling workers' behavior: A human factors taxonomy and a fuzzy analysis in the case of industrial accidents. *International Journal of Industrial Ergonomics*, 69, 29–47.

Mascarenhas, R. F., Pimentel, C., & Rosa, M. J. (2019). The way lean starts: A different approach to introduce lean culture and changing process with people's involvement. *Procedia Manufacturing*, 38, 948–956.

Meilleur, A. A. S., Jelenic, P., & Mottron, L. (2015). Prevalence of clinically and empirically defined talents and strengths in autism. *Journal of Autism and Developmental Disorders*, 45, 1354–1367.

Rodríguez, D., Buyens, D., Van Landeghem, H., & Lasio, V. (2016). Impact of lean production on perceived job autonomy and job satisfaction: An experimental study. *Human Factors and Ergonomics in Manufacturing & Service Industries*, 26(2), 159–176.

Singer, J. (1998). Odd people in: The birth of community amongst people on the "autistic spectrum": A personal exploration of a new social movement based on neurological diversity. Sydney: Faculty of Humanities and Social Science University of Technology, Sydney.

Stern, H. & Becker, T. (2019). Concept and evaluation of a method for the integration of human factors into human-oriented work design in cyber-physical production systems. *Sustainability*, 11(16), 4508.

Volk, H. E., Hertz-Picciotto, I., Delwiche, L., Lurmann, F., & McConnell, R. (2011). Residential proximity to freeways and autism in the CHARGE study. *Environmental Health Perspectives*, 119(6), 873–877.

Von Karolyi, C., Winner, E., Gray, W., & Sherman, G. F. (2003). Dyslexia linked to talent: Global visual-spatial ability. *Brain and Language*, 85(3), 427–431.

Zanchi, M., Gaiardelli, P., & Pezzotta, G. (2023). The role of lean management practices in the valorisation of neurodiverse people in production. In O. McDermott, A. Rosa, J. C. Sá, & A. Toner (eds.), *Lean, Green and Sustainability: 8th IFIP WG 5.7 European Lean Educator Conference*. Cham: Springer International Publishing, pp. 14–22.

8 Does lean lead to resilient or fragile firms? An empirical investigation and a research agenda

Andrea Furlan

Introduction

Lean management creates value for customers by focusing on continuous improvement, respect for people, and the elimination of non-value-added activities. Resilience refers to the ability of organizations to withstand and recover from unexpected disruptions or challenges. It involves building adaptive capacities, fostering flexibility, and being prepared to respond effectively to change or adversity.

Several scholars have studied the relationship between lean and resilience with contrasting results. A stream of studies argues for a complementarity between the two. Combining lean and resilience allows organizations to achieve operational excellence while also being prepared to navigate unforeseen events and disruptions. By implementing lean practices, organizations can optimize their processes, minimize waste, and create a culture of continuous improvement. At the same time, integrating resiliency principles enables them to build robust systems, proactively identify risks, and develop strategies to mitigate them.

Quite contrary, several papers suggest a possible trade-off between lean and resiliency. Some detractors argue that lean practices, with their focus on standardization and efficiency, may hinder adaptability and responsiveness to unpredictable events or changing customer needs. They claim that excessive reliance on predefined processes can limit the ability to quickly adjust to new circumstances. Critics also argue that lean initiatives often prioritize cost reduction and may lead to short-term thinking. They contend that a sole focus on cutting costs could sacrifice long-term investments, innovation, and other important aspects necessary for sustained growth and success.

In short, there is no agreement about the effect of lean on resiliency. There are also methodological issues to consider. Most studies focus on perceptive measures of resiliency aimed at capturing the abilities of the firm to monitor and respond to a disruptive event. While insightful, these measures suffer from desirability biases typical of survey-based measures. Few studies adopt objective measures of resiliency based on economic and financial indicators that signal how well a firm can weather a disruptive event.

After reviewing the relevant literature on resiliency and the relationship between lean and resiliency, we present an empirical study on a sample of Italian manufacturing firms. This study measures resiliency of the firms during 2020 ("the Covid year") using two indicators based on financial and economic data. Results show a positive (although weak) relationship between lean and resiliency. We conclude the chapter outlining a research agenda to better study the important connection between lean and resiliency.

Resilience in management literature

Resilience can be defined as the "systemic capacity of the supply chain to absorb the negative external disturbances and restore the operational regularity" (Ivanov, 2022). It is a continuous process (Bryce et al., 2020) because it requires companies to constantly find new adaptive solutions to the multiple pressures coming from their external and internal environment. Resilience combines the capability to minimize the destructive effects of a crisis and the ability to return to an acceptable level of performance afterward.

According to Meyer (1982), resilience presents three main subsequent phases: anticipatory, responsive, and readjustment. The anticipatory phase involves identifying and analyzing potential disruptions in advance, including developing risk management plans to minimize their impact. The responsive phase focuses on the immediate reaction to a crisis and requires network flexibility. The readjustment phase pertains to the recovery of the organization after the crisis. Similarly, Li et al. (2017) claim that to build supply chain resilience capabilities, organizations must adopt a proactive approach (corresponding to the anticipatory phase) and a reactive strategy (corresponding to the responsive and recovery stages).

To develop resilient capabilities and systems, the current literature proposes different strategies and practices. On the procurement side, the creation of a flexible supplier base helps to face unexpected externalities. Some examples are the geographical segregation of contractors or the establishment of backup suppliers (Hosseini et al., 2019), multi-sourcing and replacement options for raw materials, contract flexibility and incentive agreements, risk pooling, and delayed commitment (Pettit et al., 2010). Flexibility on the logistic side is reached through multiplicity of distribution channels and rerouting options (Hosseini et al., 2019) and tracking systems to enhance transportation visibility (Ruiz-Benítez et al., 2018). Finally, on the capacity side, the preservation of buffers of production capacity and/or inventory (Hosseini et al., 2019; Ruiz-Benítez et al., 2018) are practices that can support the ability of the organization to deal with unexpected variations of the market.

The relationship between resiliency and lean: substitutes or complementors?

Resilience and lean management

As anticipated in the introduction, there is a lack of consensus in the literature about the relationship between lean and resiliency (Habibi Rad et al., 2021).

Lean and resilience may appear as contrasting forces, requiring a trade-off for the organization (Alemsan et al., 2022). Lean is focused on flow efficiency and aims at eliminating buffers and stock through a logic of "pull" demand. Waste minimization makes supply chains more exposed to unforeseen disruptions. On the other hand, authors have argued how redundancy represents one of the most cited factors supporting resilience, which is achieved mainly through the investment in safety buffers and backup suppliers (de Sá et al., 2020).

Other scholars find a mixed relationship between lean and resiliency. Birkie (2016) shows that resilience and lean practices have significant complementarities, and that lean implementation is usually complemented with high levels of resiliency. However, the author notes that total productive maintenance (TPM) and just in time (JIT) exhibit an inverse relation with resilience. It is argued that these practices are strictly related to the manufacturing part of the operations, and therefore can have only a limited role in the anticipation and mitigation of external disturbances.

Ruiz-Benítez et al. (2018) show in the aerospace manufacturing sector that lean and resilience are closely connected, as some lean practices enable resilience capabilities. The authors additionally argued that both lean and resilience are concurrent to the improvement of supply chain sustainability. Similar results were confirmed by Ivanov and Dolgui (2019), who claim that the precondition to effective lean management is the adoption of a resilience paradigm, and by Uhrin et al. (2020), who argue that lean should be implemented together with resilience practices to face uncertainty and unexpected events. Hills (2015) argues that the lean represents a useful approach to face crises, highlighting the role of human respect and valorization, as well as decentralized decision-making, which foster employees' continuous training and learning, creating an organizational environment more robust to disruptions.

Other authors claim that the redundancy feature that is distinctive of resilience may coexist with lean and its inventory-minimization objective. Many lean companies introduce emergency stocks in critical nodes of their supply chains as a backup in case of crises (Hosseini et al., 2019). Christopher and Rutherford (2004) argue that supply chain resilience can be achieved through six sigma methodology by placing spare capacity in critical steps of the process (bottlenecks), in order to reduce the exposure to risk without compromising efficiency.

Our review reveals that often the conclusion about the relationship between lean and resilience depends on the specific lean and resilience practices that are implemented within the organization (Habibi Rad et al., 2021). While synergies between lean and resilience are related to practices such as customer-supplier integration, replenishment frequency, reduced production and transportation lead time, there are other practices (e.g. inventory level and capacity surplus) which have opposing effects therefore causing discrepancies.

Resilience and lean management in the Covid-19 pandemic

The topic of resilience gained importance and urgency in the context of the recent Covid-19 pandemic, an example of a low-risk, high-impact disruptive event that put many supply chains under considerable risk (Ivanov and Das, 2020). Several authors analyze whether lean has helped companies and their supply chains to maintain reactivity to such a crisis. Again, results are contrasting.

Alemsan et al. (2022) conduct a review centered on the healthcare supply chain, observing how lean practices show a highly positive relationship with resilience. More specifically, visual management techniques and work standardization can help to improve the clarity and the knowledge of the state of the operations, therefore increasing its visibility, while value stream mapping and inventory management improve the communication between actors in the supply chain, promoting collaboration. Similar conclusions were reached in other industries such as the construction industry (Parameswaran and Ranadewa, 2021).

Trabucco and De Giovanni (2021) argue that during the Covid-19 crisis lean improved firms' business sustainability (defined as the firm's capacity to mitigate performance losses in the event of a disruption), which in turn was positively correlated to resilience. However, their analysis shows that some factors (e.g. delivery time, customer service, and inventory availability) are not connected to resiliency.

Dolgui and Ivanov (2021) argue that lean supply chains (based on single sourcing and JIT) have been one of the primary factors of the negative ripple effects during the pandemic alongside global sourcing and global production. However, the authors note that this does not necessarily imply that JIT supply chains are less resilient than high-level inventory supply chains since a significant factor to consider is represented by the accessibility of such supply chains and their location.

Ivanov and Das (2020) highlight how the pandemic has brought unique implications for supply chains. Measures like subcontracting and inventory accumulation, which are typically employed for resilience, can only mitigate disruptions for a limited period. The prolonged closures of facilities and suppliers eventually lead to stoppages and performance losses thus rendering these measures ineffective in the long run. The authors suggest that resilience strategies should instead focus on real-time adjustments, such as quickly opening and closing facilities at different nodes of the supply chain.

In light of the Covid-19 pandemic, recent research has pointed out the inadequacy of existing theoretical frameworks surrounding the concept of resilience. Previous studies focus on reactive plans that only come into play after a disruption occurs. However, this approach has proven insufficient. As a result, a new perspective has emerged, i.e. the AURA (Active Usage of Resilience Assets) approach. AURA emphasizes the proactive utilization of redundancies, contingent recovery plans, and visibility systems as active resilience assets.

Considering the contrasting findings on the relationship between lean and resilience, in the next section we will show the results of a study carried out on a sample of Italian manufacturing firms during 2020, the worst year of the pandemic. Since the pandemic represented a disruptive crisis that abruptly affected the economics of firms across industries, we use objective measures of resiliency based on economic indicators.

Research methodology

Sample

We carried out a quantitative study on a sample of 454 Italian manufacturing firms (184 small firms, 221 medium firms, 49 large firms). Most of the companies are located in the northern region of Italy (80 percent, 362 firms). Most of the firms (66 percent) adopt either a design to order or make to order production system. The sample is almost equally divided between lean and non-lean adopters. Of the 454 companies of the sample, 221 (49 percent) employ at least one lean technique. Most of the lean adopters have been implementing lean for less than ten years (69 percent). The most widely applied techniques are 5S, Pull/Kanban, and value stream mapping. Most of the firms adopt lean in operations and logistics (96 percent) while less than 30 percent implement lean in other functions such as Sales & Marketing, Accounting, or IT.

Dependent variable

As said previously, literature lacks studies that use resilience indexes based on economic/financial data. We measure resilience of the sampled firms during the Covid-19 pandemic using objective data based on financial reports. We develop two original resiliency indexes.

Resilience index 1. Figure 8.1 shows the variation in revenues in 2020 for all manufacturing industries considered in our sample. The numbers of the x-axis are the two-digit ISTAT (Italian national statistics institute) codes of manufacturing industries.

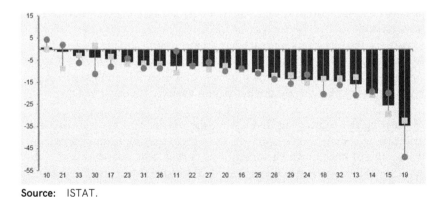

Source: ISTAT.

Figure 8.1   Revenues variation by manufacturing sector, 2020

For each industry and each firm, we calculated the 2020 variation of revenues. The first resilience index is the ratio between these two variations:

$$RESILIENCE\ INDEX_1 = \frac{REV\ VARIATION_{firm}}{REV\ VARIATION_{industry}} \qquad (1)$$

Since all industries (except one) show negative revenues' variation in 2020, the more resilient the firm is (i.e. a firm that has lower negative revenues' variation relative to the variation of the revenues of the industry or a firm that has positive revenues' variation relative to a negative industry variation of revenues), the lower this index will be.

Resilience index 2. Since resilience entails the ability of a firm to face disruptions without significant impacts in performance, we calculated for each sampled firm its "theoretical" 2020 revenue (based on the compounded annual growth rate-CAGR of the last ten years), and we compare this theoretical level to its actual revenue, as detailed in the equation below.

$$RESILIENCE\ INDEX_2 = \frac{(THEORETICAL\ REVENUE_{2020} - ACTUAL\ REVENUE_{2020})}{THEORETICAL\ REVENUE_{2020}} \qquad (2)$$

where $THEORETICAL\ REVENUE_{2020} = CAGR*ACTUAL\ REVENUE_{2019}$

A firm with actual revenues lower than theoretical revenues will show a positive index. A firm with actual revenues equal to the theoretical revenues will show an index of 0. A firm with actual revenues higher than the theoretical revenues will have a negative index. Like the first resilience index, also this one is negatively related to the resiliency of the firm.

Independent variable

Our independent variable is whether a company adopts lean or not. This is a dichotomous variable adopting value 1 if the firm has adopted lean before 2019 (221 firms) and 0 if a firm has not adopted lean before 2019 (233 firms). We also use a second independent variable that captures the extent to which firms implement lean (lean intensity). We identified two categories of lean firms depending on the numbers of lean techniques employed. By graphically analyzing the distribution of the number of adopted lean techniques across firms, we identify 25 as the cut-off number that discriminates the advanced firms (44 firms) that adopt at least 25 techniques and the beginners (177 firms) that adopt less than 25 techniques. We use two dummy variables, one for the advanced firms and one for the beginners (non-adopters is the reference group).

Control variables

We control our results for a set of variables that could affect the resilience of the firm.

- *Geographical location*: categorical variable which assumes the value "0" if the company belongs to north-east of Italy, "1" if it belongs to north-west of Italy, and "2" if it belongs to center or south of Italy.
- *Family business*: Dummy variable which assumes the value "1" if the company is a family business, or "0" otherwise.
- *Size*: number of employees.
- *Age*: the difference between the current year and the year of foundation of each company.
- *Foreign plant*: Dummy variable which assumes the value "1" if the company owns a plant abroad, or "0" otherwise.
- *Main market*: Dummy variable which assumes the value "1" if the company has Italy as its main market, or "0" otherwise.

Results

Table 8.1 shows the results of the regression analysis for the two resilience indexes. Before running the regression, we perform data trimming excluding about 10 percent of the firms with outliers' indexes. We show only the results of the model using the second independent variable ("advanced", "beginners" and "not lean" as the reference group) since regression analysis with the dichotomous variable (lean and not lean) does not show significant results.

The model with resilience index$_2$ as the dependent variable shows significant results only for the group "advanced". The relationship is negative, meaning that advanced firms have a lower resilience index than the reference group (non-lean). In other words, advanced firms have a revenue growth in 2020 closer to the one based on the CAGR, therefore showing better resilience relative to the reference group (non-lean).

We perform additional analysis as a robustness check. The extensive data trimming performed on resilience indexes suggested that the condition of normal distribution was not entirely respected. During the preliminary analysis of the variables, we observed a strong abnormality in distribution. This was confirmed also by the skewness and kurtosis which are strongly outside the suggested intervals for normal distribution (Table 8.2) as well as by the Q-Q plots.

Table 8.1   Multiple linear regressions

	RESILIENCE INDEX$_1$ (N=352)	RESILIENCE INDEX$_2$ (N=335)
Intercept	0.9693* (0.178)	0.16127* (0.0271)
LEAN CATEGORIES	(Reference level: Non-lean)	
Advanced	-0.2408 (0.260)	-0.08012* (0.0284)
Beginners	-0.0367 (0.153)	-0.01066 (0.0167)
Age	-5.53e-4 (6.33e-4)	-6.88e-4 (5.73e-4)
Size	-3.40e-5 (3.20e-4)	-4.28e-7 (4.61e-5)
Family business	-0.0509 (0.147)	0.00553 (0.0166)
GEOGRAPHICAL LOCATION	(Reference level: North-east)	
North-west	0.3858* (0.180)	0.02650 (0.0204)
Center-south	0.1882 (0.254)	0.02702 (0.0278)
Foreign plant	-0.1341 (0.178)	-0.00200 (0.0197)
Main market	-0.0546 (0.143)	-0.02074 (0.0162)
R-squared	*0.0226*	*0.0446*

Note: Standard error in parenthesis; *significance at 0.05 level.

Table 8.2   Skewness and kurtosis values for resilience indicators

	RESILIENCE INDEX$_1$	RESILIENCE INDEX$_2$
N	399	369
Skewness	-2.77	-2.09
Kurtosis	27.6	13.3
Shapiro-Wilk p	<0.001	<0.001

Table 8.3   Independent samples for Mann-Whitney test (lean vs
                   non-lean)

	N	Median	Statistic	p
RESILIENCE INDEX$_1$				
Lean	195	0.734	18.035	0.100*
Non-lean	204	0.921		
RESILIENCE INDEX$_2$				
Lean	180	0.101	14.236	0.007**
Non-lean	189	0.135		

Note: *Significance at 0.10 level; **significance at 0.05 level.

Table 8.4   Independent samples for Mann-Whitney test (advanced vs
                   non- lean+beginners)

	N	Median	Statistic	p
RESILIENCE INDEX$_1$				
Non-lean + Beginners	358	0.867	5.987	0.053*
Advanced	41	0.414		
RESILIENCE INDEX$_2$				
Non-lean + Beginners	330	0.126	4.435	0.002**
Advanced	39	0.0543		

Note: *Significance at 0.10 level; **significance at 0.05 level.

For this reason, we adopt a different approach, i.e. the Mann-Whitney test. This test is a non-parametric test (which is an alternative to the parametric t test for independent samples), and it allows to get more robust analysis in case of anomalies or asymmetries. We performed two analyses. In the first one we compare lean vs non-lean firms. In the second analysis, we compare "non-lean"+"beginners" vs "advanced firms". Results are shown in Tables 8.3 and 8.4 respectively.

For Resilience Index$_1$ results are significant at 0.10 level while results for index$_2$ are significant at 0.05 level. In both cases, lean firms show lower indexes implying higher resiliency. For example, for resilience index$_2$, lean and advanced firms show a lower median (more accentuated for the latter group), meaning that they tend to have actual revenues for 2020 closer to their theoretical revenues based on CAGR.

Discussion and research opportunities

The effect of lean on firm resilience has been discussed in recent literature with contrasting results. The objective of this chapter is to assess whether being lean helps an organization to better survive crisis and disruptive events. We carried out a study on Italian manufacturing firms during the recent Covid-19 pandemic.

Results of our study are not conclusive. We find some evidence that lean reinforces the resiliency of firms, but this evidence is rather weak. The limitations of our study and our review on lean and resilience open several avenues for future research.

We divide these research opportunities into three sections: (1) how to measure resilience using economic or financial indicators, (2) how to measure the degree of lean (lean intensity and lean maturity), and (3) the relationship between lean and resiliency.

Resilience indexes

The first important research opportunity concerns the development of sound resilience indexes both at the firm and at the supply chain level.

Most of the resilience indexes are based on survey and provide subjective measures of the resilience capabilities of the firm. Literature lacks empirical research regarding the relation between resilience capabilities and firms' economic and financial indicators (Bhamra et al., 2011). Pettit et al. (2010) and Li et al. (2017) show a positive correlation between the resilience and performance of firms. However, resilience comes at a cost connected to maintaining flexibility and to ensure redundancy (Ivanov and Dolgui, 2019).

In this study, we advance two resilience indexes based on economic indicators. The first one is the ratio between the variation of revenues of the firm and the variation of the revenues of the industry during the pandemic year. The second one is based on the difference between the theoretical revenues and the actual revenues during the pandemic year.

Our indexes suffer from several limitations. First, the economic and financial indicators for the organizations of the sample were available only for one year (2020). Future research should consider more years before and after the disruptive event to capture not just the capacity of the firm to absorb the crisis but also its capacity to react to it. Following Tortorella et al. (2022), a resilience index should capture both the ability of the firm to anticipate and monitor the crisis and the ability to adapt to (and restore from) it. Second, our indexes are based only on revenues. We invite future scholars to develop indexes based on other economic or financial performances (e.g. EBITDA, Dept/Equity). Third, our indexes measure resilience of a single firm neglecting the resilience of the supply chain in which this firm operates. The resilience of a firm (especially downstream firms) in a supply chain depends on how resilient the whole supply chain is. Future research should develop indicators that identify the weak upstream nodes (or firms) in the supply chain leading to low resilient indicators of the downstream firms.

Lean intensity and lean maturity

In our study we use two measures of lean. The first one is a dummy variable of lean/non-lean while the second one uses two dummies to capture whether the firm adopts (or not) extensively lean management. We welcome future research that develops measures that combine both the intensity of lean and the maturity of lean.

Lean intensity refers to the extent to which lean practices are adopted by the firm. Several studies find a positive relationship between financial performance and lean intensity (e.g. Fullerton and McWatters, 2001). As a measure of lean intensity some authors consider the number of lean practices adopted by the firms while others rely on experts' assessment. These are sound methodological approaches as long as they take into consideration the systemic nature of lean since lean bundles complement each other as they reinforce each other's impact on performance (Furlan et al., 2011; Shah and Ward, 2003).

Lean maturity refers to the amount (number of years) of experience with lean of the firm. Developing a lean system takes time and the financial benefits deriving from it are probably low at the beginning and increase over time. As Netland and Ferdows (2015) show, the effect of lean on operational performance follows an S-curve (low at the beginning and higher at later stages). We can assume that this "law" applies also to the relationship between lean and financial performance. However, the hypothesis that lean maturity leads to better performance (and higher resiliency) is challenged by Kinney and

Wempe (2002) who show that ROA (return on assets) improvements are mainly concentrated in the earliest years of lean adoption.

These contrasting results lead us to question how fast a firm should invest in lean. Future research can test theories like the time compression diseconomies (TCD) to answer this question. Cool et al. (2016) defined TCD as "the additional costs incurred by firms seeking to quickly reach a given level of an asset stock when this stock could be accumulated more economically over a longer period of time". According to this theory, the existence of TCD would mean that any acceleration in lean investments will likely inflate costs at an increasing rate.

Relationship between lean and resilience

We find a positive (although weak) relationship between lean and resilience. However, this relationship needs to be analyzed using a more fine-grained lens. In this study we investigate the impact of lean on resiliency regardless of the different configuration of lean bundles adopted by the firm. As Galeazzo and Furlan (2017) show, different configurations of lean practices can be equifinal with respect to a firm's financial performance.

We urge scholars to adopt a contingency approach and study the relationships between specific configurations of lean practices and different types of disruptions. Several studies suggest that different sets of lean practices show their benefits on performance depending on the characteristics of the external context. Similarly, one can argue that the effect of different configurations of lean bundles on a firm's resiliency can be contingent on the type of external disruption. As Dolgui et al. (2020) maintain, disruptions can be of different nature (operational vs strategic), different intensity (low, medium, high), and with permanent or temporary effects. We welcome studies that test relationships between specific configurations of lean bundles and specific types of disruptions.

References

Alemsan, N., Tortorella, G., Rodriguez, C. M. T., Jamkhaneh, H. B., & Lima, R. M. (2022). Lean and resilience in the healthcare supply chain: A scoping review. *International Journal of Lean Six Sigma*, 13(5), 1058–1078.

Bhamra, R., Dani, S., & Burnard, K. (2011). Resilience: The concept, a literature review and future directions. *International Journal of Production Research*, 49(18), 5375–5393.

Birkie, S. E. (2016). Operational resilience and lean: In search of synergies and tradeoffs. *Journal of Manufacturing Technology Management*, 27(2), 185–207.

Bryce, C., Ring, P., Ashby, S., & Wardman, J. K. (2020). Resilience in the face of uncertainty: Early lessons from the COVID-19 pandemic. *Journal of Risk Research*, 23(7–8), 880–887.

Christopher, M. & Rutherford, C. (2004). Creating supply chain resilience through agile six sigma. *Critical Eye*, 7(1), 24–28.

Cool, K., Dierickx, I., & Almeida, C. L. (2016). Diseconomies of time compression. In M. Augier & D. J. Teece (Eds.), *The Palgrave Encyclopedia of Strategic Management*. London: Palgrave Macmillan.

de Sá, M. M., Laczynski, P., de Souza Miguel, P. L., de Brito, P. R., & Pereira, S. (2020). Supply chain resilience: The whole is not the sum of the parts. *International Journal of Operations & Production Management*, 40(1), 92–115.

Dolgui, A. & Ivanov, D. (2021). Ripple effect and supply chain disruption management: New trends and research directions. *International Journal of Production Research*, 59(1), 102–109.

Dolgui, A., Ivanov, D., & Rozhkov, M. (2020). Does the ripple effect influence the bullwhip effect? An integrated analysis of structural and operational dynamics in the supply chain. *International Journal of Production Research*, 58(5), 1285–1301.

Fullerton, R. R. & McWatters, C. S. (2001). The production performance benefits from JIT implementation. *Journal of Operations Management*, 19(1), 81–96.

Furlan, A., Vinelli, A., & Dal Pont, G. (2011). Complementarity and lean manufacturing bundles: An empirical analysis. *International Journal of Operations & Production Management*, 31(8), 835–850.

Galeazzo, A. & Furlan, A. (2017). Lean bundles and configurations: A fsQCA approach. *Journal of Operations & Production Management*, 38(2), 513–533.

Habibi Rad, M., Mojtahedi, M., & Ostwald, M. J. (2021). The integration of lean and resilience paradigms: A systematic review identifying current and future research directions. *Sustainability*, 13(16), 8893.

Hills, M. (2015). Assuring organizational resilience with lean scenario-driven exercises. *International Journal of Emergency Services*, 4(1), 37–49.

Hosseini, S., Ivanov, D., & Dolgui, A. (2019). Review of quantitative methods for supply chain resilience analysis. *Transportation Research Part E: Logistics and Transportation Review*, 125, 285–307.

Ivanov, D. (2022). Lean resilience: AURA (active usage of resilience assets) framework for post-COVID-19 supply chain management. *The International Journal of Logistics Management*, 33(4), 1196–1217.

Ivanov, D. & Das, A. (2020). Coronavirus (COVID-19/SARS-CoV-2) and supply chain resilience: A research note. *International Journal of Integrated Supply Management*, 13(1), 90–102.

Ivanov, D. & Dolgui, A. (2019). Low-certainty-need (LCN) supply chains: A new perspective in managing disruption risks and resilience. *International Journal of Production Research*, 57(15–16), 5119–5136.

Kinney, M. R. & Wempe, W. F. (2002). Further evidence on the extent and origins of JIT's profitability effects. *The Accounting Review*, 77(1), 203–225.

Li, X., Wu, Q., Holsapple, C. W., & Goldsby, T. (2017). An empirical examination of firm financial performance along dimensions of supply chain resilience. *Management Research Review*, 40(3), 254–269.

Meyer, A. D. (1982). Adapting to environmental jolts. *Administrative Science Quarterly*, 27(4), 515–537.

Netland, T. H. & Ferdows, K. (2015). Implementing corporate lean programs: The effect of management control practices, *Journal of Operational Management*, 36(1), 90–102.

Parameswaran, A. & Ranadewa, K. A. T. O. (2021). Resilience to COVID-19 through lean construction. *FARU Journal*, 8(1), 35–45.

Pettit, T. J., Fiksel, J., & Croxton, K. L. (2010). Ensuring supply chain resilience: Development of a conceptual framework. *Journal of Business Logistics*, 31(1), 1–21.

Ruiz-Benítez, R., López, C., & Real, J. C. (2018). The lean and resilient management of the supply chain and its impact on performance. *International Journal of Production Economics*, 203, 190–202.

Shah, R. & Ward, P. T. (2003). Lean manufacturing: Context, practice bundles, and performance. *Journal of Operations Management*, 21(2), 129–149.

Tortorella, G., Fogliatto, F., Gao, S., & Chan, T.-K. (2022). Contributions of Industry 4.0 to supply chain resilience. *The International Journal of Logistics Management*, 33(2), 547–566.

Trabucco, M. & De Giovanni, P. (2021). Achieving resilience and business sustainability during COVID-19: The role of lean supply chain practices and digitalization. *Sustainability*, 13(22), 12369.

Uhrin, Á., Moyano-Fuentes, J., & Cámara, S. B. (2020). Firm risk and self-reference on past performance as main drivers of lean production implementation. *Journal of Manufacturing Technology Management*, 31(3), 458–478.

PART IV

Lean leadership and behaviors

9 How to drive proactivity in lean settings

Michela Carraro and Ambra Galeazzo

Introduction

Current research increasingly recognizes that the understanding of firm-level phenomena such as lean practices and continuous improvement initiatives should pay attention to the workforce, whose behavior determines the performance of macro-level phenomena (Barney and Felin, 2013).

An increasing number of studies demonstrate that the successful implementation of lean management relies on employees' behavior toward continuous improvement[1] (CI) initiatives (Furlan et al., 2019; Lantz et al., 2015; Rebelo et al., 2016). Indeed, to foster CI, all members of the organization are continuously encouraged to adopt proactive behaviors at work to challenge the status quo and identify opportunities for improvement, irrespective of their role in the hierarchy.

However, few studies investigate what characteristics of the lean context encourage employees to adopt proactive behaviors. The purpose of this chapter is to review the extant literature to provide a comprehensive model that links lean management to the antecedents of proactive behaviors.

---

[1] In this chapter, CI is defined as a dynamic capability that enables companies to continually change internal processes through stepwise adjustments and modifications to adapt the lean setting to new challenges and enhance several operational performance dimensions such as productivity, efficiency, quality, dependability, and flexibility (Anand et al., 2009; Fullerton et al., 2014).

A literature review on lean and proactivity

According to the organizational psychology and organizational behavior (OB) literature, individuals can perform different forms of behavior in the workplace. Griffin et al. (2007) classified these forms as proficiency, adaptivity, and proactivity. Proficiency refers to employee behaviors that closely follow the known requirements described in job roles. Adaptivity reflects behaviors that take on more dynamic roles in the workplace, including dealing with change. Proactivity refers to such behaviors as: "taking initiative in improving current circumstances or creating new ones; it involves challenging the status quo rather than passively adapting to present conditions" (Crant, 2000, p. 436).

Extant literature suggests that proactive behaviors can take several forms (Parker and Bindl, 2016; Parker and Collins, 2010). For instance, taking charge refers to those proactive behaviors that are actively involved in the change of the work environment (Morrison and Phelps, 1999). Also, personal initiative is an example of proactive behavior that employees perform when they identify, introduce, and promote new ideas within the organization to anticipate challenges and foster change (Bateman and Crant, 1993). Problem-solving is another form of proactive behavior that consists of systematically investigating causes and barriers to change and developing solutions aimed at preventing problems (Furlan et al., 2019). Further examples of proactive behaviors include voice, helping behavior, and seeking feedback (Cantor and Jin, 2019). Expressing voice refers to employees speaking up, sharing ideas for improvement, and encouraging others to do the same. Helping behaviors are performed by employees who step in and support others. Seeking feedback implies that employees ask for advice from co-workers and supervisors to improve their work performance. Overall, these forms of proactivity share three common features: they are self-initiated, indicating employees take the initiative when a problem or opportunity arises; they are future-focused, indicating employees seek to identify solutions to prevent problems and to make long-term improvement opportunities; and they are change-oriented, meaning employees aim to bring about change rather than react to a situation.

The relationship between lean management and proactivity has received increasing attention in the operations management (OM) literature in the last few years, mainly addressing two research issues. The first issue aims to understand the role of proactive behaviors in CI initiatives, demonstrating a positive relationship between proactivity and performance improvements (e.g., Choo et al., 2015; Tucker, 2016; Tucker et al., 2002). For example, Choo et al. (2015) demonstrate that managers showing a propensity to adopt a systematic problem-solving behavior are likely to enhance the level of the firm's knowledge stock and, ultimately, the number of manufacturing improvements. Similarly, in the context of hospitals, Tucker et al. (2002) highlight that nurses performing proactive problem-solving behaviors are more likely to learn from failures and identify opportunities for improvement.

The second issue explores the antecedents of proactive behaviors in lean contexts and examines how lean practices influence such behaviors. Previous research has yielded conflicting findings on this topic. Some authors have identified a negative association between lean practices and proactivity. For instance, Morrison (2015) demonstrates that lean settings characterized by time and resource shortages inhibit employees from collaborating within their teams, leading them to prefer relying on workarounds to address issues, which hampers proactive behavior. Moreover, Mazzocato et al. (2016) highlight that employees primarily use suggestion systems to recommend ideas in reaction to a problem they have encountered rather than utilizing them to test and evaluate new ideas, thereby fostering reactive behaviors instead of proactive ones. Finally, Parker (2003) shows that lean teams reported decreased job autonomy and diminished utilization of skills, which in turn were found to diminish employees' organizational commitment and proactivity.

On the contrary, other studies shed light on how lean practices can actually facilitate proactivity. Lantz et al. (2015) provide an explanation for the negative association between low autonomy and proactivity. They demonstrate that even when employees have limited autonomy in task execution due to high levels of standardization, proactive behaviors can still be nurtured through their involvement in defining work procedures and goals, as well as their collaboration with support functions. Similarly, Escrig-Tena et al. (2018) delve into the relationship between quality management (QM) practices and proactivity. They find that soft QM, which emphasizes the adoption of social practices such as top management commitment, training, and employee involvement, encourages employees' proactivity in driving improvements. However, the authors do not find support for a positive relationship between hard QM and proactivity.

Overall, the literature review highlights two main outcomes. First, proactive behaviors are recognized as individual antecedents of CI. Second, the effectiveness of lean contexts in fostering proactive behaviors remains uncertain. This raises an important issue, suggesting that lean practices may not be effectively fostering proactivity, thereby hindering the implementation of a virtuous and recursive cycle between lean, proactivity, and CI. Indeed, CI is a needed capability to leverage for a relentless strengthening of lean management. Without

CI, lean practices may struggle to adapt to changing external environments and sustain long-term operational performance.

To address this issue, we propose a theoretical model that aims to reconcile the mixed findings from our literature review regarding lean contexts and proactivity. Specifically, our model suggests an indirect relationship between lean practices and proactive behaviors, arguing that lean practices transform a firm's organizational structure and infrastructure, thereby triggering proactive behaviors in support of CI.

The theoretical model

Linking together the literature on lean management and proactive behavior, we propose a model to explain how lean practices and proactivity are related (Figure 9.1). We maintain that lean management affects proactivity by changing a firm's organizational structure and infrastructure.

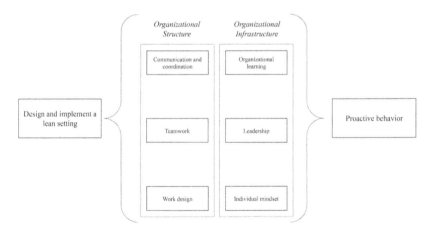

Figure 9.1   Model

Referring to organizational structure, Simon (1997, pp. 18–19) defines it as "the pattern of communications and relations among a group of human beings, including the processes for making and implementing decision". Child (1972, p. 2) delineates it as "the formal allocation of work roles and the administrative mechanisms to control and integrate work activities including those which cross formal organizational boundaries." Building upon these definitions, we refer to organizational structure as the formal design of communication and coordination practices, control mechanisms, and allocation of work roles among employees that influence the work context's configuration. The literature on lean management highlights that lean practices intervene in all these structural elements. Specifically, they impact communication and coordination mechanisms by simplifying and expediting the exchange of information and materials. They affect control mechanisms by replacing hierarchical systems of management control with more bottom-up, output-oriented control, and team-based organizations. Lastly, they influence job design by empowering employees with the skills and competencies necessary for successfully implementing lean practices.

Referring to organizational infrastructure, organization theorists define it as the systems, protocols, and processes that an organization adopts for managing and directing work (Schein, 1992; Scott, 1981). It encompasses all the decisions and practices that the organization embraces to operate effectively within its competitive environment. OM literature emphasizes that lean management provides a consistent and comprehensive set of decisions and practices crucial for developing dynamic capabilities that support CI. In particular, lean practices affect organizational learning by fostering an organizational culture of constant adaption and improvement. They impact leadership styles by encouraging managers to provide the appropriate support and stimuli to employees. Lastly, they shape individual mindsets by developing cognitive capabilities that contribute significantly to identifying improvement opportunities and stimulating proactivity.

In the following sections, we elaborate on how lean practices intervene in changing organizational and infrastructural factors to foster proactive behaviors.

Organizational structure

Communication and coordination

Lean management is characterized by the development of formal communication and coordination mechanisms that aim to identify, standardize, and streamline the flow of information and materials, aligning all members of the organization toward common objectives. Lean practices such as value stream mapping and visual management systems assist top management in identifying processes that improve coordination and communication among functions within and across organizational boundaries. This coordination enhances employees' understanding of task interdependencies and the chain of command, facilitating interactions, communication, and cooperation (Yen and Teng, 2013; Zeng et al., 2017). Consequently, lean contexts exhibit improved information quality and broader information flow. This enhanced information equips employees with better knowledge to address problems and enhance their job skills and work methods. By constantly assimilating new and valuable knowledge, employees are therefore more likely to exhibit behaviors such as voicing their opinions, engaging in helping behaviors, and proactive problem-solving (Cantor and Macdonald, 2009; Furlan et al., 2019).

Furthermore, Total Preventive Maintenance (TPM) and lean practices like SMED (Single Minute Exchange of Die), kanban, poka-yoke, and heijunka contribute to reducing variability, increasing standardization, and promoting synchronization of processes. This fosters the development of stable and well-organized working environments. Stability and order provide employees with a clear understanding of their tasks, strengthening their engagement in improvement initiatives and demonstrating their task competency (Bandura, 1988), thereby fostering proactive behaviors.

Teamwork

Proactivity is closely linked to teamwork, which creates a psychologically safe working environment where employees can freely share knowledge, openly discuss errors, and assist one another in diagnosing and solving problems (Choo et al., 2007; Galeazzo et al., 2017; Lantz et al., 2015). Such teamwork environments can effectively trigger proactivity. However, motivating employees to effectively join forces toward a common goal is a challenging capability to achieve. For example, in a 22-year study on 308 companies, Birdi et al. (2008) demonstrate that teamwork practices take six to nine years to generate productivity improvements. The authors explain that this delay is due to the time required for employees to learn how to work together effectively.

Lean settings are considered successful in fostering teamwork (Liker, 2004; Monden, 1994) as they are organized into small teams of multiskilled operators periodically involved in team-based improvement activities and kaizen events (Kobayashi, 1995). Team-based improvement activities and kaizen events fall under Vough and colleagues' definition of proactivity routine: "a socially constructed and accepted process by which individual employees [can] initiate team- or unit-level changes in their work processes" (2017, p. 1193). Proactivity routines play a crucial role in supporting teamwork toward the implementation of changes, especially in social contexts characterized by low autonomy.

By providing employees with a specific pattern of action to follow during change implementation, proactivity routines aim to facilitate the coordination of employees' improvement efforts and enable the team to achieve changes effectively. It is worth noting that proactivity routines describe how teams should pursue improvement opportunities, but do not specify which issues to raise, when to raise them, or which targets to work toward (Kobayashi, 1995; Vough et al., 2017). In essence, proactivity routines promote teamwork toward CI while enabling employees to determine their own improvement goals.

Work design

Proactive behaviors are influenced by employees' job characteristics. According to the job design literature, jobs can be described using various models such as the job characteristics model by Hackman and Oldham (1975), the job demands-resources model by Bakker and Demerouti (2007), and the work design questionnaire by Morgeson and Humphrey (2006), which shed light on how tasks should be designed across dimensions like social, motivational, cognitive, and physical to foster proactive behaviors.

Lean management is defined as a socio-technical system that requires firms to implement technical practices such as TQM, TPM, and JIT, along with human-related practices such as training and coaching programs. This highlights the need for organizations to develop employees' skills and competencies to support the implementation of lean practices (Bortolotti et al., 2015; Galeazzo and Furlan, 2018). To foster skills and competencies, employees' job characteristics need to be revised. For instance, training programs in lean organizations that enable employees to assume flexible roles by working on multiple workstations (Cimini et al., 2023) foster job enrichment and job enlargement. This endows employees with a broader and deeper understanding of internal processes compared to traditional organizations. Additionally, lean practices such as kaizen events and PDCA cycles reshape employees' job characteristics. These practices require employees to take part in problem-solving processes and behave proactively to find new improvement opportunities. As a result, employees exercise a certain degree of autonomy in decision-making processes and introduce complexity and variety into their daily tasks compared to employees in traditional working settings (Cullinane et al., 2014). Moreover, past studies demonstrate that lean organizations foster social support through practices such as Gemba walks, U-cell layout, and the placement of technical staff and line managers close to the shop floor, which increase work engagement, employee active participation, responsibility, and psychological ownership toward the organization (Eaidgah et al., 2016; Huo and Boxall, 2018). These personal attitudes and behaviors are traditionally associated with various forms of proactivity, such as organizational citizenship behavior, stewardship behavior, helping behavior, and voice behavior (Dawkins et al., 2017).

Finally, although some lean practices may have negative impacts on job characteristics and proactivity, the implementation of other lean practices can offset these effects. For example, JIT may increase the work pace in employees' jobs because tasks need to be performed more quickly. Similarly, TQM may increase workload as employees need to pay greater attention and perform additional tasks to minimize errors and improve quality. These practices can act as a hindrance to demands on employees, with an overall reduction of engagement and an increase in exhaustion (Cullinane et al., 2014). However, human-related lean practices endow employees with resources that make employees perceive hindrances as challenges instead. As a result, employees perceive the implementation of JIT and TQM as motivating conditions (Beraldin et al., 2019), thereby increasing their well-being and proactivity.

Organizational infrastructure

Organizational learning

Organizational learning should be developed to motivate employees to adopt proactive behaviors at work. Organizational learning can be defined as the process of generating and integrating new organizational knowledge to modify and adapt operating routines to shifting competitive conditions (Zollo and Winter, 2002), thereby enabling the organization to maintain a sustainable competitive advantage.

Past studies suggest that belonging to an organization that stimulates organizational learning is an important lever for employees' proactivity at work. For instance, Furlan et al. (2019) show that when employees feel that they are involved in meaningful learning mechanisms, they are more prone to dynamically adapt organizational knowledge to the changing environment and to identify better solutions to problems. Furthermore, Bakker and Demerouti (2007) stress that employees who perceive learning from past successes and failures as a key element of their work role tend to be more engaged with their job and suggest more ideas for improving current circumstances. Finally, Saabye and Powell (2022) demonstrate that action learning interventions aimed at teaching employees to experiment and critically reflect on their experiences stimulate proactivity at work.

Lean management fosters organizational learning (Ballé and Régnier, 2007; Kristensen et al., 2022). As one of the core principles of lean is striving for perfection (Womack and Jones, 1996), employees in lean contexts are expected to be continuously challenging current practices and looking for better ways of doing things, and both failure and success experiences are connotated as learning opportunities that constitute part of the employee's work role. Based on the "striving for perfection" principle, lean contexts aim to create an organizational framework that promotes inquiry and experimentation and empowers employees to take an active role in adapting and continuously improving current practices.

More recent research emphasizes that lean management acts as an education system that stimulates employees to engage in learning opportunities and, at the same time, helps them learn how to learn (see Part II of this book). Accordingly, successful lean transformations are generally achieved through action learning interventions that develop a learning-to-learn capability (Powell and Coughlan, 2020; Saabye and Powell, 2022). This capability empowers employees by enabling them to employ lean tools to experiment independently, reflect on their experiences, and develop improved solutions to problems, thereby stimulating their proactivity at work.

Leadership

Lean managers modify the typical command and control management practices to engage employees in lean transformations (Netland et al., 2020). It is important for them to become role models, communicate a positive vision, provide individualized consideration, stimulate innovation and creativity, respect people, celebrate and recognize success, and build motivation and engagement (e.g., Van Assen, 2018) in order to support teams in the successful implementation of lean management. Overall, these leadership characteristics describe the lean leadership style (Liker and Convis, 2011).

Lean leadership style has many similarities with other well-known leadership styles. For example, lean leadership has features in common with the transformational leadership style described by Bass (1990). They both engender changes in employees' beliefs, attitudes, and values in order to motivate them to perform tasks beyond expectations. It also shares some elements with the servant leadership style because they both aim to grow employees to their full potential (Stone et al., 2004). Finally, lean leadership is similar to empowering leadership because they both try to develop employees' self-leadership capabilities, participative decision-making processes, and innovative performance (Konczak et al., 2000).

In general, Tortorella and Fogliatto (2017) warn managers to adapt their lean leadership styles to the level of lean maturity and their hierarchical positioning in the organization. Despite the need to understand when and how lean leadership styles should be adopted, extant research extensively agrees that lean leadership and other similar leadership styles (e.g., transformational, empowering) positively influence any form of proactive behavior (Liker and Convis, 2011; López-Domínguez et al., 2013).

Individual mindset

One of the most difficult challenges to CI is to mitigate the "we have always done it this way" attitude. This attitude is embedded in the mindset of individuals who tend to over-rely on historical experience to fix problems with minimum cognitive efforts rather than proactively engaging in analytical reasoning (Mohaghegh and Furlan, 2020; Wu et al., 2014). Fostering proactive behaviors, therefore, encompasses a shift in individual mindsets that must embrace change as improvement opportunities. To do so, organizations need to induce employees to develop the cognitive capabilities that enable them to engage in intentional, rational, and cognitively effortful activities to improve their workplace.

Cognitive capabilities can be defined as an individual's capacity to perform one or more mental activities that support human agency (Bandura, 2001; Helfat and Peteraf, 2015). Several theories have been developed to explain how cognitive capabilities affect employees' proactivity at work. For instance, drawing on expectancy theory (Vroom, 1964), some scholars suggest that individuals employ cognition to anticipate the consequences of their actions and to assess the likelihood that their actions will yield the expected results before implementing changes (Morrison and Phelps, 1999). Other researchers explain the relationship between cognitive capabilities and proactivity by drawing on social cognitive theory (Bandura, 2001), according to which individuals regulate their motivation and actions based on their self-efficacy beliefs about being in control of their actions (Frese and Fay, 2001; Parker et al., 2006). Contrary to approaches that rely on waiting for instructions or implementing potentially obsolete solutions to react to problems, cognitive capabilities stimulate individuals to anticipate and diagnose problems, specify their root causes, and develop mental simulations to evaluate potential solutions and improvements to current processes (Mohaghegh and Furlan, 2020; Wu et al., 2014). In other words, the amount of effort that employees devote to performing mental activities is positively related to their learning abilities. As a result, it is important to foster employees' cognitive capabilities to stimulate proactivity at work.

Lean settings rely on different tools and techniques that encourage employees to develop their cognitive capabilities through their engagement in structured thinking activities. For instance, A3 thinking facilitates the development of cognitive capabilities by asking employees to specify the current situation, determine the root cause of a problem, and develop and implement adequate countermeasures (Shook, 2008). Furthermore, techniques to perform root causes analysis have been developed to help employees reason about and address problems at the source. Sakichi Toyoda suggested addressing the question "Why is this problem occurring?" repeatedly until identifying the source of the problem (Ohno, 1988). Kaoru Ishikawa proposed a fishbone diagram to investigate the possible causes of a problem by brainstorming on six main categories, namely methods, machines, manpower, materials, measurements, and environment (Ishikawa, 1982). These examples demonstrate how lean tools and practices engage employees in structured thinking activities, thereby stimulating the development of cognitive capabilities. Cognitive capabilities, in turn, help employees to self-regulate their motivation and actions to proactively enact changes and tackle improvement opportunities.

Future research

The increasing recognition of employees as the pivotal drivers of macro-level operational phenomena, such as CI, highlights the importance of further exploring the interplay between lean contexts and employee proactivity at work. This exploration is crucial to address and reconcile the mixed empirical findings of previous studies (e.g., Anand et al., 2009; Lantz et al., 2015; Mazzocato et al., 2016; Parker, 2003). In this regard, we propose that adopting a multilevel approach similar to the one employed in our model provides a comprehensive theoretical lens. Our proposed model emphasizes that lean management influences proactivity through organizational structures and infrastructures at three levels. Specifically, macro-level factors impact organizational learning and communication and coordination mechanisms, meso-level factors influence teamwork and leaders, and micro-level factors shape shopfloor employees' jobs and mindsets, ultimately influencing proactivity. By uncovering and understanding the interconnectedness of these macro-, meso-, and micro-level factors influenced by lean management, we can gain deeper insights into the link between lean practices and proactive behaviors. Figure 9.2 presents several research questions that can guide future investigations to a better understanding and testing of our proposed theoretical model in real-world settings.

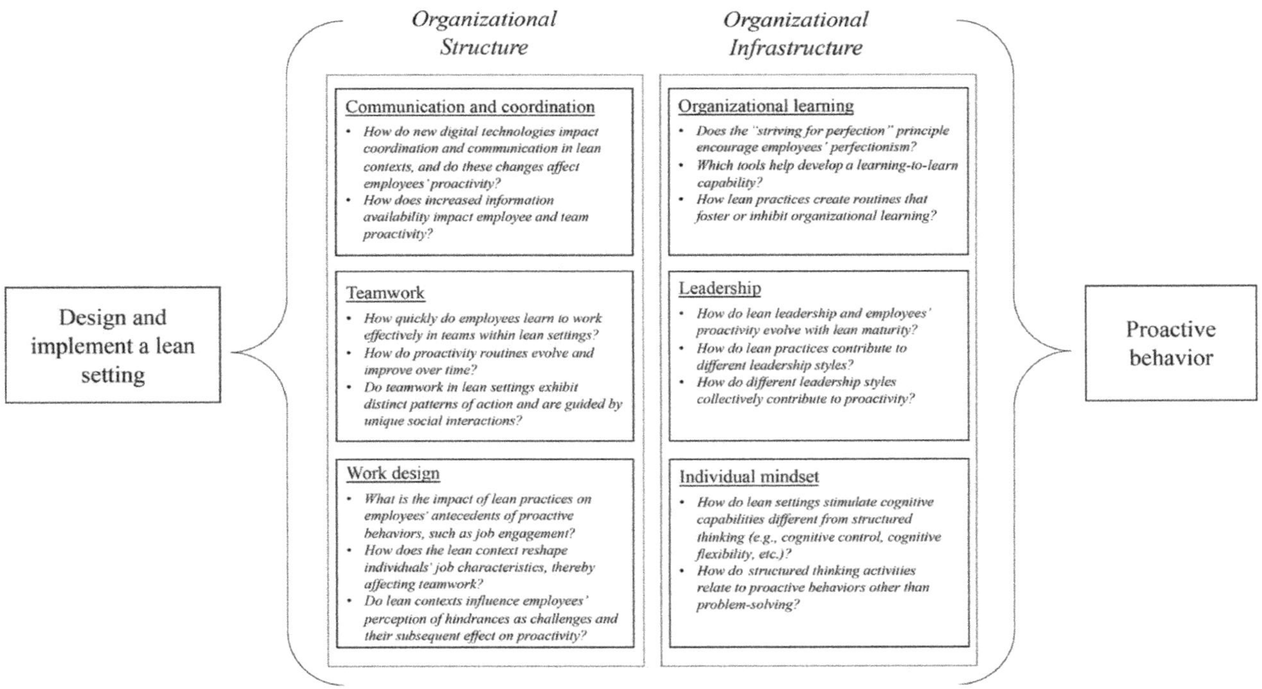

Figure 9.2   A future agenda for lean practices and proactive behaviors

Proactive behavior

Organizational Infrastructure

Organizational learning
- *Does the "striving for perfection" principle encourage employees' perfectionism?*
- *Which tools help develop a learning-to-learn capability?*
- *How lean practices create routines that foster or inhibit organizational learning?*

Leadership
- *How do lean leadership and employees' proactivity evolve with lean maturity?*
- *How do lean practices contribute to different leadership styles?*
- *How do different leadership styles collectively contribute to proactivity?*

Individual mindset
- *How do lean settings stimulate cognitive capabilities different from structured thinking (e.g., cognitive control, cognitive flexibility, etc.)?*
- *How do structured thinking activities relate to proactive behaviors other than problem-solving?*

Organizational Structure

Communication and coordination
- *How do new digital technologies impact coordination and communication in lean contexts, and do these changes affect employees' proactivity?*
- *How does increased information availability impact employee and team proactivity?*

Teamwork
- *How quickly do employees learn to work effectively in teams within lean settings?*
- *How do proactivity routines evolve and improve over time?*
- *Do teamwork in lean settings exhibit distinct patterns of action and are guided by unique social interactions?*

Work design
- *What is the impact of lean practices on employees' antecedents of proactive behaviors, such as job engagement?*
- *How does the lean context reshape individuals' job characteristics, thereby affecting teamwork?*
- *Do lean contexts influence employees' perception of hindrances as challenges and their subsequent effect on proactivity?*

Design and implement a lean setting

References

Anand, G., Ward, P. T., Tatikonda, M. v., & Schilling, D. A. (2009). Dynamic capabilities through continuous improvement infrastructure. *Journal of Operations
Management*, 27(6), 444–461.

Bakker, A. B. & Demerouti, E. (2007). The job demands-resources model: State of the
art. *Journal of Managerial Psychology*, 22(3), 309–328.

Ballé, M. & Régnier, A. (2007). Lean as a learning system in a hospital ward. *Leadership
in Health Services*, 20(1), 33–41.

Bandura, A. (1988). Self-efficacy conception of anxiety. *Anxiety Research*, 1, 77–98.

Bandura, A. (2001). Social cognitive theory: An agentic perspective. *Annual Review of
Psychology*, 52, 1–26.

Barney, J. B. & Felin, T. (2013). What are microfoundations? *Academy of Management
Perspectives*, 27(2), 138–155.

Bass, B. M. (1990). From transactional to transformational leadership: Learning to
share the vision. *Organizational Dynamics*, 18(3), 19–31.

Bateman, T. S. & Crant, J. M. (1993). The proactive component of organizational behavior: A measure and correlates. *Journal of Organizational Behavior*, 14(2), 103–118.

Beraldin, A. R., Danese, P., & Romano, P. (2019). An investigation of the relationship between lean and well-being based on the job demands-resources model.
International Journal of Operations & Production Management, 39(12), 1295–1322.

Birdi, K., Clegg, C., Patterson, M., Robinson, A., Stride, C. B., Wall, T. D., & Wood, S.
J. (2008). The impact of human resource and operational management practices on
company productivity: A longitudinal study. *Personnel Psychology*, 61(3), 467–501.

Bortolotti, T., Boscari, S., & Danese, P. (2015). Successful lean implementation:
Organizational culture and soft lean practices. *International Journal of Production
Economics*, 160, 182–201.

Cantor, D. E. & Jin, Y. (2019). Theoretical and empirical evidence of behavioral and
production line factors that influence helping behavior. *Journal of Operations
Management*, 65(4), 312–332.

Cantor, D. E. & Macdonald, J. R. (2009). Decision-making in the supply chain:
Examining problem solving approaches and information availability. *Journal of
Operations Management*, 27(3), 220–232.

Child, J. (1972). Organizational structure, environment, and performance: The role of
strategic choice. *Sociology*, 6, 2–22.

Choo, A. S., Linderman, K. W., & Schroeder, R. G. (2007). Method and context perspectives on learning and knowledge creation in quality management. *Journal of
Operations Management*, 25(4), 918–931.

Choo, A. S., Nag, R., & Xia, Y. (2015). The role of executive problem solving in
knowledge accumulation and manufacturing improvements. *Journal of Operations
Management*, 36(1), 63–74.

Cimini, C., Lagorio, A., & Gaiardelli, P. (2023). The evolution of operators' role in
production: How lean manufacturing and Industry 4.0 affect job enlargement and
job enrichment. *International Journal of Production Research*, 61(24), 8493–8511.

Crant, J. M. (2000). Proactive behavior in organizations. *Journal of Management*, 26(3),
435–462.

Cullinane, S. J., Bosak, J., Flood, P. C., & Demerouti, E. (2014). Job design under lean
manufacturing and the quality of working life: A job demands and resources perspective. *International Journal of Human Resource Management*, 25(21), 2996–3015.

Dawkins, S., Tian, A. W., Newman, A., & Martin, A. (2017). Psychological ownership: A review and research agenda. *Journal of Organizational Behavior*, 38(2), 163–183.

Eaidgah, Y., Maki, A. A., Kurczewski, K., & Abdekhodaee, A. (2016). Visual management, performance management and continuous improvement: A lean manufacturing approach. *International Journal of Lean Six Sigma*, 7(2), 187–210.

Escrig-Tena, A. B., Segarra-Ciprés, M., García-Juan, B., & Beltrán-Martín, I. (2018). The impact of hard and soft quality management and proactive behaviour in determining innovation performance. *International Journal of Production Economics*, 200, 1–14.

Frese, M. & Fay, D. (2001). Personal initiative: An active work for the 21st century. *Research in Organizational Behavior*, 23, 133–187.

Fullerton, R. R., Kennedy, F. A., & Widener, S. K. (2014). Lean manufacturing and firm performance: The incremental contribution of lean management accounting practices. *Journal of Operations Management*, 32(7–8), 414–428.

Furlan, A., Galeazzo, A., & Paggiaro, A. (2019). Organizational and perceived learning in the workplace: A multilevel perspective on employees' problem solving. *Organization Science*, 30(2), 280–297.

Galeazzo, A. & Furlan, A. (2018). Lean bundles and configurations: A fsQCA approach. *International Journal of Operations & Production Management*, 38(2), 513–533.

Galeazzo, A., Furlan, A., & Vinelli, A. (2017). The organizational infrastructure of continuous improvement: An empirical analysis. *Operations Management Research*, 10(1–2), 33–46.

Griffin, M. A., Neal, A., & Parker, S. K. (2007). A new model of work role performance: Positive behavior in uncertain and interdependent contexts. *The Academy of Management Journal*, 50(2), 327–347.

Hackman, J. R. & Oldham, G. R. (1975). Development of the job diagnostic survey. *Journal of Applied Psychology*, 60(2), 159–170.

Helfat, C. E. & Peteraf, M. A. (2015). Managerial cognitive capabilities and the microfoundations of dynamic capabilities. *Strategic Management Journal*, 36(6), 831–850.

Huo, M.-L. & Boxall, P. (2018). Are all aspects of lean production bad for workers? An analysis of how problem-solving demands affect employee well-being. *Human Resource Management Journal*, 28(4), 569–584.

Ishikawa, K. (1982). *Guide to Quality Control*, 2nd edition. Tokyo: Asian Productivity Organization.

Kobayashi, I. (1995). *20 Keys to Workplace Improvement*. New York: Productivity Press.

Konczak, L. J., Stelly, D. J., & Trusty, M. L. (2000). Defining and measuring empowering leader behaviors: Development of an upward feedback instrument. *Educational and Psychological Measurement*, 60(2), 301–313.

Kristensen, T. B., Saabye, H., & Edmondson, A. (2022). Becoming a learning organization while enhancing performance: The case of LEGO. *International Journal of Operations & Production Management*, 42(13), 438–481.

Lantz, A., Hansen, N., & Antoni, C. (2015). Participative work design in lean production: A strategy for dissolving the paradox between standardized work and team proactivity by stimulating team learning? *Journal of Workplace Learning*, 27(1), 19–33.

Liker, J. K. (2004). *Toyota Way: 14 Management Principles from the World's Greatest Manufacturer*. New York: McGraw-Hill Education.

Liker, J. & Convis, G. (2011). *The Toyota Way to Lean Leadership: Achieving and Sustaining Excellence through Leadership Development*. New York: McGraw-Hill.

López-Domínguez, M., Enache, M., Sallan, J. M., & Simo, P. (2013). Transformational leadership as an antecedent of change-oriented organizational citizenship behavior. *Journal of Business Research*, 66(10), 2147–2152.

Mazzocato, P., Stenfors-Hayes, T., von Thiele Schwarz, U., Hasson, H., & Nyström, M. E. (2016). Kaizen practice in healthcare: A qualitative analysis of hospital employees' suggestions for improvement. *BMJ Open*, 6. https://doi.org/10.1136/bmjopen-2016-012256.

Mohaghegh, M. & Furlan, A. (2020). Systematic problem-solving and its antecedents: A synthesis of the literature. *Management Research Review*, 43(9), 1033–1062.

Monden, Y. (1994). *Toyota Production System*, 2nd edition. London: Chapman & Hall.

Morgeson, F. P. & Humphrey, S. E. (2006). The Work Design Questionnaire (WDQ): Developing and validating a comprehensive measure for assessing job design and the nature of work. *Journal of Applied Psychology*, 91(6), 1321–1339.

Morrison, B. (2015). The problem with workarounds is that they work: The persistence of resource shortages. *Journal of Operations Management*, 39(1), 79–91.

Morrison, E. W. & Phelps, C. C. (1999). Taking charge at work: Extrarole efforts to initiate workplace change. *Academy of Management Journal*, 42(4), 403–419.

Netland, T. H., Powell, D. J., & Hines, P. (2020). Demystifying lean leadership. *International Journal of Lean Six Sigma*, 11(3), 543–554.

Ohno, T. (1988). *Toyota Production Systems: Beyond Large Scale Production*. New York: Productivity Press.

Parker, S. K. (2003). Longitudinal effects of lean production on employee outcomes and the mediating role of work characteristics. *Journal of Applied Psychology*, 88(4), 620–634.

Parker, S. K. & Bindl, U. K. (2016). Proactivity at work: A big picture perspective on a construct that matters. In S. K. Parker and U. K. Bindl (eds.), *Proactivity at Work: Making Things Happen in Organizations*. New York: Routledge, pp. 1–20.

Parker, S. K. & Collins, C. G. (2010). Taking stock: Integrating and differentiating multiple proactive behaviors. *Journal of Management*, 36(3), 633–662.

Parker, S. K., Williams, H. M., & Turner, N. (2006). Modeling the antecedents of proactive behavior at work. *Journal of Applied Psychology*, 91(3), 636–652.

Powell, D. & Coughlan, P. (2020). Corporate lean programs: Practical insights and implications for learning and continuous improvement. *Procedia CIRP*, 93, 820–825.

Rebelo, M. F., Santos, G., & Silva, R. (2016). Integration of management systems: Towards a sustained success and development of organizations. *Journal of Cleaner Production*, 127, 96–111.

Saabye, H. & Powell, D. J. (2022). Fostering insights and improvements from IIoT systems at the shop floor: A case of industry 4.0 and lean complementarity enabled by action learning. *International Journal of Lean Six Sigma*. https://doi.org/10.1108/IJLSS-01-2022-0017.

Schein, E. H. (1992). *Organizational Culture and Leadership*. San Francisco: Jossey-Bass.

Scott, W. R. (1981). *Organizations: Rational, Natural, and Open Systems*. Upper Saddle River, NJ: Prentice-Hall.

Shook, J. (2008). *Managing to Learn: Using the A3 Management Process to Solve Problems, Gain Agreement, Mentor and Lead*. Cambridge, MA: Lean Enterprise Institute.

Simon, H. A. (1997). *Administrative Behavior*, 4th edition. New York: Macmillan.

Stone, A. G., Russell, R. F., & Patterson, K. (2004). Transformational versus servant leadership: A difference in leader focus. *Leadership & Organization Development Journal*, 25(4), 349–361.

Tortorella, G. & Fogliatto, F. (2017). Implementation of lean manufacturing and situational leadership styles: An empirical study. *Leadership & Organization Development Journal*, 38(7), 946–968.

Tucker, A. L. (2016). The impact of workaround difficulty on frontline employees' response to operational failures: A laboratory experiment on medication administration. *Management Science*, 62(4), 1124–1144.

Tucker, A. L., Edmondson, A. C., & Spear, S. (2002). When problem solving prevents organizational learning. *Journal of Organizational Change Management*, 15(2), 122–137.

Van Assen, M. F. (2018). Exploring the impact of higher management's leadership styles on lean management. *Total Quality Management and Business Excellence*, 29(11–12), 1312–1341.

Vough, H. C., Bindl, U. K., & Parker, S. K. (2017). Proactivity routines: The role of social processes in how employees self-initiate change. *Human Relations*, 70(10), 1191–1216.

Vroom, V. H. (1964). *Work and Motivation*. Hoboken, NJ: Wiley.

Womack, J. & Jones, D. (1996). *Lean Thinking: Banish Waste and Create Wealth in Your Corporation*. London: Simon & Schuster.

Wu, C. H., Parker, S. K., & de Jong, J. P. J. (2014). Need for cognition as an antecedent of individual innovation behavior. *Journal of Management*, 40(6), 1511–1534.

Yen, C. H. & Teng, H. Y. (2013). The effect of centralization on organizational citizenship behavior and deviant workplace behavior in the hospitality industry. *Tourism Management*, 36, 401–410.

Zeng, J., Zhang, W., Matsui, Y., & Zhao, X. (2017). The impact of organizational context on hard and soft quality management and innovation performance. *International Journal of Production Economics*, 185, 240–251.

Zollo, M. & Winter, S. G. (2002). Deliberate learning and the evolution of dynamic capabilities. *Organization Science*, 13(3), 339–351.

10 Leading lean transformations: towards a 3D view of lean leadership

Desirée H. van Dun

Introduction

In the previous two decades, increasingly scholars have addressed the "soft" or leadership aspects of effective lean implementation. One of the seminal papers in this regard was written by Pauline Found and Rebecca Harvey at Cardiff Business School's Lean Enterprise Research Centre. They explored Jeffrey Liker's proposition that lean requires "leaders who live the system from top to bottom" (Found & Harvey, 2006, p. 36; 2007). Since then, a plethora of papers have examined "lean leadership" from a variety of angles. This development was also driven by the call from practitioners who struggled their way through lean implementation and who discovered that, in their effort to copycat Toyota, a mere lean tool application orientation was not a panacea to their operational issues.

Lean leadership can and should exist at different levels and behaviours (Netland et al., 2019; Van Beers et al., 2022), of which the leadership of lean work-floor teams[1] (van Dun & Wilderom, 2012), departments (van Dun et al., 2017), as well as whole organisations (Netland et al., 2019) are prominent examples. Because lean in essence requires a transformation of the entire organisational system (Åhlström et al., 2021), it is important to take a holistic approach to the concept of lean leadership. This chapter therefore reviews the available empirical lean leadership literature and drafts a broad, practice-relevant research agenda guided by the question: What do we know about leading organisational lean transformations, and what should we know?

---

[1] Not to be confused with Kaizen groups (Franken et al., 2021) or internal/corporate lean teams (van Dun & Wilderom, 2017).

Theoretical foundations of lean leadership: what do we know?

The leadership section of the general Organisational Behaviour (OB) literature is quite large and still growing, to date. It has evolved from the early effective leadership behaviour, trait, and "Great Man" theories, via more situational and social-cognitive theories, to transformational and charismatic leadership theories (Lord et al., 2017). In other words, besides defining specific effective leader behaviours and personal characteristics, leadership scholars explored the role of context and defined a large variety of specific leadership styles. Hence, it is for a reason that scholars have critiqued the coining of lean leadership as yet another leadership style in the Operations Management (OM) literature. As a countermeasure, lean scholars have pleaded for the return to generic leadership theory in examining the role of leaders in lean transformations (Seidel et al., 2019). This section therefore reviews the theories that are most prominent in lean leadership studies to date, of which the majority happens to entail general OB theories. Table 10.1 provides an overview of those theories, which can be distinguished as what I called here as more *description*, *dependence*, and *development* focused theories.

Description focused theories

The first category concerns, first of all, leadership style theories (Anderson & Sun, 2017; Da Costa Nogueira et al., 2018; Seidel et al., 2019), which elaborate on the (effective) behaviours, traits, and characteristics of lean leaders in more descriptive dimensions. Among those styles the transformational leadership theory of follower transformation is one of the most prominent ones (Siangchokyoo et al., 2020). Given the continuous improvement mantra of lean, it is no surprise that in the past many scholars have linked this particular leadership style to lean leaders (Poksinska et al., 2013; van Dun et al., 2017), although others have also questioned this link (Da Costa Nogueira et al., 2018). Transformational leaders are considered the drivers of organisational change and innovation (Tan et al., 2014), especially through offering values-driven inspiration, motivation, stimulation, and consideration for their followers. While immensely popular among scholars, in the general leadership literature transformational leadership theory has also been critiqued for not always "delivering its promises" of follower transformation, in other words, calling for more inductive studies to further explore and theorise the transformational leadership mechanisms (Siangchokyoo et al., 2020).

Table 10.1   Theoretical underpinnings of lean leadership: description, dependence, and development focused theories applied in lean leadership studies

Theory	Rationale	Example articles
Description focused theories		
Transformational leadership	Lean leaders adopt transformational leadership, which is a process through which leaders "broaden and elevate the interests of their employees ... generate awareness and acceptance of the purposes and mission of the group, and ... stir their employees to look beyond their own self-interests for the good of the group" (Bass, 1990, p. 21). And "the extent to which leaders are considered transformational is a function of four leader dimensions: (1) Idealized influence (role modeling attributes and behaviors); (2) Inspirational motivation (articulations of compelling and inspiring visions of the future); (3) Intellectual stimulation (challenging existing assumptions and stimulating new ways of thinking); and (4) Individualized consideration (attending to followers' needs and concerns)" (Siangchokyoo et al., 2020, p. 3).	Poksinska et al., 2013; Reynders et al., 2020; van Dun et al., 2017; Van Elp et al., 2022; Van Rossum et al., 2016
Values-behaviours	A lean leader's values influences their (observable) behaviours, whereby values are defined as: "(1) beliefs intrinsically related to emotion that, when activated, generate positive and negative feelings; (2) a motivational construct that drives people to act in an appropriate manner; (3) something that transcends specific situations and actions, differing from social attitudes and norms, in addition to guiding people in various social contexts; (4) something that guides the selection and evaluation of actions, policies, people and events and that composes criteria for judgements; (5) something that is ordered according to the relative importance given to the other values, and, thus, forming an ordered system of axiological priorities" (Torres et al., 2016, p. 342).	van Dun et al., 2017; van Dun & Wilderom, 2016, 2021

Theory	Rationale	Example articles
Dependence focused theories		
Contingency	The effectiveness of certain lean leader behaviours "is contingent upon the specific, situational context in which the leader operates" (Fiedler, 1964, p. 154; Lorsch, 2010). Examples of such contingencies include: "the external context, the firm's strategy, culture and size, and the stage of implementation of the lean system" (Camuffo & Gerli, 2018, p. 418) but also "team size" and individual level factors like "leader's age" (Tortorella et al., 2018, p. 1205).	Camuffo & Gerli, 2018; Gelei et al., 2015; Tortorella et al., 2017; Tortorella & Fogliatto, 2017; Tortorella et al., 2018
Substitute for leadership	The impact of a lean leader's behaviours depends on "a wide variety of individual, task, and organizational characteristics" that in some cases tend "to negate the leader's ability to either improve or impair subordinate satisfaction and performance" (Kerr & Jermier, 1978, p. 377). When lean leaders stimulate their subordinates' self-management capabilities this reduces "the need for close supervision because it can indeed be a 'substitute for leadership'" (Manz & Sims Jr., 1980, p. 366).	Niepce & Molleman, 1996
Situational leadership	A lean leader's behaviours depend on their subordinates. To be precise, "the primary situational determinant of leader behavior is the task-relevant maturity of the subordinate(s)" (Graeff, 1983, p. 285).	Tortorella & Fogliatto, 2017

Theory	Rationale	Example articles
Development focused theories		
Social learning	Lean leaders are inclined to learn from successful superiors given that "behavior is learned, at least in rough form, before it is performed. By observing a model of the desired behavior, an individual forms an idea of how response components must be combined and temporally sequenced to produce new behavioral configurations" (Bandura, 1977, p. 8).	Tortorella et al., 2020; Van Beers et al., 2022; van Dun & Wilderom, 2021
Coactive vicarious learning-by-doing	Lean leaders develop their leadership through "a discursive learning process where individuals (i.e., a model and learner) intentionally share and jointly process a model's work experience(s) in interpersonal interactions to co-construct an emergent, situated understanding of the experience(s)" (Myers, 2018, pp. 613–614; 2021) and "a 'doing' type of learning that matched their reflexive type of 'talking'" (van Dun & Wilderom, 2021, p. 88).	van Dun & Wilderom, 2021

Other studies have identified particular patterns of values and linked objectively observable behaviours to describe effective leadership of lean transformations (van Dun et al., 2017; van Dun & Wilderom, 2016, 2021). These studies were grounded in the idea that lean is inherently values-driven (e.g., continuous improvement and respect for people), assuming that effective lean leaders should explicitly espouse such (lean) values and adopt values-congruent behaviours. The lean leadership studies grounded in this type of more descriptive theories have laid the foundation for offering better insight into the "content" of effective lean leadership, as well as identifying the largely subtle differences between such lean leaders and generally effective/non-lean leaders. Taking it one level deeper, Schwartz's universal individual values theory (Schwartz et al., 2012) and Yukl's leader-behavioural taxonomy (Yukl, 2012; Yukl et al., 2002) have been instrumental in developing this more descriptive line of lean leadership research.

Dependence focused theories

Nevertheless, despite being built on universal theories, especially effective leader behaviours may be quite context-specific, which brings me to the second category of leadership theories applied in lean leadership studies: dependency type theories. These theories have in common that they point to the influence of external factors such as organisational context or the role of followers on how lean leadership takes shape. For example, contingency theory has, among others, been applied by Guilherme Tortorella and colleagues (Tortorella et al., 2017; Tortorella & Fogliatto, 2017; Tortorella et al., 2018). Contingency theory basically states that the effective implementation of OM practices is dependent upon organisational characteristics, whereby each organisation has its own specific variables and constraints (Lorsch, 2010). As such, what constitutes effective lean leadership is rather dependent on situational factors, like organisational or team size (Tortorella et al., 2018), lean maturity (Tortorella et al., 2020), national culture (Erthal & Marques, 2018), etc. In addition, this category encompasses theories that relate to the dependency of leadership style on followers who, throughout the lean transformation process, are suggested to start adopting more proactive, self-managing types of behaviours themselves rather than relying solely on their leaders for instruction. These theories are grounded in substitute for leadership theory (Héon et al., 2017; Manz & Sims Jr., 1980; McMackin & Flood, 2019), which, in turn, find their origin in Marie Parker Follett's philosophy of effective leadership and relational team functioning (van Dun & Wilderom, 2021). The key tenet is that employees take over tasks and responsibilities from their lean leaders, by taking charge of, for instance, continuous improvement cycles and task and/or performance monitoring. As such, a lean leader's behaviour is also dependent upon the behaviours displayed by their followers, e.g., by filling the gap and supporting their team wherever needed. This also aligns with the ideas behind situational leadership theory, as studied by some lean scholars (Tortorella & Fogliatto, 2017).

Development focused theories

A third and final category of leadership theories used in somewhat more recent lean studies focuses on how lean leaders develop and emerge over time. Two prominent theories fitting this category concern the social learning and coactive vicarious learning-by-doing theories (van Dun & Wilderom, 2021). The first theory states that people are inclined to learn from observing the behaviours of successful superiors (Bandura, 1977), like higher-level leaders' exemplary lean leadership behaviour. An example of how an action-learning type lean training intervention led to the development of effective leadership that boosted, through social learning, employees' work process improvement idea sharing and implementation is documented by Tan et al. (2024). The second theory, coactive vicarious learning-by-doing, extends this idea by adding that also leaders can learn from and together with their subordinates, not only by observing their behaviours but also by talking about and reflecting on other's actions, i.e., vicarious learning. A key aspect in this category of developmental lean leadership theories is a leader's experience level, or maturity (Tortorella et al., 2020). It is assumed that more novice lean leaders might apply different behaviours from those leaders who are in a more advanced stage of lean adoption. Although longitudinal lean leadership studies are still scarce, there already exists some (qualitative) evidence of the evolving nature of lean leadership, which fits the continuous improvement principle of lean.

Overall, the three categories of lean leadership theories (description, dependence, and development focused) offer a perspective on the diverse types of lean leadership studies conducted so far, whereby the first, descriptive category is more advanced compared to the more recent developmental type of lean leadership studies.

Developments in practice

Naturally, the (global) socio-economic context and workforce is continuously evolving, spurring many other related strategic developments which greatly influence what is expected of modern-day organisational leaders. In recent years, most lean-aspiring organisations have also taken up additional strategic ambitions, including boosting organisational agility, producing in a more green/pro-environmental way, digitalising (parts of) the work processes through smart technologies, and enabling remote working for attracting and retaining talent. In many ways these new developments have also intensified organisations' awareness of and interest in knowing more about the key human side of those transformations, enabling their employees and managers to effectively adapt to them.

To dive deeper into the first development: organisational agility was promoted to enable faster operational adjustment and resources reallocation to meet fast-changing customer demands in a volatile market (Teece et al., 2016; Walter, 2021). With the popularisation of agility, or agile, some organisations have either fully transformed their ways of working from lean to agile or have adopted agile practices in parallel to lean (often in different departments or business units). For instance, a large international bank like ING which had initially adopted lean, made the shift to adopting agile instead (Birkinshaw, 2018). Agile was born as an approach to software development, such as at Spotify, that is based on iterative and incremental improvement in collaborative, self-organising teams which aim "to dynamically adjust to changing customer requirements, needing to balance freedom and responsibility, learning and performance" (Bäcklander, 2019, p. 42). Given that agile abandons formal leadership roles and instead is based on self-management principles with rotating leadership functions like product owners and agile coaches (Birkinshaw, 2018), this does require a rethink of the leadership role. In particular, agile brings in the idea of complexity leadership theory of "balancing order and disorder" which requires the parallel development of operational, entrepreneurial, and enabling leadership competences (Bäcklander, 2019, p. 43).

Another key development is the increasing attention of both governments and organisations given to the Sustainable Development Goals (SDGs) and to their contribution to tackling climate change (George et al., 2016). But even well before the introduction of the SDGs in 2015, lean organisations had started to put more emphasis on their "green" performance (King & Lenox, 2001). Given the resemblance with the key lean principle of waste reduction, "lean and green" has gained more traction, whereby the adoption of lean practices is thought to lead to greener outcomes. The adoption of both lean and green may require additional skills from the leaders involved, in that lean leaders might need to start adopting environmentally specific transformational leadership (Robertson & Barling, 2013). For example, leaders must start to convey pro-environmental values to inspire their employees' green behaviours (Wang et al., 2018). In line with this, organisations have started to embrace certifications like "B Corp" to not only attend to their environmental performance and accountability but also meet the standards for decent work conditions and societal performance (Hasle & Vang, 2021; Pollack et al., 2020). These developments challenge lean leaders to define lean's principles of "customer value" and "respect for people" in much broader terms.

With the transition towards "Industry 4.0", many lean organisations have also started to experiment with the adoption of advanced, smart technologies on their lean shopfloors (Tortorella et al., 2019). On the one hand, smart technology adoption might further optimise and increase the quality of (already) lean processes (Tortorella et al., 2019). On the other hand, the digital transformation towards cyber-physical systems and interconnected, autonomous monitoring systems may completely change work-floor operations, making the majority of current operational staff redundant or (feel they) work like robots (Schneider, 2018; Schneider & Sting, 2020). Apart from the immediate impacts on operators' daily work, these developments certainly also depend on how leaders introduce this digitalisation agenda among their workforce, as well as how they are sensitive to and can deal with their staff's potential feelings of job insecurity in emotionally intelligent ways (van Dun & Kumar, 2023), in line with lean's "respect for people" principle. In fact, there is a wider shared call for studies on the impact of the adoption of Industry 4.0 technologies on lean work teams and their members (Frank et al., 2022; Rosin et al., 2020). Whereas some technologies might reduce the need for collaboration and interaction between operators, other technologies could in fact facilitate and boost the collaboration between operators across different sites. For instance, a large maintenance organisation in the Netherlands currently experiments with the use of virtual and augmented reality goggles for their maintenance workers to allow remote monitoring and expert peer consultation between geographically spread locations.

Finally, accelerated through the COVID-19 pandemic, globalisation, and the need to attract and retain talents by enabling healthier work-life balances, the last decade has witnessed a shift to more remote work and, thus, a reduction of face-to-face communication. These developments have various implications for lean leaders who have been stimulated before, through lean practices like leader standard work, to engage in daily "Gemba walks" as well as visual management (Poksinska et al., 2013; van Dun & Wilderom, 2021). First of all, the (forced) remote working arrangements have reduced leaders' direct access to employees, and vice versa, which on the one hand has led to reduced perceived leader controlling type behaviours, but also decreased their delegation behaviours (Stoker et al., 2022). In addition, the reduced level of face-to-face interactions may impact opportunities for participation in problem solving and decision making, as well as the coactive vicarious learning-by-doing that is a key mechanism for lean leadership development (van Dun & Wilderom, 2021). Second, it may increase barriers for building close relationships among staff, which is typically seen as detrimental to team psychological safety and team conflict management (Fenner et al., 2023; Klonek et al., 2022). Hence, employee and team well-being and affect may require more lean leader attention (Åhlström et al., 2021), especially in such remote working conditions. Third, remote working policies go hand-in-hand with an increasingly international workforce. This means that lean leaders may need to start taking cross-cultural differences into account, both in terms of their team's functioning as well as how they can effectively lead culturally diverse teams. Cross-cultural differences have previously been mentioned as a key influential factor of lean implementation success across countries (Erthal & Marques, 2018; van Dun et al., 2023). However, a novel aspect is that current-day workplaces are far more multi-cultural than before, which opens up the need to explore the leading of lean teams and transformations in multi-cultural factories or offices (Danese et al., 2017).

These four practical developments are thus key in informing a future research agenda that links effective (lean) leadership and team functioning to digital and green transformation of organisations. This opens up whole new pathways to explore in future empirical studies, as elaborated in the next section.

Future research agenda: what should we know?

Building on the current state of the field and the four key developments in practice, there are vast research opportunities that will help answer lean leaders' (future) big questions.

Primarily, there is a need for further convergence within each of the three different theoretical angles, the three D's, to be able to give better directions to lean leaders on how they can effectively lead their organisation's (or unit's) lean initiatives. Although the first studies of lean leadership and their teams were more inductive and qualitative in nature, fitting the nascent stage of the field (Edmondson & McManus, 2007), the field rather quickly moved to more quantitative hypotheses-testing type studies using generic leadership scales. Although on the one hand, the connection with general OB literature is key to advancing the field, there is a risk in looking for such solutions rather than building more in-depth understanding of what it takes for leaders to effectively lead their lean transformation. To boost the field as a whole, I therefore call for developing a deeper understanding of the three theoretical perspectives, both independently as well as in connection with one another, which will altogether allow us to develop a more sophisticated '3D' view of lean leadership (see Figure 10.1).

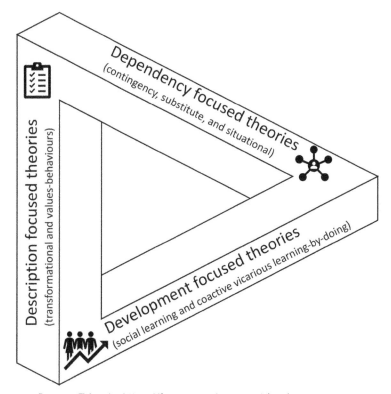

Source: Penrose Triangle, https://freesvg.org/penrose-triangle.

Figure 10.1   3D model of lean leadership theories

Methodologically, this also means initiating more cutting-edge and creative qualitative field study approaches that benefit from the state of the art in OB, including video-observation (Christianson, 2018), visual management studies (Bell & Davison, 2013), organisational ethnography and shadowing approaches (Czarniawska, 2007, 2008; McDonald, 2005), action learning research (Coughlan & Coghlan, 2002; Saabye et al., 2023), physiological measurements among leaders and employees (Hoogeboom et al., 2021), and (retrospective) process studies (van Dun et al., 2022). Such field studies require scholars to "go to the Gemba" and, although more time-intensive, will offer more precise 3D insight into what lean leadership comprises. It will also make us better understand how lean leadership is impacted by and, vice versa, impacts contextual factors. In addition, it will tell us more about how lean leadership can be developed across organisational levels, both by those that hold formal as well as those with informal leadership positions given that also employees can assume leading roles.

Then, because lean in practice was merged with other strategic developments, scholars need to examine how lean and agile, lean and green (or SDGs), lean and digital transformation, and lean and remote (cross-cultural) work go together and what this implies for effective leadership and teamwork. As described in the previous section, these global developments are expected to impact what is required of leaders and their teams in many ways. For example, while most studies on lean leadership and team functioning were conducted in single countries, a next step would be to develop cross-cultural comparative studies (Erthal & Marques, 2018). Also, examining how leaders could strengthen organisational resilience by integrating lean practices with initiatives to boost the agility, greenness, and digital transformation of work-floor operations is a fruitful and societally important avenue.

Conclusion

This chapter reviewed the current state of what we know about effectively leading lean transformations. Three theoretical foci emerged, which are grounded in the general OB literature, namely description, dependence, and development focused lean leadership theories. Whereas lean scholars mainly focused their studies on the leadership of lean implementation, organisations have moved with the "flow" and started embracing also other strategies including organisational agility, green transformation, digital transformation, and remote working. To embrace this complexity and allow for more impactful insights regarding the effective leadership of major organisational transformations, future studies should develop a 3D image of lean leadership.

References

Åhlström, P., Danese, P., Hines, P., Netland, T. H., Powell, D. J., Shah, R., Thürer, M., & van Dun, D. H. (2021). Is lean a theory? Viewpoints and outlook. *International Journal of Operations & Production Management*, 41(12), 1852–1878.

Anderson, M. H. & Sun, P. Y. T. (2017). Reviewing leadership styles: Overlaps and the need for a new "full-range" theory. *International Journal of Management Reviews*, 19(1), 76–96.

Bäcklander, G. (2019). Doing complexity leadership theory: How agile coaches at Spotify practise enabling leadership. *Creativity and Innovation Management*, 28(1), 42–60.

Bandura, A. (1977). *Social Learning Theory*. Upper Saddle River, NJ: Prentice Hall.

Bass, B. M. (1990). From transactional to transformational leadership: Learning to share the vision. *Organizational Dynamics*, 18(3), 19–31.

Bell, E. & Davison, J. (2013). Visual management studies: Empirical and theoretical approaches. *International Journal of Management Reviews*, 15(2), 167–184.

Birkinshaw, J. (2018). What to expect from agile. *MIT Sloan Management Review*, 59(2), 39–42.

Camuffo, A. & Gerli, F. (2018). Modeling management behaviors in lean production environments. *International Journal of Operations & Production Management*, 38(2), 403–423.

Christianson, M. K. (2018). Mapping the terrain: The use of video-based research in top-tier organizational journals. *Organizational Research Methods*, 21(2), 261–287.

Coughlan, P. & Coghlan, D. (2002). Action research for operations management. *International Journal of Operations & Production Management*, 22(2), 220–240.

Czarniawska, B. (2007). *Shadowing, and other Techniques for Doing Fieldwork in Modern Societies*. Malmö: Liber AB.

Czarniawska, B. (2008). Organizing: How to study it and how to write about it. *Qualitative Research in Organizations and Management: An International Journal*, 3(1), 4–20.

Da Costa Nogueira, D. M., Sousa, P. S. A., & Moreira, M. R. A. (2018). The relationship between leadership style and the success of lean management implementation. *Leadership & Organization Development Journal*, 39(6), 807–824.

Danese, P., Romano, P., & Boscari, S. (2017). The transfer process of lean practices in multi-plant companies. *International Journal of Operations & Production Management*, 37(4), 468–488.

Edmondson, A. C. & McManus, S. E. (2007). Methodological fit in management field research. *Academy of Management Review*, 32(4), 1155–1179.

Erthal, A. & Marques, L. (2018). National culture and organisational culture in lean organisations: A systematic review. *Production Planning & Control*, 29(8), 668–687.

Fenner, S. V., Arellano, M. C., Von Dzengelevski, O., & Netland, T. H. (2023). Effect of lean implementation on team psychological safety and learning. *International Journal of Operations & Production Management*, 43(2), 308–331.

Fiedler, F. E. (1964). A contingency model of leadership effectiveness. *Advances in Experimental Social Psychology*, 1, 149–190.

Found, P. A. & Harvey, R. (2006). The role of leaders in the initiation and implementation of manufacturing process change. *The International Journal of Knowledge, Culture & Change Management*, 6(8), 35–46.

Found, P. A. & Harvey, R. (2007). Leading the lean enterprise. *IET Engineering Management*, 17(1), 40–43.

Frank, A. G., Marodin, G. A., Godinho Filho, M., & Thürer, M. (2022). Beyond industry 4.0: Integrating lean, digital technologies and people. Call for papers, *International Journal of Operations & Production Management*. Retrieved 23 February 2023 from https://www.emeraldgrouppublishing.com/calls-for-papers/beyond-industry-40-integrating-lean-digital-technologies-and-people.

Franken, J. C. M., van Dun, D. H., & Wilderom, C. P. M. (2021). Kaizen event process quality: Towards a phase-based understanding of high-quality group problem-solving. *International Journal of Operations & Production Management*, 41(6), 962–990.

Gelei, A., Losonci, D., & Matyusz, Z. (2015). Lean production and leadership attributes: The case of Hungarian production managers. *Journal of Manufacturing Technology Management*, 26(4), 477–500.

George, G., Howard-Grenville, J., Joshi, A., & Tihanyi, L. (2016). Understanding and tackling societal grand challenges through management research. *Academy of Management Journal*, 59(6), 1880–1895.

Graeff, C. L. (1983). The situational leadership theory: A critical review. *Academy of Management Review*, 8(2), 285–291.

Hasle, P. & Vang, J. (2021). Designing better interventions: Insights from research on decent work. *Journal of Supply Chain Management*, 57(2), 58–70.

Héon, F., Damart, S., & Nelson, L. A. T. (2017). Mary Parker Follett: Change in the paradigm of integration. In D. B. Szabla, W. Pasmore, M. Barnes, & A. N. Gipson (Eds.), *The Palgrave Handbook of Organizational Change Thinkers*, 1, London: Palgrave Macmillan, pp. 471–492.

Hoogeboom, A. M. G. M., Saeed, A., Noordzij, M. L., & Wilderom, C. P. M. (2021). Physiological arousal variability accompanying relations-oriented behaviors of effective leaders: Triangulating skin conductance, video-based behavior coding and perceived effectiveness. *The Leadership Quarterly*, 32, 101493.

Kerr, S. & Jermier, J. M. (1978). Substitutes for leadership: Their meaning and measurement. *Organizational Behavior and Human Performance*, 22(3), 375–403.

King, A. A. & Lenox, M. J. (2001). Lean and green? An empirical examination of the relationship between lean production and environmental performance. *Production and Operations Management*, 10(3), 244–256.

Klonek, F. E., Kanse, L., Wee, S., Runneboom, C., & Parker, S. K. (2022). Did the COVID-19 lock-down make us better at working in virtual teams? *Small Group Research*, 53(2), 185–206.

Lord, R. G., Day, D. V., Zaccaro, S. J., Avolio, B. J., & Eagly, A. H. (2017). Leadership in applied psychology: Three waves of theory and research. *Journal of Applied Psychology*, 102(3), 434–451.

Lorsch, J. (2010). A contingency theory of leadership. In N. Nohria & R. Khurana (Eds.), *Handbook of Leadership Theory and Practice*. Boston: Harvard Business Press, pp. 411–432.

Manz, C. C. & Sims Jr., H. R. (1980). Self-management as a substitute for leadership: A social learning theory perspective. *Academy of Management Review*, 5(3), 361–367.

McDonald, S. (2005). Studying actions in context: A qualitative shadowing method for organizational research. *Qualitative Research*, 5(4), 455–473.

McMackin, J. & Flood, P. (2019). A theoretical framework for the social pillar of lean. *Journal of Organizational Effectiveness: People and Performance*, 6(1), 39–55.

Myers, C. G. (2018). Coactive vicarious learning: Toward a relational theory of vicarious learning in organizations. *Academy of Management Review*, 43(4), 610–634.

Myers, C. G. (2021). Performance benefits of reciprocal vicarious learning in teams. *Academy of Management Journal*, 64(3), 926–947.

Netland, T. H., Powell, D. J., & Hines, P. (2019). Demystifying lean leadership. *International Journal of Lean Six Sigma*, 11(3), 543–554.

Niepce, W. & Molleman, E. (1996). Characteristics of work organization in lean production and sociotechnical systems: A case study. *International Journal of Operations & Production Management*, 16(2), 77–90.

Poksinska, B., Swartling, D., & Drotz, E. (2013). The daily work of lean leaders: Lessons from manufacturing and healthcare. *Total Quality Management & Business Excellence*, 24(8), 886–898.

Pollack, J. M., Garcia, R., Michaelis, T. L., Hanson, S., Carr, J. C., & Sheats, L. (2020). Pursuing B Corp certification: Exploring firms' entrepreneurial orientation and prosocial motivation. *Academy of Management Discoveries*, 7(2), 294–316.

Reynders, P., Kumar, M., & Found, P. A. (2020). "Lean on me": An integrative literature review on the middle management role in lean. *Total Quality Management & Business Excellence*, 33(3–4), 318–354.

Robertson, J. L. & Barling, J. (2013). Greening organizations through leaders' influence on employees' pro-environmental behaviors. *Journal of Organizational Behavior*, 34(2), 176–194.

Rosin, F., Forget, P., Lamouri, S., & Pellerin, R. (2020). Impacts of Industry 4.0 on lean principles. *International Journal of Production Research*, 58(6), 1644–1661.

Saabye, H., Powell, D. J., & Coughlan, P. (2023). Lean and action learning: Towards an integrated theory? *International Journal of Operations & Production Management*, 43(13), 128–151.

Schneider, P. (2018). Managerial challenges of Industry 4.0: An empirically backed research agenda for a nascent field. *Review of Managerial Science*, 12(3), 803–848.

Schneider, P. & Sting, F. J. (2020). Employees' perspectives on digitalization-induced change: Exploring frames of industry 4.0. *Academy of Management Discoveries*, 6(3), 406–435.

Schwartz, S. H., Cieciuch, J., Vecchione, M., Davidov, E., Fischer, R., Beierlein, C., Ramos, A., Verkasalo, M., Lönnqvist, J., Demirutku, K., Dirilen-Gumus, O., & Konty, M. (2012). Refining the theory of basic individual values. *Journal of Personality and Social Psychology*, 103(4), 663–688.

Seidel, A., Saurin, T. A., Tortorella, G. L., & Marodin, G. A. (2019). How can general leadership theories help to expand the knowledge of lean leadership? *Production Planning & Control*, 30(16), 1322–1336.

Siangchokyoo, N., Klinger, R. L., & Campion, E. D. (2020). Follower transformation as the linchpin of transformational leadership theory: A systematic review and future research agenda. *The Leadership Quarterly*, 31(1), 1–18.

Stoker, J. I., Garretsen, H., & Lammers, J. (2022). Leading and working from home in times of COVID-19: On the perceived changes in leadership behaviors. *Journal of Leadership & Organizational Studies*, 29(2), 208–218.

Tan, A. B. C., van Dun, D. H., & Wilderom, C. P. M. (2024). Lean innovation training and transformational leadership for employee creative role identity and innovative work behavior in a public service organization. *International Journal of Lean Six Sigma*, 15(8), 1–33.

Teece, D. J., Peteraf, M. A., & Leih, S. (2016). Dynamic capabilities and organizational agility: Risk, uncertainty, and strategy in the innovation economy. *California Management Review*, 58(4), 13–35.

Torres, C. V., Schwartz, S. H., & Nascimento, T. G. (2016). The refined theory of values: Associations with behavior and evidences of discriminative and predictive validity. *Psicologia USP*, 27(2), 341–356.

Tortorella, G. L., Fetterman, D., Anzanello, M., & Sawhney, R. (2017). Lean manufacturing implementation, context and behaviors of multi-level leadership:

A mixed-methods exploratory research. *Journal of Manufacturing Technology Management*, 28(7), 867–891.

Tortorella, G. L., & Fogliatto, F. (2017). Implementation of lean manufacturing and situational leadership styles: An empirical study. *Leadership & Organization Development Journal*, 38(7), 946–968.

Tortorella, G. L., Fetterman, D., Frank, A., & Marodin, G. A. (2018). Lean manufacturing implementation: Leadership styles and contextual variables. *International Journal of Operations & Production Management*, 38(5), 1205–1227.

Tortorella, G. L., Giglio, R., & van Dun, D. H. (2019). Industry 4.0 adoption as a moderator of the impact of lean production practices on operational performance improvement. *International Journal of Operations & Production Management*, 39(6–8), 860–886.

Tortorella, G. L., van Dun, D. H., & De Almeida, A. G. (2020). Leadership behaviors during lean healthcare implementation: A review and longitudinal study. *Journal of Manufacturing Technology Management*, 31(1), 193–215.

Van Beers, J. J. C. A. M., van Dun, D. H., & Wilderom, C. P. M. (2022). Effective hospital-wide lean implementation: Top-down, bottom-up or through co-creative role modeling? *International Journal of Lean Six Sigma*, 13(1), 46–66.

van Dun, D. H., & Kumar, M. (2023). Social enablers of Industry 4.0 technology adoption: Transformational leadership and emotional intelligence. *International Journal of Operations & Production Management*, 43(13), 152–182.

van Dun, D. H., Hicks, J. N., & Wilderom, C. P. M. (2017). Values and behaviors of effective lean managers: Mixed-methods exploratory research. *European Management Journal*, 35(2), 174–186.

van Dun, D. H., Tortorella, G. L., & Carminati, L. (2023). Lean leadership across different national cultures: A comparative study. *Production Planning & Control*, DOI: 10.1080/09537287.2023.2223541.

van Dun, D. H. & Wilderom, C. P. M. (2012). Human dynamics and enablers of effective lean team cultures and climates. In G. P. Hodgkinson & J. K. Ford (Eds.), *International Review of Industrial and Organizational Psychology*, 27, Hoboken, NJ: John Wiley and Sons, pp. 115–152.

van Dun, D. H. & Wilderom, C. P. M. (2016). Lean-team effectiveness through leader values and members' informing. *International Journal of Operations & Production Management*, 36(11), 1530–1550.

van Dun, D. H. & Wilderom, C. P. M. (2017). Lean teams. In T. H. Netland & D. J. Powell (Eds.), *The Routledge Companion to Lean Management*. New York: Routledge, pp. 106–117.

van Dun, D. H. & Wilderom, C. P. M. (2021). Improving high lean team performance through aligned behaviour-value patterns and coactive vicarious learning-by-doing. *International Journal of Operations & Production Management*, 41(13), 65–99.

van Dun, D. H., Wijnmaalen, J. R., & Wilderom, C. P. M. (2022). Mapping team dynamics through retrospective team events analysis. *International Journal of Qualitative Methods*, 21, 1–14.

Van Elp, B., Roemeling, O., & Aij, K. H. (2022). Lean leadership: Towards continuous improvement capability in healthcare. *Health Services Management Research*, 35(1), 7–15.

Van Rossum, L., Aij, K. H., Simons, F. E., Van der Eng, N., & Ten Have, W. D. (2016). Lean healthcare from a change management perspective: The role of leadership and workforce flexibility in an operating theatre. *Journal of Health Organization and Management*, 30(3), 475–493.

Walter, A. T. (2021). Organizational agility: Ill-defined and somewhat confusing? A systematic literature review and conceptualization. *Management Review Quarterly*, 71, 343–391.

Wang, X., Zhou, K., & Liu, W. (2018). Value congruence: A study of green transformational leadership and employee green behavior. *Frontiers in Psychology*, 9(1946), 1–8.

Yukl, G. (2012). Effective leadership behavior: What we know and what questions need more attention. *Academy of Management Perspectives*, 26(4), 66–85.

Yukl, G., Gordon, A., & Taber, T. (2002). A hierarchical taxonomy of leadership behavior: Integrating a half-century of behavior research. *Journal of Leadership and Organizational Studies*, 9(1), 15–32.

11 Searching for the magic formula of lean leadership

Marte D. Q. Holmemo

Introduction

The last decade we have increased our attention towards lean leadership in both research and managerial practice. The importance of leadership is emphasized by a large volume of reports on failed lean transformations. Leadership is to blame for failure (e.g., Jadhav et al., 2014) as well as the most important factor of success (e.g., Bortolotti et al., 2015).

Being one of the scholar voices of lean management and change processes in Norway, I have been invited and challenged in several arenas where managerial professionals within different industries meet, discussing the topic of lean leadership. For the sake of clear communication and spirit of lean lingo, I constructed a "5C" concept grounded on my own research and current literature on the topic. The message was that management needed core competence, communication, coordination, a coaching style and caring for both customers, employees, and surroundings. The five C-words have been met with recognition, but during a few of the following conversations with the audience the question "what is the difference between this concept of lean leadership and just pure good leadership?" has been posed. I find this comment brilliant as it demonstrates the vagueness of both lean and leadership in research and practice.

In this chapter I will present some of the challenges we face in trying to define a concept of lean leadership, and I suggest three future directions for the research agenda on the topic.

What is lean leadership?

As researchers we embark on understanding the characteristics and efficiency of a concept we call "lean leadership". In the dawn of the fascination of the Toyota Production System, one always talked about lean *management*. The term *leadership* appeared in explanations of failures based on aspects that were lost in translation, illustrated by Liker and Convis (2011, p. 7): "[R]eplicating Toyota's technical system without understanding their source – the engine that drives the system, you might say – has largely proved futile … Why? Because tools and blitz events don't ingrain the leadership needed to coach and sustain a large process change within the existing company culture".

In the Scandinavian languages we have the same term for "management" and "leadership" (Norwegian and Danish: "ledelse"). Nonetheless, Scandinavians at work are not unfamiliar with the content and the discourse on the meanings of the two English terms. In the literature, this has been debated since 1977 when Zaleznik (2004) coined the opposing purposes: management towards rationality and control and leadership as creative and relational, non-compatible with control and structure. There is an established consensus of the two both overlapping and complementing each other, yet managers identify themselves as better when performing leadership compared to management (boring necessity), whatever that could mean – leadership is a vague concept (Carroll and Levy, 2008; Yukl, 1989).

Leadership could be understood as different forms, traits, behaviors, skills, roles, and practices to mention only some (Clegg et al., 2019). The scholarly field on leadership is dominated by understandings from psychology, searching for the ideal personality, one is born with or could possibly reinforce or grow, depending on which perspective you claim to (Clegg et al., 2019). Regarding lean leadership, one could find some anecdotal examples of preferable characteristics of employees and leaders, like *humble* and *trainable* (Liker and Convis, 2011, p. 101). Emiliani and Stec (2005) would claim that lean leaders are respectful too. Aij and Teunissen (2017) performed systematic research on attributes of lean leadership. Characteristics such as honesty, trust, engagement, and emotional intelligence were the attributes that linked the most to personal characteristics. As a Western reader, one could believe that the archetype of Japanese sensei (Ballé et al., 2019; Ohno, 2013) is an introverted, critical, and charmless character, but at a closer look, most descriptions or summarized attributes (Aji and Teunissen, 2017) are rather styles, or practices of lean leaders.

More challenging is the description of the invisible aspects of these principles, norms, and values (that at least could be espoused) or the underlying assumptions – the ideal beliefs and mindsets. van Dun et al. (2017) enhance certain values which were ranked highest by the most effective lean middle managers and their associates: *honesty, participation, teamwork, and responsibility.*

Traits of lean leadership are less represented in the literature (Seidel et al., 2019). Values are often referred to, but are intangible, while examples of behaviors and practices of lean leadership are thoroughly described. In defining lean leadership Poksinska et al. (2013) draw our attention to a set of competencies, practices, and behaviors to successfully implement and exploit lean. This more actionable way of seeing lean leadership is supported by Spear (2004) who gave an early contribution on lean leadership by describing his journey as a leader in Toyota. He shared how he gradually was coached and supported by expectations of improvement and self-development from bottom and upwards in the system.

Several authors have followed up here. Liker and Convis (2011) presented their diamond model of lean leadership from Toyota, consisting of the four actionable principles: *commit to self-development, coach and develop others, support daily kaizen,* and *create vision and align goals,* all these built on *true north values* (Liker and Convis, 2011, p. 39). In similar normative fashion, Dombrowski and Mielke (2013) build on Toyota when they suggest five fundamental principles for lean leadership: *improvement culture, self-development, qualification, Gemba,* and *hoshin kanri.* Netland et al. (2020) summarize good lean leadership as a set of practices: *go and see* (Gemba walks), *daily layered accountability* (typically standup meetings), *structured problem solving, continuous improvement* (engage in and apply suggestion systems and hoshin kanri), *coaching* (hierarchical coach the coach), and *strategy deployment* (adapted to current managerial level). In addition, Van Assen (2018) showed that communication is particularly effective in lean leadership.

Bringing the debate further from normative or empirical descriptions of attributes and practice, some authors have theorized lean leadership considering contemporary leadership theories. Despite different grounds and origins, lean seems to have similarities with general theories. For instance, Poksinska et al. (2013) built on the practice of coaching and empowering and facilitating teams towards development and characterized lean leadership as similar to servant leadership, transformative leadership, and situational leadership. Aij and colleagues supported that transformative (Aij et al., 2015) and servant (Aij and Teunissen, 2017) leadership were aligned with lean and stated that these leadership ideas brought the philosophical understanding of lean rather than tool-oriented approaches that were more likely to fail. Nuanced by Tortorella et al. (2020) not only people orientation, but also task oriented behaviors were recommendable, especially in an early stage of lean implementation with short-term goals. Seidel et al. (2019) confirm that the lean leadership literature tends towards transformative, situational, and servant leadership, but conclude by emphasizing the balance between leadership and management and stating the importance of a surrounding system compatible with the internal and external context of the firm.

This alerts us to the view that leadership is not an individual matter, but part of a social system with established structures and collective responsibility. Holmemo et al. (2023) showed that building lean leadership is not just a matter of hard or soft managerial skills of a group of individual managers, but also organizational systems and structures supporting behaviors aligned with a lean practice.

Bringing additional complexity to the discourse on lean leadership is claiming that an organizational leader cannot be characterized by a general description. Separating different leadership roles shows that lean leadership is also contextual. Netland et al. (2020) show that there should be differences in lean leadership between senior management and operating supervisors. Leaders have different roles in the hierarchy. It might be right for the top manager to be visionary, and transformation oriented as the strategic and external force, while a servant and coaching style could suit better at the operational level. In-between, there could be several layers of mid-management, which Holmemo and Ingvaldsen (2016) showed to have an important role of communication and coordination that should not be bypassed in lean implementation or practice.

Muddling through towards lean leadership

As demonstrated through this presentation of the lean leadership literature, we are faced with a wide and vague concept of lean leadership. This is challenging for both academics and managerial practitioners (both leaders and other practitioners in the field of lean implementation and organizational change, for instance internal or external consultants; Holmemo et al., 2018). When I constructed the 5C label for dissemination purposes, my agenda was to summarize a literature that pointed in several directions and help systemize it into something actionable, but still lift managers up from their (at the time) customary conception of lean as 5S.

One might say I made an eclectic selection of words with reference to the literature presented above. For instance: coordination is the main message from Holmemo and colleagues (e.g., Holmemo and Ingvaldsen 2016), communication is highlighted by Van Assen (2018), most authors advocate coaching (Seidel et al., 2019), core competence is about understanding the whole process as described by Spear (2004), but also a precondition for the kata system and Gemba practice (e.g., Netland et al., 2020), and one could credit Emiliani and Stec (2005) and other proponents of "soft values" (e.g., van Dun et al., 2017) for enhancing the importance of caring.

Another explanation for the 5C slogan is building argumentation based on known mechanisms within lean and management. To avoid the most ambiguous understanding of lean, which would include every interpretation of lean, we can approach this from a more intersectional approach. As we all know by now, there is no clear definition of the core of lean, but I would probably not be mistaken claiming that most conceptions of lean include some kind of movement – continuous improvement and learning from practice on one hand, and an interwoven structured system for processes guiding standardized, collective practice on the other (actually not very different from the Toyota house model with just-in-time, jidoka, and continuous improvement at its center) (Liker, 2004). One wants to build systematic and collective competence through experimentation and reflection on practice, which could be facilitated through Socratic methods of coaching from a friendly senior (Nonaka, 1994; Schein and Schein, 2018). However, this demands acknowledgment and understanding of the system as a whole, both from the coach and the coachees. To be able to improve and learn from experience and participation, people need psychological safety (Edmondson, 2018). This is dependent on contextual culture, but we have reasons to believe that the leader should have some form of empathic behavior – or they should actually care. Laissez faire leadership is known to be the worst (Skogstad et al., 2007). Communication is at the core in both coaching and also for learning and understanding the holism of the system. Finally, changing one thing in a system could and should affect others. In addition, empowering changes from operators, bottom-up or middle-bottom-up (Nonaka, 1994), puts a huge responsibility on coordination within the structure. Thus, coordination, communication, care, coaching, and core competence would be areas to support and develop in leadership of a lean organization.

So, when the clever comment on the five C's representing just "good leadership" came up, one should not be surprised. There are two ways to construct such a bullet-list concept from the existing literature. One is to summarize the reports that in most cases empirically investigate the leadership characteristics of leading lean companies. The other is to combine normative descriptions of lean management and leadership. In addition, one can, like me, do a little bit of both, and then end up with something wide and vague that is not wrong, but not scientifically specific or clear.

Challenges in search of the magic formula

Making a scientific formula for lean leadership is challenging, maybe even impossible. The main reason for this is the fact that combining two vague concepts does not make the new concept clearer. Putting this together into a theoretical concept called "lean leadership" is arduous. As an attempt to explain this, I allow myself to disassemble lean leadership into its two components, aware of the risk in this reductionistic approach of losing crucial synergies, which could be overlooked in attempts to reassemble the concept.

Regarding lean, the moving concept has been one reason why Toyota never feared being copied due to their openness towards the production system (Liker and Convis, 2011). Movement and change of concept have been the essence of the lean genealogy (Holweg, 2007). The very essence of lean is continuous change where organizations interpret and develop their own version of lean (Hines et al., 2004). This has brought the concept to the point that Browning and de Treville (2021, p. 644) ask: "What is Lean? A phenomenon? An ideal? A philosophy? A way of thinking? A collection of practices? A strategy? Widespread agreement is lacking." Browning and de Treville (2021) suggest narrowing (or to lean (*sic*)) the lean concept to a list of operation management practices to prolong the life of the concept. On the other hand, founded on institutional theory Benders and van Veen (2001) have claimed that interpretability is the very reason that lean has survived the fashion cycles.

The problem arises when the lean concept is to guide a poor manager in decision making or development. What does it mean to "commit to the true north" (Liker and Convis, 2011)? Where to begin in reality? Take leadership philosophies claiming that one should begin with communicating a vision and values (Kotter, 2012). The problem is that when we try to make single-word descriptions detached from practice or context, we tend to lose some meaning in the translation. For instance, when Emiliani and Stec (2005) remind us of the *respect for people* issue, this could differ in practice from Toyota to Volvo. In Ohno's (2013, p. 107) own words: "The gemba is a convenient place to get angry at people. There is a lot of noise so they can't really hear what I am saying. When I scold the supervisors on the gemba, the workers see that their boss is being yelled at and they sympathize with their boss. Then it becomes easier for that supervisor to correct the workers." Understanding "respect" this way is something totally different in a Scandinavian culture where: "The micromanagement, the authoritarian leadership style and the patriarchal culture that demands stringent commitment, is perceived as brainwashing in our culture" (Björkman and Lundqvist, 2013, p. 33). This example of how to interpret "respect" demonstrates the importance of understanding mindsets or values in leadership in terms of contexts and situations. Lean practices would be more easily transferrable across cultures and industries (Browning and de Treville, 2021), for instance doing Gemba walks or visual management.

The trouble continues for us lean academics in search of evidence of good or bad lean leadership, as we strive in making theories by comparing apples and pears. As researchers we are challenged in our search for academic evidence on efficiency in empirically separating mechanisms corresponding to a concept of lean from all other concurrent factors in an organizational environment (e.g., Kuipers et al., 2004; Mackelprang and Nair, 2010). It is even harder to define the lean concept by only comparing one single case of lean leadership practice with another.

What can we conclude from "anything goes"? Have some of us come to erroneous conclusions? Can we formulate a clear concept of lean leadership (understood as something good and effectual) from this research?

Looking at the collection on lean leadership publications beyond normative postulations deduced from observed practices and espoused principles of Toyota (e.g., Liker and Convis, 2011; Spear, 2004), much of our work is based on empirical descriptions of good, bad, or missing leadership in lean production contexts (e.g., Holmemo and Ingvaldsen, 2016; Netland et al., 2020). Others are constructions from literature on good leadership and good lean practice (e.g., Dombrowski et al., 2013), or comparisons of lean leadership descriptions to leadership theories (e.g., Seidel et al., 2019). In addition, many authors have presented meta studies based on the previous sources, generating theories on what the existing literature has in common (e.g., Aji and Teunissen, 2017; Reynders et al., 2020). Despite being disparate, the lean leadership literature risks being self-referring and self-confirming. For example, asking a group of leaders what good lean leadership is when they might all have read the same books could be a source of bias.

The discourse on leadership is not any easier. In Yukl's (1989) thorough review on managerial leadership the comprehensiveness of the concept is well documented, as well as the methodological challenges this will cause. What the understandings have in common might be some kind of influence. According to Blom and Alvesson (2015) leadership has uncritically become something all and nothing in its ambiguity. Or as they recently put it: "It may be about influencing, instructing, inspiring, meanings, attitudes, behaviors, results etc. It may be leader-driven, follower-driven, combined, group-based, a style, a relationship, an act, a framework, an espoused belief, a set of beliefs enacted, a fantasy, an identity support mechanism, or a language game. It may be about having followers, or not having followers, as all are involved in the social leadership process" (Alvesson and Blom, 2022, p. 64). Alvesson and Blom (2022) introduce the acronym "hembig" concerning concepts that are hegemonic, ambiguous, and big, and demonstrate this by the examples of leadership, strategy, and institution. There is reason to suggest that the concept of lean could be included as another example.

Alvesson and Blom's (2022) appeal is to approach such concepts more carefully and critically and to discuss the matter more closely. I would claim that we as scholars within lean could have followed up as we are not sufficiently precise regarding "leadership". In our attempt to "soften up" and pay attention to the human dimensions of lean (Bouranta et al., 2022; Magnani et al., 2019), many of us turn our backs on familiar areas of management and embark on some understanding of leadership. We describe practices and sort and share different categories of attributes associated with leadership or try to define a holistic concept of it. What would be more interesting would be to lose the fluffy term and concentrate on what is essential to understanding organizational behavior related to the lean concept. We could embark deeply on discussions of personal characteristics and preferences, such as what could be enhanced and what could be trained on the individual level; the role of power, responsibilities, authority, and influence; how leaders communicate to drive followers towards certain actions; how to understand practice and embedded routines on individual and collective levels; how to understand leadership as social structures that interact with the individual lean leader.

What intrigues me is not when academics like Seidel et al. (2019) fit lean leadership into the concurrent leadership theories, but when they are able to reflect on the importance of keeping the understanding of management, as nicely summarized: "general leadership theories do not bear the managerial emphasis that Lean does, which is based on continuous improvement (demanding leaders' self-development skill) and changes in managerial paradigms (demanding problem solving and risk management)" (Seidel et al., 2019, p. 1331). They also emphasize the importance of context in adapting leadership ideas into managerial practice. Again, this reminds us of the importance of management issues, aligned with Holmemo et al. (2018) enhancing the importance of structures and Netland et al. (2020) on managerial roles and responsibilities. However, there is a need to elaborate this further. As ongoing research, I collaborate with a large production company and a public service organization that both have organized management differently than the classical hierarchy known from Toyota (Ingvaldsen and Benders, 2016). Combining lean with matrix or project organization, with separated responsibility for development, production, and human aspects, unveils challenges for leaders and followers that are yet to be understood extensively.

When we acknowledge that leadership, lean, and other relevant concepts to understand and approach organizational challenges can be vague, ambiguous, and context dependent, one must find support from theoretical perspectives that recognize these fundamental views of the world, for instance processual or critical perspectives, providing room for sensemaking and reflexivity (Sveningsson and Sörgärde, 2019). Understanding leadership as "less spectacular and consisting of more mundane actions; the everyday managers ... portrayed as humble and hardworking heroes who manage to accomplish change – or maintain high quality and efficiency – and business success incrementally" (Alvesson et al., 2016, p. 5) should bring us down to earth without blaming us for being less concerned about scientific knowledge.

Can we make a magic formula?

I do not believe there is any magic here, only hard work. Given the clear findings of managerial challenges in implementing and keeping organizations lean, and the problems I have presented concerning lean leadership research, I believe we need to keep trying to build our knowledge base within the field. I have three main suggestions for the future research agenda:

1. Shifting focus from making a definition of lean leadership different from (just) good leadership, to finding characteristics of leadership that work in a lean management context.

This argument is based on both scientific rigor and managerial relevance. Separating ordinary leadership from lean leadership is not important for a leader or an organizational practitioner. How to lead whatever they lead better would be relevant, and this deserves focus and reflection. Most organizations have had some influence of lean management, or at least share some essential characteristics in common with a lean organization. Further, the vagueness and flux of lean might lead to the internal variation of lean organizations bigger than the differences between lean and non-lean. What we search for more insight on is how leadership actions, behaviors, and practices influence the continuous development and improved outcome of an organization (and vice versa), and we should do this with academic sound methods, rather than referring to what Toyota has done. And, from the comment of my clever audience of the 5C concept: It might be true that lean leadership is good for all types of managerial situations, let's take that as an extra benefit.

2. Unwrapping the hegemonic, ambiguous, big concepts (HEMBIGs) and being precise and specific in what we are studying.

With a wide understanding of lean it is hard to picture a non-lean organization or work environment, and with our understanding of leadership it is hard to not be general. To be able to be more scientifically oriented and present evidence, we need to narrow the scope of our research. As stated by Wulff et al. (2023), the scientific field of leadership suffers from several weak building bricks of methodological and empirical mistakes. What I recognize from the collection of literature on lean leadership is especially clarifications of variables and their relationships. In this sense we might just create building bricks (to use the metaphor of Wulff et al., 2023) when we want to create temples. But temples could be built by combining solid bricks.

We might benefit more from a collaboration of different disciplines involved in leadership research, rather than mistrusting (often with good reason) the level of detail and precision when we cross each other's fields of knowledge. Engineers and economists should respect the expertise of psychology and psychologists should listen to the knowledge on organization structures from engineers or social scientists. We all have a lot to learn from joint precision in cross-disciplinary studies. As scientists we have a responsibility to present our research with moderation and reflexivity. We should keep the faith in research to provide more precise answers, but also to present an openness and honesty to methodological and practical challenges towards the discourse on lean leadership (or ought we again talk about *management and leadership*?). The lean leadership research should be self-critical and challenge some of our hegemonies on both leadership and lean.

3. Studying practices and consequences in processual logics, rather than interpretations of coexisting characteristics.

We tend to measure perceptions of behaviors as behaviors and be less specific if relations are causal or coexisting (Wulff et al., 2023). Unlike Wulff et al. (2023), I think we can create strong bricks of qualitative case studies by a sound theory building (e.g., Eisenhardt, 2021). However, I share Wulff et al.'s (2023) concern over a lack of timeliness in studies concerned with processes as lean and leadership need, unpacking the concepts to specific practices and behaviors that should be studied as processes (Langley, 1999). Shifting focus from looking for leadership characteristics like styles or traits or leadership theories like servant or transformational leadership, I support Browning and de Treville (2021) in focusing more on actions and practices. Methodologically I miss more process studies, where one understands how things evolve over time, estimating the complexity of contextual factors (Langley, 1999). Hence, we need to acknowledge that leadership is not only a personal characteristic or a strategic choice of single individuals, but also part of larger structures. As lean is an evolving concept concerning improving ways of working, the understanding of how managerial choices lead to consequences in performance should be more evolved. Unwrapped, the fuzziness of leadership, through more rigorous research and consciousness of ceteris paribus relationships, our scientific knowledge and suggested magic formulas would be more reliable.

References

Aij, K. H. & Teunissen, M. (2017). Lean leadership attributes: A systematic review of the literature. *Journal of Health Organization and Management*, 31(7/8), 713–729.

Aij, K. H., Visse, M., & Widdershoven, G. A. (2015). Lean leadership: An ethnographic study. *Leadership in Health Services*, 28(2), 119–134.

Alvesson, M. & Blom, M. (2022). The hegemonic ambiguity of big concepts in organization studies. *Human Relations*, 75(1), 58–86.

Alvesson, M., Blom, M., & Sveningsson, S. (2016). *Reflexive Leadership: Organising in an Imperfect World*. London: Sage.

Ballé, M., Chartier, N., Coignet, P., Olivencia, S., Powell, D., & Reke, E. (2019). *The Lean Sensei: Go See Challenge*. Boston: Lean Enterprise Institute.

Benders, J. & van Veen, K. (2001). What's in a fashion? Interpretative viability and management fashions. *Organization*, 8(1), 33–53.

Björkman, T. & Lundqvist, K. (2013). Lean ur historiskt perspektiv. In P. Sederblad (ed.), *Lean i arbetslivet*. Stockholm: Liber, pp. 18–47.

Blom, M. & Alvesson, M. (2015). All-inclusive and all good: The hegemonic ambiguity of leadership. *Scandinavian Journal of Management*, 31(4), 480–492.

Bortolotti, T., Boscari, S., & Danese, P. (2015). Successful lean implementation: Organizational culture and soft lean practices. *International Journal of Production Economics*, 160, 182–201.

Bouranta, N., Psomas, E., & Antony, J. (2022). Human factors involved in lean management: A systematic literature review. *Total Quality Management & Business Excellence*, 33(9–10), 1113–1145.

Browning, T. R. & de Treville, S. (2021). A lean view of lean. *Journal of Operations Management*, 67, 640–652.

Carroll, B. & Levy, L. (2008). Defaulting to management: Leadership defined by what it is not. *Organization*, 15(1), 75–96.

Clegg, S. R., Pitsis, T. S., & Mount, M. (2019). *Managing and Organizations: An Introduction to Theory and Practice*. London: Sage.

Dombrowski, U. & Mielke, T. J. P. C. (2013). Lean leadership: Fundamental principles and their application. *Procedia CIRP*, 7, 569–574.

Edmondson, A. C. (2018). *The Fearless Organization: Creating Psychological Safety in the Workplace for Learning, Innovation, and Growth*. Hoboken, NJ: John Wiley & Sons.

Eisenhardt, K. M. (2021). What is the Eisenhardt method, really? *Strategic Organization*, 19(1), 147–160.

Emiliani, M. L. & Stec, D. J. (2005). Leaders lost in transformation. *Leadership & Organization Development Journal*, 26(5), 370–387.

Hines, P., Holweg, M., & Rich, N. (2004). Learning to evolve. *International Journal of Operations & Production Management*, 24(10), 994–1011.

Holmemo, M. D. Q. & Ingvaldsen, J. A. (2016). Bypassing the dinosaurs? How middle managers become the missing link in lean implementation. *Total Quality Management & Business Excellence*, 27(11–12), 1332–1345.

Holmemo, M. D. Q., Ingvaldsen, J. A., & Powell, D. (2023). Beyond the lean manager: Insights on how to develop corporate lean leadership. *Total Quality Management & Business Excellence*, 34(1–2), 19–31.

Holmemo, M. D. Q., Powell, D. J., & Ingvaldsen, J. A. (2018). Making it stick on borrowed time: The role of internal consultants in public sector lean transformations. *The TQM Journal*, 30(3), 217–231.

Holweg, M. (2007). The genealogy of lean production. *Journal of Operations Management*, 25(2), 420–437.

Ingvaldsen, J. A. & Benders, J. (2016). Lost in translation? The role of supervisors in lean production. *German Journal of Human Resource Management*, 30(1), 35–52.

Jadhav, J. R., Mantha, S. S., & Rane, S. B. (2014). Exploring barriers in lean implementation. *International Journal of Lean Six Sigma*, 5(2), 122–148.

Kotter, J. P. (2012). *Leading Change*. Boston: Harvard Business Review Press.

Kuipers, B. S., De Witte, M. C., & van der Zwaan, A. H. (2004). Design or development? Beyond the LP-STS debate: Inputs from a Volvo truck case. *International Journal of Operations & Production Management*, 24(8), 840–854.

Langley, A. (1999). Strategies for theorizing from process data. *Academy of Management Review*, 24(4), 691–710.

Liker, J. K. (2004). *Toyota Way: 14 Management Principles from the World's Greatest Manufacturer*. New York: McGraw-Hill Education.

Liker, J. & Convis, G. (2011). *The Toyota Way to Lean Leadership: Achieving and Sustaining Excellence through Leadership Development*. New York: McGraw-Hill.

Mackelprang, A. W. & Nair, A. (2010). Relationship between just-in-time manufacturing practices and performance: A meta-analytic investigation. *Journal of Operations Management*, 28(4), 283–302.

Magnani, F., Carbone, V., and Moatti, V. (2019). The human side of lean: A literature review. *Supply Chain Forum: An International Journal*, 20(2), 132–144.

Netland, T. H., Powell, D. J., & Hines, P. (2020). Demystifying lean leadership. *International Journal of Lean Six Sigma*, 11(3), 543–554.

Nonaka, I. (1994). A dynamic theory of organizational knowledge creation. *Organization Science*, 5(1), 14–37.

Ohno, T. (2013). *Taiichi Ohno's Workplace Management, Special 100th Birthday Edition*. New York: McGraw-Hill.

Poksinska, B., Swartling, D., & Drotz, E. (2013). The daily work of lean leaders: Lessons from manufacturing and healthcare. *Total Quality Management & Business Excellence*, 24(8), 886–898.

Reynders, P., Kumar, M., & Found, P. A. (2020). "Lean on me": An integrative literature review on the middle management role in lean. *Total Quality Management & Business Excellence*, 33(3–4), 318–354.

Schein, E. H. & Schein, P. A. (2018). *Humble Leadership: The Power of Relationships, Openness, and Trust*. Oakland, CA: Berrett-Koehler Publishers.

Seidel, A., Saurin, T. A., Tortorella, G. L., & Marodin, G. A. (2019). How can general leadership theories help to expand the knowledge of lean leadership? *Production Planning & Control*, 30(16), 1322–1336.

Skogstad, A., Einarsen, S., Torsheim, T., Aasland, M. S., & Hetland, H. (2007). The destructiveness of laissez-faire leadership behavior. *Journal of Occupational Health Psychology*, 12(1), 80–92.

Spear, S. J. (2004). Learning to lead at Toyota. *Harvard Business Review*, 82(5), 78–91.

Sveningsson, S. & Sörgärde, N. (2019). *Managing Change in Organizations: How, What and Why?* London: Sage Publications.

Tortorella, G. L., van Dun, D. H., & De Almeida, A. G. (2020). Leadership behaviors during lean healthcare implementation: A review and longitudinal study. *Journal of Manufacturing Technology Management*, 31(1), 193–215.

Van Assen, M. F. (2018). The moderating effect of management behavior for lean and process improvement. *Operations Management Research*, 11(1), 1–13.

van Dun, D. H., Hicks, J. N., & Wilderom, C. P. M. (2017). Values and behaviors of effective lean managers: Mixed-methods exploratory research. *European Management Journal*, 35(2), 174–186.

Wulff, J. N., Sajons, G. B., Pogrebna, G., Lonati, S., Bastardoz, N., Banks, G. C., & Antonakis, J. (2023). Common methodological mistakes. *The Leadership Quarterly*, 34(1), 101677.

Yukl, G. (1989). Managerial leadership: A review of theory and research. *Journal of Management*, 15(2), 251–289.

Zaleznik, A. (2004). Managers and leaders: Are they different? *Harvard Business Review*, 82(1), 74–81.

12 Anxiety that drives kaizen: a strategic blueprint for kaizen implementation across borders

Kodo Yokozawa

Introduction

Kaizen is a continuous improvement process within organizations that aims to eliminate waste from business processes (Imai, 1986). It relies on the knowledge and ideas of employees and is a central value of the Toyota Production System (Liker, 2004). Despite its recognized effectiveness and simplicity, implementing and sustaining kaizen can be challenging (Bessant & Caffyn, 1997; Brunet & New, 2003). Research on kaizen also reveals variations in its performance between Japan and other nations (Robinson & Stern, 1998). For instance, European factories generate only 0.4 suggestions per worker per year, whereas Toyota produces an average of 61.6 suggestions annually (Womack et al., 1990). Additionally, in 1995, the average number of suggestions submitted per employee in the US and Japan was 0.16 and 18.5, respectively (Robinson & Stern, 1998). Yokozawa et al. (2010) conducted in-depth interview research among 30 Japanese production managers who have experience working in overseas manufacturing bases. Seventy-three percent of them answered that they cannot develop a kaizen mind among overseas local employees. These statistics imply that while the kaizen concept aligns well with the Japanese context, its implementation in different countries and contexts can be challenging.

Many factors play a role in the international transfer of kaizen, such as cultural differences (Lagrosen, 2003; Naor et al., 2008; Recht & Wilderom, 1998), the influence of labor unions (Humphrey, 1995), and job security (Young, 1992). However, an intriguing aspect worth exploring is the impact of "anxiety" on kaizen performance, as suggested by Imai (1986). Imai recounts a conversation with a European diplomat in Japan, who highlighted a stark contrast between Western complacency and overconfidence versus Japanese feelings of anxiety and imperfection. The concept of imperfection and the experience of anxiety among the Japanese workforce may serve as significant driving forces for kaizen (Imai, 1986, p. 32). Similarly, Parker and Slaughter (1988) observed that workers at NUMMI plant, a joint venture between General Motor (GM) and Toyota Motor, were consistently motivated to enhance their performance through kaizen, leading to its characterization as "the factory that runs on anxiety." These insights challenge the prevailing belief that anxiety has a negative impact on work performance (Martens et al., 1990), making them particularly thought-provoking. However, Imai (1986) does not delve deeper into the reasons behind Japanese workers' feelings of anxiety, nor does he explain how or why this emotion contributes as a driving force for kaizen.

To understand why kaizen is widely practiced in Japan but difficult to transfer to other countries, we must address two crucial questions: (1) Does higher personal anxiety contribute to improved kaizen performance? and (2) Do Japanese individuals experience higher levels of anxiety compared to people in other nations? Answering these questions helps uncover the cultural and psychological factors influencing kaizen implementation globally. If higher personal anxiety does lead to enhanced kaizen performance and Japanese workers experience more anxiety than individuals in other nations, this could explain kaizen's success in Japan and its limitations in other countries. Organizations aiming to implement kaizen effectively in diverse cultural contexts must understand these factors.

Kaizen and lean

Kaizen and lean are two management approaches aimed at enhancing business process efficiency and reducing waste. While they share a common goal, they differ in their origins, emphasis, and focus.

Introduced in 1986 by Massaki Imai in his book *Kaizen: The Key to Japan's Competitive Success*, the concept of kaizen originated in Japan and was initially discussed from a Japanese perspective. It encompassed various elements such as philosophy, management systems, and organizational culture, which were deeply ingrained in Japanese companies. These elements played a pivotal role in motivating employees to actively participate in continuous improvement initiatives within the Japanese context. However, when implementing kaizen principles outside of Japan, it becomes necessary to evaluate which of these factors can be adapted to suit the non-Japanese context. Previous research on kaizen has aimed to identify the cultural factors that can be effectively applied in non-Japanese settings (Lillrank, 1995; Recht & Wilderom, 1998).

In contrast, the lean concept introduced by Womack et al. (1990) takes a more universal approach to management, prioritizing the elimination of waste and ensuring quality across all business aspects, from design to production to distribution. The lean concept primarily emphasizes the use of tools and techniques to improve efficiency and eliminate waste, with a specific focus on enhancing processes and eliminating non-value-added activities. Lean research has recently shifted its focus towards examining the role of organizational infrastructure (Galeazzo et al., 2017) and culture (Bortolotti et al., 2015; Erthal & Marques, 2018; Losonci et al., 2017), leadership (Holmemo et al., 2023; Netland et al., 2020; Tortorella & Fogliatto, 2017; Tortorella et al., 2018, 2020; van Dun & Wilderom, 2021) and management practice (Netland et al., 2015) in sustaining lean initiatives. This shift is due to the recognition that lean initiatives often fail to deliver sustained improvements over the long term, and a lack of attention to these factors is identified as a potential reason for this. In contrast, recent research indicates that kaizen is often viewed as one of the tools under lean production, such as kaizen blitz and kaizen events. The chapter uses the term "kaizen" instead of "lean" because it places emphasis on the cultural and psychological aspects associated with Japan.

Imai (1986) identified three distinct components of kaizen: management-oriented, group-oriented, and individual-oriented. Management-oriented kaizen focuses on improving the systems and procedures within an organization, primarily involving managers and professionals. Group-oriented kaizen aims to enhance work procedures and standards through small group activities, such as quality control circles. Individual-oriented kaizen concentrates on improving one's own work area, typically through individual suggestion systems.

This chapter highlights the importance of individual kaizen, which is considered equally vital as organization-level kaizen. Individual kaizen improves knowledge, problem-solving skills (Kerrin & Oliver, 2002), and communication within the workplace (Imai, 1986), leading to increased motivation and morale (Bessant & Caffyn, 1997; Cheser, 1998), and overall corporate performance. Implementing individual kaizen can result in significant and long-term quality improvements and cost savings for organizations (Bessant & Caffyn, 1997; Brunet & New, 2003).

Personal factors affecting individual kaizen performance

Few studies have examined individual-oriented kaizen, with most research focusing on factors influencing the implementation and sustainability of suggestion systems. Lasrado et al. (2015, 2016) identified determinants for sustaining an employee suggestion system, including leadership, work environment, system capability, effectiveness, organizational encouragement, and system barriers. However, previous research has mainly focused on organizational-level factors.

Although Axtell et al. (2000) suggest that organizational factors and individual characteristics impact individual kaizen performance, limited studies have examined the individual-level factors influencing improvement activities. Feist (1998) indicates that individual creativity is influenced by autonomy, introversion, openness to new experiences, norm-doubting, and self-confidence. Frese et al. (1999) confirm that idea generation is affected by proactivity, ambition, and self-efficacy. Axtell et al. (2000) find that self-efficacy and interest in workplace issues increase the likelihood of making proposals. Rapp and Eklund (2007) proposed that employees who desire a better working environment and employees with only some of their suggestions rejected are more likely to be active in submitting suggestions compared to employees whose suggestions are mostly rejected or accepted. It is important for employees to feel encouraged, knowing that their suggestions are being evaluated properly by their first-line managers and that they receive feedback with good reasons for implementation or rejection. Lipponen et al. (2008) discovered that strong organizational identification and openness to change lead to successful suggestion-making outcomes. Verworn (2009) verifies that older employees provide higher-quality suggestions. Woods et al. (2018) reveal that employees with high levels of openness and longer tenures generate more ideas. To the best of our knowledge, none of the previous research has empirically verified the relationship between personal anxiety and the individual kaizen performance.

Anxiety and kaizen performance

Anxiety refers to a psychological state characterized by intense feelings of tension, worry, or apprehension regarding potential adverse events that may occur in the future (Saviola et al., 2020, p. 1). Unlike fear, which arises in response to immediate threats, anxiety is a more diffuse and future-oriented form of fear (Barlow, 2014; Freud, 1920). Anxiety is a common emotion caused by stress or threats. Severe and persistent anxiety can lead to anxiety disorders that greatly affect one's quality of life (Dennis-Tiwary, 2022). In this chapter, we will focus on understanding anxiety as an emotion.

Limited research exists on the relationship between personal anxiety and individual kaizen performance, but literature on anxiety's impact on general job performance reveals three patterns. First, anxiety can have a negative effect on performance, as highly anxious individuals perceive many situations as threats and struggle to concentrate, resulting in poor performance (Cassady & Johnson, 2002; Chapell et al., 2005; Culler & Holahan, 1980; Derakshan & Eysenck, 2009). Second, a positive relationship between anxiety and performance is observed, as high anxiety individuals tend to focus on negative aspects and become more sensitive to problems and threats, which can energize them to achieve their goals (Mughal et al., 1996; Strack & Esteves, 2015; Strack et al., 2014, 2017). Finally, an inverted U-shaped relationship is found, indicating that manageable levels of anxiety can help individuals stay focused, motivated, and improve task performance (Chamberlain & Hale, 2007; Dennis-Tiwary, 2022; Yerkes & Dodson, 1908).

Yokozawa et al. (2021) examined the impact of state and trait anxiety on kaizen performance, building on Imai's recognition that anxiety can drive kaizen. State anxiety refers to situational feelings, while trait anxiety reflects dispositional personality traits (Spielberger et al., 1983). The study explored how these anxieties influence behaviors associated with kaizen, including rule adherence, initiative, and perseverance. The research surveyed 552 employees from four Japanese companies and used structural equation modeling for analysis. The study's findings revealed that state anxiety has a significantly positive effect on rule adherence and kaizen performance. Conversely, trait anxiety positively influences employees' initiative and perseverance but is negatively associated with both dimensions of kaizen performance. By differentiating between these two types of anxiety, the research underscores that state anxiety primarily influences short-term kaizen performance, whereas trait anxiety has a greater influence on long-term performance. This temporal aspect aligns with theoretical discussions but lacked empirical support until this study. In summary, these findings provide empirical support for Imai's recognition.

Research findings suggest that managers can enhance kaizen activities by increasing employees' state anxiety and creating an urgent work environment. Injecting urgency, implementing benchmarking practices, and setting challenging goals contribute to improved kaizen performance. Employees with higher trait anxiety show more initiative and perseverance, making them valuable for smoother kaizen implementation. However, for complex challenges, the relationship between anxiety and performance may follow an inverted U-shaped pattern (Yerkes & Dodson, 1908). Excessive anxiety can induce fear and negatively impact performance, so managers should exercise caution.

Japanese and anxiety

Imai (1986, p. 32) acknowledges that Japanese individuals tend to exhibit higher levels of anxiety compared to Westerners. Cross-national studies examining anxiety-related personality traits have consistently shown that the Japanese display a higher degree of anxiety when compared to other ethnic groups. In a comprehensive international research study encompassing 53 countries, Japan scored the lowest in terms of self-esteem (Schmitt & Allik, 2005), which refers to an individual's overall positive self-evaluation (Rosenberg, 1965), and has a negative correlation with anxiety (Sowislo & Orth, 2013). Furthermore, in the domain of neuroticism, which is closely associated with anxiety (Vittengl, 2017; Widiger & Mullins-Sweatt, 2009), the Japanese also obtained the highest scores (Chatard et al., 2009).

Moreover, research findings from a genetic perspective indicate a predisposition towards anxiety-related traits among the Japanese population. Serotonin, a neurotransmitter that contributes to feelings of well-being and happiness (Lesch et al., 1996; Murakami et al., 1999), has been identified as a contributing factor. The serotonin transporter gene, responsible for encoding the serotonin transporter involved in neuron communication has been studied in relation to anxiety-related traits. Lesch et al. (1996) discovered that the short version of the serotonin transporter gene, known as the S allele, is associated with anxiety-related traits compared to the long version, known as the L allele. Esau et al. (2008) conducted a comparison of genotypes across different ethnic groups and found that the prevalence of the S allele among the Japanese was the highest among all the groups studied, further supporting the notion of a higher propensity for anxiety among the Japanese population (see Table 12.1).

Table 12.1   Allelic distribution in normal populations in different
countries

Population group	Allele (%)	
	L	S
European Caucasian	60.85	39.15
Americans	56.47	43.53
British Caucasians	47.14	52.86
Indians	31.47	68.53
Chinese	29.91	70.09
Japanese	19.06	80.94

Source: Adapted from Chiao and Blizinsky (2010) and Esau et al. (2008), and
modified by the author.

Discussion: challenges in international transfer of kaizen

Yokozawa et al. (2021) present compelling evidence supporting the idea that
personal anxiety can actually have a positive impact on personal kaizen performance. This is particularly noticeable when it comes to individual kaizen
suggestions, which are usually relatively simple in nature. These findings
suggest a positive correlation between anxiety and performance. However, as
workplace challenges become more complex and employees need to tap into
their creative abilities it can be inferred that the relationship between anxiety
and kaizen performance follows an inverted U-shaped pattern. Additionally,
as mentioned earlier, the data indicates a higher level of anxiety among the
Japanese population. Based on these two assumptions, we can offer some
insightful explanations for the differences in kaizen performance among
countries.

Japanese companies with predominantly Japanese employees, who often experience higher levels of trait anxiety, require human resource (HR) management
strategies to reduce anxiety and improve kaizen performance. Conversely, in
countries with lower anxiety levels and a higher sense of complacency, management strategies should focus on generating a sense of urgency (see Figure
12.1).

Japan's prevailing HR management system emphasizes long-term employment, seniority-based promotions (Abegglen, 1958), a collective mindset
(Ouchi, 1981), supportive bureaucratic structures (Adler, 1999), and a man-

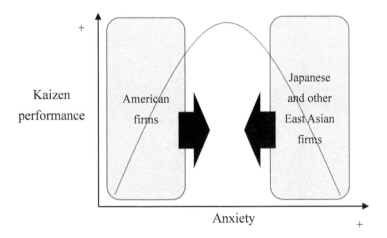

Figure 12.1   Strategy for managing national-level anxiety to achieve optimal kaizen performance

agerial familism (Ishikawa, 1982). These can be seen as aiming to deliberately alleviate employee anxiety. In contrast, the commonly described US system emphasizes individualism, performance-based promotions and salary increases, and there is a prevalence of short-term employment (Ouchi, 1981). This system frequently intensifies anxiety through consistent challenges and expectations. To maximize kaizen performance, it is crucial to consider and utilize HR systems that align with the employees' anxiety levels. The differences in improvement efforts across countries can be attributed to varying levels of apprehension within each country. Simply adopting HR systems from other countries without acknowledging these differences can lead to problems. Implementing Japanese-style HR systems, designed to reduce anxiety, in an American context may result in increased relaxation and decreased performance. Similarly, blindly applying American-style HR management, which aims to increase anxiety, in a Japanese context could induce fear and panic among Japanese employees who already experience high trait anxiety.

Previous research suggests that Japanese companies operating internationally tend to utilize Japanese HR management systems in their non-Japanese locations (Abo, 1994). This practice of imposing Japanese methods may contribute to the challenges faced by Japanese companies when transferring the kaizen philosophy. It is essential to recognize the varying levels of anxiety in different countries when introducing systems and practices outside of Japan. The success of certain practices in Japan does not guarantee their effectiveness elsewhere. To ensure sustainable kaizen, it is vital to identify and implement practices that are suitable for employees in each specific country, considering their unique cultural and social contexts, including anxiety levels.

Future research directions

To enhance our understanding of the kaizen performance differences among countries, we propose several future research directions in two key research domains: behavioral operations and international operations management. These directions aim to expand our knowledge and provide valuable insights.

Behavioral operations

Enhancing sensitivity to employee feelings: strategies for managers

Employee feelings, particularly anxiety, have been shown to have a significant impact on kaizen performance (Yokozawa et al., 2021). However, managers often face challenges in recognizing and addressing these emotions due to employees' reluctance to openly discuss them. To effectively tackle employee anxiety and enhance performance, it is crucial for managers to develop heightened sensitivity towards their employees' feelings.

One valuable approach for cultivating this sensitivity is through regular Gemba walks. Gemba walks involve managers actively observing and engaging with employees in their work environment. This practice facilitates the detection of tacit information, including employee emotions, which may not be readily apparent in other contexts. By visiting the Gemba frequently, managers can familiarize themselves with the normal state of the workplace and the typical emotions exhibited by employees. Through regular Gemba walks, managers can promptly identify any deviations from the normal state. This heightened sensitivity enables them to detect anomalies and address them proactively, ultimately improving employee performance and well-being (Phung et al., 2022).

Moreover, it is essential to examine how this enhanced sensitivity impacts overall employee performance. Understanding the relationship between emotional awareness and performance can help managers refine their strategies and tailor interventions to specific needs.

Enhancing motivation: harnessing anxiety as a catalyst for kaizen activities

Managers and leaders can significantly benefit from recognizing the potential of anxiety and transforming it into a motivational force or a sense of urgency. Future research should delve into the conditions and mechanisms that facilitate this transformation, eventually fostering heightened motivation and proactive problem-solving.

By reframing anxiety as "motivational anxiety" (Strack et al., 2017), individuals can harness its energy to propel themselves forward rather than allowing it to hinder their progress. This perspective shift empowers managers and leaders to leverage anxiety as a driving force, cultivating a sense of urgency within themselves and their teams.

Furthermore, investigating the mechanisms behind this transformation can shed light on how anxiety triggers adaptive responses. By uncovering the cognitive, emotional, and behavioral processes involved, researchers can develop effective interventions and strategies to facilitate the conversion of anxiety into motivation. This knowledge will enable managers and leaders to empower their teams by providing them with the tools and resources necessary to channel anxiety productively.

Enhancing group dynamics and group-oriented kaizen performance: exploring the impact of anxiety levels

Understanding anxiety's impact on group dynamics and performance is crucial. Prioritizing research on group-level anxiety and the effectiveness of kaizen implementation can reveal the optimal anxiety level for impactful improvements. The kaizen approach applied in groups has proven effective but requires further exploration regarding its influence on group dynamics and performance. While anxiety can motivate individuals and groups, excessive anxiety hampers performance. Identifying the optimal anxiety level enables organizations to manage it effectively, enhancing group dynamics and performance in kaizen. The research findings provide practical implications for leaders to create supportive environments, manage anxiety, provide training and support, and foster psychological safety for successful group-oriented kaizen.

International operations management

Relationship between national-level anxiety and lean/kaizen performance

Investigating the relationship between national-level anxiety and lean/kaizen performance can provide valuable insights into the impact of broader societal factors on organizational improvement efforts. Understanding how national-level anxiety influences the adoption, sustainability, and success of lean practices can help organizations develop culturally and contextually appropriate strategies. This research implies that the prevalence of kaizen in Japan may be influenced by higher anxiety levels, posing challenges for its transfer to countries with lower anxiety levels. Future studies could explore whether the average trait anxiety level of a country's population can predict the ease or difficulty of transferring kaizen across nations.

Addressing these future research directions will contribute to a deeper understanding of behavioral operations and international operations management. The findings will inform the development of more effective strategies and practices for organizations to achieve continuous improvement and optimize operational performance.

Conclusion

Our study explores two questions on kaizen performance across countries: Does higher personal anxiety boost kaizen performance? Are Japanese individuals more anxious than others? Understanding the answers to these questions is crucial for uncovering cultural and psychological factors in diverse countries. Previous research shows a positive correlation between personal anxiety and kaizen performance, and higher levels of trait anxiety among Japanese individuals. These insights shed light on kaizen in Japanese corporations and challenges in non-Japanese contexts. Further research is needed to strengthen this perspective. To advance our understanding in this area, we propose the following future research directions:

- Examining management sensitivity to employee feelings: investigating how managers can better understand and address the anxiety levels of employees in order to create an environment conducive to kaizen implementation.
- Enhancing motivation: harnessing anxiety as a catalyst for kaizen activities; exploring how anxiety can be utilized as a motivational factor to drive and improve kaizen initiatives.

- Enhancing group dynamics and performance through group-oriented kaizen: investigating the impact of group-oriented kaizen approaches on group dynamics and overall performance, considering the influence of anxiety levels within the group.
- Relationship between national-level anxiety and lean/kaizen performance.

By pursuing these research directions, we can enhance our knowledge of the factors contributing to successful kaizen implementation and address performance gaps among different countries.

References

Abegglen, J. G. (1958). *The Japanese Factory: Aspects of Its Social Organization.* New York: Free Press.

Abo, T. (Ed.) (1994). *Hybrid Factory: The Japanese Production System in the United States.* New York: Oxford University Press.

Adler, P. (1999). Building better bureaucracies. *Academy of Management Executive,* 13(4), 36–49.

Axtell, C. M., Holman, D. J., Unsworth, K. L., Wall, T. D., Waterson, P. E., & Harrington, E. (2000). Shopfloor innovation: Facilitating the suggestion and implementation of ideas. *Journal of Occupational and Organizational Psychology,* 73(3), 265–285.

Barlow, D. H. (2014). *Clinical Handbook of Psychological Disorders: A Step-by-Step Treatment Manual.* New York: Guilford Press.

Bessant, J. & Caffyn, S. (1997). High-involvement innovation through continuous improvement. *International Journal of Technology Management,* 14(1), 7–28.

Bortolotti, T., Boscari, S., & Danese, P. (2015). Successful lean implementation: Organizational culture and soft lean practices. *International Journal of Production Economics,* 160, 182–201.

Brunet, A. P. & New, S. (2003). Kaizen in Japan: An empirical study. *International Journal of Operations & Production Management,* 23(12), 1426–1446.

Cassady, J. C. & Johnson, R. E. (2002). Cognitive test anxiety and academic performance. *Contemporary Educational Psychology,* 27(2), 270–295.

Chamberlain, S. & Hale, B. (2007). Competitive state anxiety and self-confidence: Intensity and direction as relative predictors of performance on a golf putting task. *Anxiety, Stress, & Coping,* 20(2), 197–207.

Chapell, M. S., Blanding, Z. B., Silverstein, M. E., Takahashi, M., Newman, B., Gubi, A., & McCann, N. (2005). Test anxiety and academic performance in undergraduate and graduate students. *Journal of Educational Psychology,* 97(2), 268–274.

Chatard, A., Selimbegović, L., & Konan, P. N. D. (2009). Self-esteem and suicide rates in 55 nations. *European Journal of Personality,* 23(1), 19–32.

Cheser, R. N. (1998). The effect of Japanese kaizen on employee motivation in U.S. manufacturing. *International Journal of Organizational Analysis,* 6(3), 197–217.

Chiao, J. Y. & Blizinsky, K. D. (2010). Culture-gene coevolution of individualism-collectivism and the serotonin transporter gene. *Proceedings of the Royal Society B: Biological Sciences,* 277(1681), 529–537.

Culler, R. E. & Holahan, C. J. (1980). Test anxiety and academic performance: The effects of study-related behaviors. *Journal of Educational Psychology*, 72(1), 16–20.

Dennis-Tiwary, T. (2022). *Future Tense: Why Anxiety is Good for You (even Though it Feels Bad)*. London: Hachette.

Derakshan, N. & Eysenck, M. W. (2009). Anxiety, processing efficiency, and cognitive performance. *European Psychologist*, 14(2), 168–176.

Erthal, A. & Marques, L. (2018). National culture and organisational culture in lean organisations: A systematic review. *Production Planning & Control*, 29(8), 668–687.

Esau, L., Kaur, M., Adonis, L., & Arieff, Z. (2008). The 5-HTTLPR polymorphism in South African healthy populations: A global comparison. *Journal of Neural Transmission*, 115(5), 755–760.

Feist, G. J. (1998). A meta-analysis of personality in scientific and artistic creativity. *Personality and Social Psychology Review*, 2(4), 290–309.

Frese, M., Teng, E., & Wijnen, C. J. D. (1999). Helping to improve suggestion systems: Predictors of making suggestions in companies. *Journal of Organizational Behavior*, 20(7), 1139–1155.

Freud, S. (1920). *A General Introduction to Psychoanalysis*. New York: Liveright.

Galeazzo, A., Furlan, A., & Vinelli, A. (2017). The organizational infrastructure of continuous improvement: An empirical analysis. *Operations Management Research*, 10(1–2), 33–46.

Holmemo, M. D. Q., Ingvaldsen, J. A., & Powell, D. (2023). Beyond the lean manager: Insights on how to develop corporate lean leadership. *Total Quality Management & Business Excellence*, 34(1–2), 19–31.

Humphrey, J. (1995). The adaption of Japanese management techniques in Brazilian industry. *Journal of Management Studies*, 32(6), 767–787.

Imai, M. (1986). *Kaizen: The Key to Japan's Competitive Success*. New York: McGraw-Hill.

Ishikawa, A. (1982). A survey of studies in the Japanese style of management. *Economic and Industrial Democracy*, 3(1), 1–15.

Kerrin, M. & Oliver, N. (2002). Collective and individual improvement activities: The role of reward systems. *Personnel Review*, 31(3), 320–337.

Lagrosen, S. (2003). Exploring the impact of culture on quality management. *International Journal of Quality & Reliability Management*, 20(4), 473–487.

Lasrado, F., Arif, M., & Rizvi, A. (2015). The determinants for sustainability of an employee suggestion system. *International Journal of Quality & Reliability Management*, 32(2), 182–210.

Lasrado, F., Arif, M., Rizvi, A., & Urdzik, C. (2016). Critical success factors for employee suggestion schemes: A literature review. *International Journal of Organizational Analysis*, 24(2), 315–339.

Lesch, K. P., Bengel, D., Heils, A., Sabol, S. Z., Greenberg, B. D., Petri, S., Benjamin, J., Muller, C. R., Hamer, D. H., & Murphy, D. L. (1996). Association of anxiety-related traits with a polymorphism in the serotonin transporter gene regulatory region. *Science*, 274(5292), 1527–1531.

Liker, J. K. (2004). *Toyota Way: 14 Management Principles from the World's Greatest Manufacturer*. New York: McGraw-Hill Education.

Lillrank, P. (1995). The transfer of management innovations from Japan. *Organization Studies*, 16(6), 971–989.

Lipponen, J., Bardi, A., & Haapamäki, J. (2008). The interaction between values and organizational identification in predicting suggestion-making at work. *Journal of Occupational and Organizational Psychology*, 81(2), 241–248.

Losonci, D., Kása, R., Demeter, K., Heidrich, B., & Jenei, I. (2017). The impact of shop floor culture and subculture on lean production practices. *International Journal of Operations & Production Management*, 37(2), 205–225.

Martens, R., Burton, D., Vealey, R. S., Bump, L. A., & Smith, D. E. (1990). Development and validation of the competitive state anxiety inventory-2. In R. Martens, R. S. Vealey, & D. Burton (Eds.), *Competitive Anxiety in Sport*. Champaign, IL: Human Kinetics, pp. 117–190.

Mughal, S., Walsh, J., & Wilding, J. (1996). Stress and work performance: The role of trait anxiety. *Personality and Individual Differences*, 20(6), 685–691.

Murakami, F., Shimomura, T., Kotani, K., Ikawa, S., Nanba, E., & Adachi, K. (1999). Anxiety traits associated with a polymorphism in the serotonin transporter gene regulatory region in the Japanese. *Journal of Human Genetics*, 44(1), 15–17.

Naor, M., Goldstein, S. M., Linderman, K. W., & Schroeder, R. G. (2008). The role of culture as driver of quality management and performance: Infrastructure versus core quality practices. *Decision Sciences*, 39(4), 671–702.

Netland, T. H., Powell, D. J., & Hines, P. (2020). Demystifying lean leadership. *International Journal of Lean Six Sigma*, 11(3), 543–554.

Netland, T. H., Schloetzer, J. D., & Ferdows, K. (2015). Implementing corporate lean programs: The effect of management control practices. *Journal of Operations Management*, 36, 90–102.

Ouchi, W. G. (1981). *Theory Z: How American Business Can Meet the Japanese Challenge*. Reading, MA: Addison-Wesley.

Parker, M. & Slaughter, J. (1988). The factory that runs on anxiety. *The Washington Post*. https://www.washingtonpost.com/archive/opinions/1988/10/09/the-factory-that-runs-on-anxiety/12a24ff1-e86e-42eb-9e9c-875a7b5386c4/.

Phung, H. T. X., Yokozawa, K., & Kimura, T. (2022). Concept, theoretical foundation, and significance of management sensitivity. Paper presented at the 6th World Conference on Production and Operations Management (P&OM), Nara, Japan.

Rapp, C. & Eklund, J. (2007). Sustainable development of a suggestion system: Factors influencing improvement activities in a confectionary company. *Human Factors and Ergonomics in Manufacturing & Service Industries*, 17(1), 79–94.

Recht, R. & Wilderom, C. (1998). Kaizen and culture: On the transferability of Japanese suggestion systems. *International Business Review*, 7(1), 7–22.

Robinson, A. & Stern, S. (1998). *Corporate Creativity: How Innovation and Improvement Actually Happen*. San Francisco, CA: Berrett-Koehler Publishers.

Rosenberg, M. (1965). *Society and the Adolescent Self-Image*. Princeton, NJ: Princeton University Press.

Saviola, F., Pappaianni, E., Monti, A., Grecucci, A., Jovicich, J., & De Pisapia, N. (2020). Trait and state anxiety are mapped differently in the human brain. *Scientific Reports*, 10(1), 1–11.

Schmitt, D. P. & Allik, J. (2005). Simultaneous administration of the Rosenberg Self-Esteem Scale in 53 nations: Exploring the universal and culture-specific features of global self-esteem. *Journal of Personality and Social Psychology*, 89(4), 623–642.

Sowislo, J. F. & Orth, U. (2013). Does low self-esteem predict depression and anxiety? A meta-analysis of longitudinal studies. *Psychological Bulletin*, 139(1), 213–240.

Spielberger, C., Gorsuch, R., Lushene, R., Vagg, P., & Jacobs, G. (1983). *Manual for the State-Trait Anxiety Inventory*. Palo Alto, CA: Consulting Psychologists Press.

Strack, J. & Esteves, F. (2015). Exams? Why worry? Interpreting anxiety as facilitative and stress appraisals. *Anxiety, Stress, & Coping*, 28(2), 205–214.

Strack, J., Lopes, P., & Esteves, F. (2014). Will you thrive under pressure or burn out? Linking anxiety motivation and emotional exhaustion. *Cognition & Emotion*, 29(4), 1–14.

Strack, J., Lopes, P., Esteves, F., & Fernández-Berrocal, P. (2017). Must we suffer to succeed? When anxiety boosts motivation and performance. *Journal of Individual Differences*, 38(2), 113–124.

Tortorella, G. L. & Fogliatto, F. (2017). Implementation of lean manufacturing and situational leadership styles: An empirical study. *Leadership & Organization Development Journal*, 38(7), 946–968.

Tortorella, G. L., Fetterman, D., Frank, A., & Marodin, G. A. (2018). Lean manufacturing implementation: Leadership styles and contextual variables. *International Journal of Operations & Production Management*, 38(5), 1205–1227.

Tortorella, G. L., van Dun, D. H., & De Almeida, A. G. (2020). Leadership behaviors during lean healthcare implementation: A review and longitudinal study. *Journal of Manufacturing Technology Management*, 31(1), 193–215.

van Dun, D. H. & Wilderom, C. P. M. (2021). Improving high lean team performance through aligned behaviour-value patterns and coactive vicarious learning-by-doing. *International Journal of Operations & Production Management*, 41(13), 65–99.

Verworn, B. (2009). Does age have an impact on having ideas? An analysis of the quantity and quality of ideas submitted to a suggestion system. *Creativity and Innovation Management*, 18(4), 326–334.

Vittengl, J. R. (2017). Who pays the price for high neuroticism? Moderators of longitudinal risks for depression and anxiety. *Psychological Medicine*, 47(10), 1794–1805.

Widiger, T. A. & Mullins-Sweatt, S. N. (2009). Five-factor model of personality disorder: A proposal for DSM-V. *Annual Review of Clinical Psychology*, 5(1), 197–220.

Womack, J. P., Jones, D. T., and Roos, D. (1990). *The Machine That Changed the World: The Story of Lean Production, Toyota's Secret Weapon in the Global Car Wars That Is Now Revolutionizing World Industry*. New York: Simon & Schuster.

Woods, S., Mustafa, M., Anderson, N., & Sayer, B. (2018). Innovative work behavior and personality traits: Examining the moderating effects of organizational tenure. *Journal of Managerial Psychology*, 33(1), 29–42.

Yerkes, R. M. & Dodson, J. D. (1908). The relation of strength of stimulus to rapidity of habit-formation. *Journal of Comparative Neurology and Psychology*, 18(5), 459–482.

Yokozawa, K., Nguyen, H. A., & Tran, T. B. H. (2021). Role of personal anxiety in individual kaizen behaviour and performance: Evidence from Japan. *International Journal of Operations & Production Management*, 41(6), 942–961.

Yokozawa, K., Steenhuis, H. J., & de Bruijn, E. J. (2010). Recent experience with transferring Japanese management systems abroad. *Journal of Strategic Management Studies*, 2(1), 1–16.

Young, S. M. (1992). A framework for successful adoption and performance of Japanese manufacturing practices in the United States. *Academy of Management Review*, 17(4), 677–700.

PART V

Lean and digitalization

13 A digital lean world: from digital lean manufacturing to Lean 4.0

Daryl Powell, David Romero, Jiju Antony and Paolo Gaiardelli

Introduction

For several decades, improvement efforts in manufacturing firms have been built on the concept of lean manufacturing and its associated ideals of continuous improvement and people development (Netland and Powell, 2017). Nevertheless, the current wave of industrial improvement is being driven by the application of key enabling (digital) technologies associated with Industry 4.0 (Lorenz et al., 2020). Hence, there is growing appreciation among academics and practitioners of the need to understand how digitalization can be successfully integrated with the principles and practices of lean production to further improve the efficiency and competitiveness of manufacturing organizations.

Digital Lean Manufacturing (DLM) refers to the application of digital technology in order to enhance the lean and learning transformation in manufacturing organizations (Ashrafian et al., 2019). Powell and Romero (2021) suggest that the term DLM first appeared in the extant literature in 2007, with an initial emphasis on Computer-Aided Design and Computer-Aided Manufacturing (CAD-CAM) and Integrated Product and Process Development (IPPD). Thereafter, DLM research has shifted its focus towards the integration of Industry 4.0 or smart manufacturing with the lean manufacturing paradigm (Cattaneo et al., 2017; Mora et al., 2017). It was Romero et al. (2018), however, that first offered the operations management (OM) research community with a definition and typology for DLM:

> DLM builds on new data acquisition, data integration, data processing and data visualization capabilities to create different descriptive, predictive, and prescriptive analytics applications to detect, fix, predict and prevent unstable process parameters

and/or avoid quality issues inside defined tolerance ranges that may lead to any type of waste within the cyber- and physical-worlds.

DLM, then, refers to established lean methods gaining a new digitally enabled edge (Romero et al., 2018). However, as the lean and digital worlds continue to converge, we move ever closer to a digital lean paradigm that we might coin *Lean 4.0*. As such, the aim of this chapter is to describe the state-of-the-art with respect to current DLM knowledge and to develop a coherent concept of the emergent Lean 4.0 ideal, providing readers with an outline for future research in this exciting, nascent field.

State-of-the-art: digital lean manufacturing

In this section, we present the current state-of-the-art (SOTA) concerning DLM, which has emerged as a renewed production management paradigm (Powell et al., 2022b) and represents the next cyber/digital frontier for lean manufacturing practices (Romero et al., 2018), such as Jidoka 4.0 (Romero et al., 2019) and digital kanban (Amrani and Powell, 2022) as well as intelligent poke-yokes (Romero et al., 2022a) and cyber-physical visual management systems (Romero et al., 2022b). Importantly, each of these works discusses not only the technical perspective of such digital lean solutions but also the learning (social) perspective. For example, Amrani and Powell (2022) indicate how the combination of lean production with I4.0 technologies leads to both increased operational performance as well as increased learning capabilities of shop floor teams, while Romero et al. (2019) present Jidoka as both an automation approach and a learning system – "Incorporating human learning gives automation its human touch".

Given that the Toyota Production System (TPS) is a learning system consisting of a set of production practices aimed at revealing problems so that people can react quickly to avoid defects or missed shipments (Ballé et al., 2019), in this section, we briefly explore the state-of-the-art of DLM using TPS as a frame (Figure 13.1).

Stability

Returning to the initial definition of Romero et al. (2018), DLM promises to provide "different data analytics applications to detect, fix, predict and prevent unstable process parameters". In this respect, digital technologies such as Industrial Internet of Things (IIoT) and big data analytics present manufac-

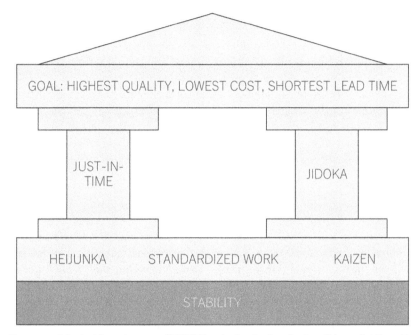

Source: Adapted from lean.org (2020) Toyota Production System "House". https://www.lean.org/wp-content/uploads/2020/11/tps-house.jpg (accessed 10 December).

Figure 13.1 The Toyota Production System

turers with means of improving the stability and reliability of equipment and machinery through digital enhancement of total productive maintenance (Saabye and Powell, 2022; Tortorella et al., 2022). Visual management builds a foundation of stability in the process (Hodge et al., 2011, p. 245), thus it can be suggested that stability can be further improved with the introduction of digitally enabled Mieruka systems (Romero et al., 2022b).

Heijunka

In following the stability perspective described previously, Heijunka, translated as *steady wave*, is a production levelling technique which aims at creating stability in the production schedule to improve production flow and eliminate both Mura and Muri (unevenness and overburden). Żywicki et al. (2017), Kjellsen et al. (2021) and Spenhoff et al. (2021) present accounts of digitalized Heijunka, from the initial data analysis requirements to the potential support functionality offered by big data analytics and the IIoT.

Standardized work

Also in line with the aforementioned stability perspective, technological advancements present opportunities for the digitalization of standardized work procedures (Magnani, 2021) in particular and shop floor management (Lorenz et al., 2019) practices in general. Furthermore Dalstam et al. (2019) suggest that "the implementation of a virtual factory relies on standardized work procedures, ensuring its use as a decision aid throughout the company" (p. 3229). Thus standardized work is an enabler of digitalization, and digitalization is an enabler of (more enhanced) standardized work practices.

Kaizen

Kaizen (improvement, or "change for the better" in Japanese), is a principle that stands to benefit from the potential offered by the key enabling technologies of Industry 4.0. Dang-Pham et al. (2022) present Digital Kaizen as "a digital transformation methodology that involves conducting a series of small yet effective digital transformation initiatives within short time frames as a means of driving business and technological transformation through people engagement" (p. 11). In a similar vein, Umeda et al. (2020) present the digital triplet concept as an extension of the digital twin, combining the physical and cyber worlds with the "intelligent activity" world to drive the continuous improvement of cyber-physical production systems (CPPSs) through "humans solving various problems using the digital twin".

Jidoka

Jidoka – or automation with a human touch – describes a set of automation systems' design principles that aim to separate human activity from machine cycles to allow a human operator to attend to multiple machines (Romero et al., 2019). As a system, it is attributed to Sakichi Toyoda, Japanese inventor and industrialist, and founder of Toyoda Automatic Loom Works and later Toyota Industries Co., Ltd. Jidoka is a mechanism that allows machines to autonomously detect abnormalities and shutdown, preventing defects from occurring. It further controls feedback to machine operators by means of Andon alarms (Baudin, 2007).

The field of *Zero Defect Manufacturing* (ZDM) (see for example Powell et al., 2022a) presents manufacturing firms with a plethora of exciting digital platforms and frameworks for the digital enhancement of quality, reliability, and maintenance management practices – pushing mechanical Jidoka practices into the Industry 4.0 era as part of smart factory and industrial ecosystem initiatives. Powell et al. (2021a) suggest that the onset of Industry 4.0 presents organizations with technologies that promise to further enhance the quality of both products and processes, but also add a third dimension to ZDM – people. For example, Arica and Powell (2021) present the concept of the digitally enhanced operator which uses augmented reality (AR) combined with sensory devices on equipment to strengthen the autonomy, situational awareness, and teamwork of production shop floor operators.

Just-in-time

The Just-in-Time (JIT) concept is attributed to Kiichiro Toyoda, son of Sakichi Toyoda and founder of Toyota Motor Company. His vision was simple: to make only what is needed, when it is needed, and in the amount needed. More recently, and in line with this original JIT vision, Akio Toyoda (previous president of Toyota Motor Co.) was recently reported to have stressed the importance of applying the concepts of TPS, specifically JIT, to digital information; ensuring that the necessary amount of data is available to those who need it, precisely when they need it.

From a visual management perspective, particular attention is also given to the new data visualization capabilities offered by novel digital technologies, which play a significant role in spreading the right information; in the right visualization type, medium, and frequency; to the right person(s); at the right time for decision-making. This is indeed aligned with the vision of Kiichiro Toyoda, providing just-in-time information to support the provision of just-in-time material.

Lean 4.0

In this section we provide an overview of more recent developments that have led to coinage of the term "Lean 4.0". This will be followed by a presentation of the benefits associated with integrating Lean and Industry 4.0 (Lean 4.0) as well as some of the rudimentary challenges in their integration. Although there are many articles available in the existing literature on the integration of Lean Production and Industry 4.0, only a handful include case studies which show how the integrated approach can work in real-world scenarios. Moreover, it was also found that the integrated approach primarily focuses on financial and operational performance indicators rather than social and environmental performance indicators (de Sousa Jabbour et al., 2018). Though the term Lean 4.0 emerged in 2017 through the work of Metternich et al. (2017) in the German language publication titled "Lean 4.0—Between Contradiction and Vision" (Gil-Vilda et al., 2021), until now there remains no formal definition of the term Lean 4.0. We therefore adopt the following definition of Lean (Industry) 4.0 as suggested in Hines et al. (2023, p. 74):

> An innovative socio-technical paradigm that uses both human- and artificial intelligence and relies on the strategic, cultural, systems, and tools of lean as well as the various Industry 4.0 digital technologies continually and discontinuously used to improve both single organizations and their supply chains with a focus on simplifying and managing complexity to benefit the triple bottom line and hence meet specific customer and organizational needs as well as the expectations of employees and wider society.

So what is Lean 4.0 and why do we need to integrate Lean with Industry 4.0? Lean 4.0 can be viewed as an approach of creating an efficient and effective network of smart machines, processes, humans, and respective technologies throughout the entire value chain – leading to smart factories and industrial ecosystems. Ciano et al. (2021) suggest that lean's high streamlined process orientation and its standardization of processes along with an emphasis on visual control and transparency facilitate the implementation and realization of the Industry 4.0 vison of connectivity, information sharing, and automation. Given the increasing complexity of operations, many companies have found that lean by itself is no longer sufficient to address their operational challenges.

Two perspectives on Lean and Industry 4.0 integration

Cifone et al. (2021) explicate two perspectives on the integration of Lean Production and Industry 4.0. The first perspective suggests that lean serves as a foundation for implementing Industry 4.0. For example, lean practices focus on minimizing waste throughout the process, making it essential to have a well-organized and efficient process before embarking on digitalization efforts. The authors find that companies that have already implemented lean to a higher degree are more likely to benefit from adopting Industry 4.0 and fully leveraging its potential (as is also reported in Buer et al., 2021). In essence, though the authors suggest that lean implementation is not an absolute requirement prior to digitalization, they state that it stands to amplify the positive outcomes of digitalization. Powell et al. (2021b) also present a *Lean First ... Then Digitalize* approach to digitalization, particularly in the context of small and medium-sized enterprises (SMEs) – which often lack knowledge and competence in both lean and Industry 4.0.

The second perspective views Industry 4.0 as a necessary addition to traditional lean practices. This perspective argues that modern market demands are becoming more complex, with customers seeking highly personalized products. These demands can pose challenges for traditional "paper-based" lean approaches, which may not be fully effective in addressing such customization requirements. Industry 4.0 offers solutions for lean to adapt and keep up with the pace of customization. By incorporating Industry 4.0 technologies, lean can leverage new manufacturing trends and allow lean manufacturers to maintain robust and resilient processes.

Both of these perspectives reflect the view presented in Powell et al. (2020) – in which "lean paves the way for successful digital transformation and digitalization enriches lean practices".

Benefits of Lean 4.0

The following benefits are found to be reported in the existing literature for Lean 4.0. We observe from the analysis of benefits that most are focused on operational and financial performance indicators, with few reports of social and environmental benefits:

- In a study carried out by Ani et al. (2018), the benefits of Lean 4.0 see productivity increase by 250 per cent.
- A number of studies report lead-time reduction benefits in the literature. For instance, Trebuna et al. (2019) show a lead-time reduction of nearly 60 per cent. In addition, the value-added index increased by almost 250 per cent, while inventories had also been reduced by 70 per cent.
- In another study carried out by Fayos-Jordan et al. (2020), the lead time decreased by almost 90 per cent following the application of Internet of Things (IoT) technology.
- Guillen et al. (2018) present a case study integrating simulation with some of the core tools of lean such as Jidoka, 5S, and Kanban. The results of this study indicated that defects and rework were reduced by 50 per cent, while raw material replenishment improved by 40 per cent and delivery schedule adherence improved by 100 per cent.
- Ito et al. (2020) also present a case study in which a firm enhances its decision-making capabilities in lean manufacturing using a combination of IoT, Andon system, and simulation. A better decision-making information flow was observed within an automotive part manufacturer showing a productivity improvement of over 170 per cent.

Challenges of Lean 4.0

Despite the reported benefits of Lean 4.0, there are also various challenges presented in the extent literature. The following are some of the fundamental challenges reported by Alsadi et al. (2023) and Yilmaz et al. (2022):

- The cost of investment in digitalization tools can be a real challenge for many organizations, in particular SMEs with limited opportunities for extensive capital investment.
- Technological readiness can be an immense challenge to many companies as this depends upon the existing organizational culture and engagement of the workforce with such new initiatives.
- Lack of management support and employees' resistance to change.
- There are no practical and useful frameworks in place which integrate the best of Lean Production and Industry 4.0.
- Lack of training from many training providers illustrating how they should be integrated with case studies.

Digital lean world: future research

Though Industry 4.0 seemed to begin its life as a competing paradigm to the long established concept of Lean Production, its key enabling technologies present exciting opportunities for advancing the lean and learning transformations of manufacturing firms. Not only do we find that such technologies promise to enhance more traditional, analogue lean best practices; we also observe that lean thinking and practice remains a prerequisite for effective (and indeed sustainable) digital transformation.

This synergistic relationship is further enriched with the onset of Industry 5.0 (I5.0), which contrary to many interpretations of Industry 4.0 as a purely *technology-centric* paradigm, places humans' well-being at the centre of *socio-technical* manufacturing systems (Leng et al., 2022). Indeed, I5.0 shifts the focus from automation and digitalization as ends in themselves to using digitalization as a means of realizing human-centricity, sustainability, and resiliency in industrial companies, networks, and ecosystems. Therefore, future research within DLM and indeed Lean 4.0 should cross-examine its effects not just on the financial and operational performance of firms, but also on social and environmental sustainability as well as organizational resilience. Indeed, as Powell et al. (2022b) suggest, "the future appears bright and promising for those who are able to think lean and use technology to achieve the triple bottom line of sustainable production".

References

Alsadi, J., Antony, J., Mezher, T., Jayaraman, R., and Maalouf, M. (2023). Lean and Industry 4.0: A bibliometric analysis, opportunities for future research directions. *Quality Management Journal*, 30(1), 41–63.

Amrani, A. Z. and Powell, D. (2022). Industry 4.0 technologies as drivers for eliminating waste in lean production: A French-Norwegian study. In *IFIP Advances in Information and Communication Technology*, Vol. 664. Berlin: Springer Science and Business Media, pp. 567–574.

Ani, M. N. C., Kamaruddin, S., and Azid, I. A. (2018). The model development of an effective triggering system of production kanban size towards just-in-time (JIT) production. *Advances in Science, Technology and Engineering Systems Journal*, 3(5), 298–306.

Arica, E. and Powell, D. (2021). Digitalization in manufacturing: Trends, drivers, challenges, and research areas in Norway. In A. Dolgui, A. Bernard, D. Lemoine, G. von Cieminski, and D. Romero (Eds.), *Advances in Production Management Systems: Artificial Intelligence for Sustainable and Resilient Production Systems*. Cham: Springer.

Ashrafian, A., Powell, D. J., Ingvaldsen, J. A., et al. (2019). Sketching the landscape for lean digital transformation. In F. Ameri, K. E. Stecke, G. von Ciemenski, and D. Kiritsis (Eds.), *IFIP Advances in Information and Communication Technology*, Vol. 566. New York: Springer, pp. 29–36.

Ballé, M., Chartier, N., Coignet, P., Olivencia, S., Powell, D., and Reke, E. (2019). *The Lean Sensei: Go See Challenge*. Boston: Lean Enterprise Institute.

Baudin, M. (2007). *Working with Machines: The Nuts and Bolts of Lean Operations with Jidoka*. New York: Productivity Press.

Buer, S. V., Strandhagen, J. W., Semini, M., and Strandhagen, J. O. (2021). The digitalization of manufacturing: Investigating the impact of production environment and company size. *Journal of Manufacturing Technology Management*, 32(3), 621–645.

Cattaneo, L., Rossi, M., Negri, E., Powell, D., and Terzi, S. (2017). Lean thinking in the digital era. In *Product Lifecycle Management and the Industry of the Future: 14th IFIP WG 5.1 International Conference on PLM 2017*. Berlin: Springer International Publishing, pp. 371–381.

Ciano, M. P., Dallasega, P., Orzes, G., and Rossi, T. (2021). One-to-one relationships between Industry 4.0 technologies and lean production techniques: A multiple case study. *International Journal of Production Research*, 59(5), 1386–1410.

Cifone, F. D., Hoberg, K., Holweg, M., and Staudacher, A. P. (2021). "Lean 4.0": How can digital technologies support lean practices? *International Journal of Production Economics*, 241, 108258.

Dalstam, A., Engberg, M., Nåfors, D., Johansson, B., and Sundblom, A. (2019). A stepwise implementation of the virtual factory in manufacturing industry. *Proceedings of the Winter Simulation Conference*, Institute of Electrical and Electronics Engineers, Vol. 2018, pp. 3229–3240.

Dang-Pham, D., Hoang, A. P., Vo, D. T., and Kautz, K. (2022). Digital kaizen: An approach to digital transformation. *Australasian Journal of Information Systems*, 26. https://doi.org/10.3127/ajis.v26i0.3851.

de Sousa Jabbour, A. B. L., Jabbour, C. J. C., Foropon, C., and Filho, M. G. (2018). When titans meet: Can industry 4.0 revolutionise the environmentally-sustainable manufacturing wave? The role of critical success factors. *Technological Forecasting and Social Change*, 132, 18–25.

Fayos-Jordan, R., Felici-Castell, S., Segura-Garcia, J., Lopez-Ballester, J., and Cobos, M. (2020). Performance comparison of container orchestration platforms with low cost devices in the fog, assisting Internet of Things applications. *Journal of Network and Computer Applications*, 69(11).

Gil-Vilda, F., Yagüe-Fabra, J. A., and Sunyer, A. (2021). From lean production to lean 4.0: A systematic literature review with a historical perspective. *Applied Sciences*, 11(21), 10318.

Guillen, K., Umasi, K., Quispe, G., and Raymundo, C. (2018). LEAN model for optimizing plastic bag production in small and medium sized companies in the plastics sector. *International Journal of Engineering Research and Technology*, 11(11), 1713–1734.

Hines, P., Tortorella, G., Antony, J., and Romero, D. (2023). Lean industry 4.0: Past, present, and future. *Quality Management Journal*, 30(1), 64–88.

Hodge, G. L., Goforth Ross, K., Joines, J. A., and Thoney, K. (2011). Adapting lean manufacturing principles to the textile industry. *Production Planning & Control*, 22(3), 237–247.

Ito, T., Abd Rahman, M. S., Mohamad, E., Abd Rahman, A. A., and Salleh, M. R. (2020). Internet of things and simulation approach for decision support system in lean manufacturing. *Journal of Advanced Mechanical Design, Systems, and Manufacturing*, 14(2), JAMDSM0027.

Kjellsen, H. S., Ramillon, Q. J. L., Dreyer, H. C., and Powell, D. J. (2021). Heijunka 4.0: Key enabling technologies for production levelling in the process industry. In *IFIP Advances in Information and Communication Technology*, Vol. 630. Berlin: Springer Science and Business Media, pp. 704–711.

Leng, J., Sha, W., Wang, B., et al. (2022). Industry 5.0: Prospect and retrospect. *Journal of Manufacturing Systems*, 65, 279–295.

Lorenz, R., Benninghaus, C., Friedli, T., and Netland, T. H. (2020). Digitization of manufacturing: The role of external search. *International Journal of Operations and Production Management*, 40(7–8), 1129–1152.

Lorenz, R., Powell, D. J., and Netland, T. (2019). Exploring the effect of digitalizing shop floor management. Paper presented at the 26th Annual EurOMA Conference, Helsinki.

Magnani, F. (2021). Digitization of operational processes: Use case of standardization in an assembly learning factory. In L. Roucoules, M. Paredes, B. Eynard, P. Morer Camo, and C. Rizzi (Eds.), *JCM 2020: Advances on Mechanics, Design Engineering and Manufacturing III*. Cham: Springer, pp. 323–328.

Metternich, J., Müller, M., Meudt, T., and Schaede, C. (2017). Lean 4.0—Zwischen Widerspruch und Vision. *ZWF Zeitschrift für Wirtschaftlichen Fabrikbetrieb*, 112, 346–348.

Mora, E., Gaiardelli, P., Resta, B., and Powell, D. (2017). Exploiting lean benefits through smart manufacturing: A comprehensive perspective. In *Advances in Production Management Systems: The Path to Intelligent, Collaborative and*

Sustainable Manufacturing: IFIP WG 5.7 International Conference, APMS 2017. Berlin: Springer International Publishing, pp. 127–134.

Netland, T. H. and Powell, D. J. (2017). A lean world. In D. J. Powell and T. H. Netland (Eds.), *The Routledge Companion to Lean Management.* New York: Routledge, pp. 465–473.

Powell, D. and Romero, D. (2021). Digital lean manufacturing: A literature review. *Proceedings of the 2021 IEEE International Conference on Industrial Engineering and Engineering Management (IEEM).* Institute of Electrical and Electronics Engineers Inc., Kuala Lumpur, pp. 659–662.

Powell, D., Eleftheriadis, R. J., and Myklebust, O. (2021a). Digitally enhanced quality management for zero-defect manufacturing. *Procedia CIRP*, 104, 1351–1354.

Powell, D., Lodgaard, E., and Dreyer, H. (2020). Investigating the challenges and opportunities for production planning and control in digital lean manufacturing. In B. Lalic, V. Majstorovic, U. Marjanovic, G. von Cieminski, and D. Romero (Eds.), *IFIP Advances in Information and Communication Technology*, Vol. 592. Berlin: Springer, pp. 425–431.

Powell, D., Magnanini, M. C., Colledani, M., and Myklebust, O. (2022a). Advancing zero defect manufacturing: A state-of-the-art perspective and future research directions. *Computers in Industry*, 136, 103596.

Powell, D., Morgan, R., and Howe, G. (2021b). Lean first … then digitalize: A standard approach for industry 4.0 implementation in SMEs. In A. Dolgui, A. Bernard, D. Lemoine, G. von Cieminski, and D. Romero (Eds.), *IFIP Advances in Information and Communication Technology*, Vol. 631. Berlin: Springer, pp. 31–39.

Powell, D., Romero, D., and Gaiardelli, P. (2022b). New and renewed manufacturing paradigms for sustainable production. *Sustainability*, 14, 1279.

Romero, D., Gaiardelli, P., Powell, D., Wuest, T., and Thürer, M. (2018). Digital lean cyber-physical production systems: The emergence of digital lean manufacturing and the significance of digital waste. In I. Moon, G. M. Lee, J. Park, D. Kiritsis, and G. von Cieminski (Eds.), *IFIP Advances in Information and Communication Technology*, Vol. 535. New York: Springer, pp. 11–20.

Romero, D., Gaiardelli, P., Powell, D., Wuest, T., and Thürer, M. (2019). Rethinking jidoka systems under automation & learning perspectives in the digital lean manufacturing world. *IFAC-Papers Online*, 52(13), 899–903.

Romero, D., Gaiardelli, P., Powell, D. J., and Zanchi, M. (2022a). Intelligent poka-yokes: Error-proofing and continuous improvement in the digital lean manufacturing world. In D. Y. Kim, G. von Cieminski, and D. Romero (Eds.), *IFIP Advances in Information and Communication Technology*, Vol. 664. Berlin: Springer, pp. 595–603.

Romero, D., Zanchi, M., Powell, D. J., and Gaiardelli, P. (2022b). Cyber-physical visual management systems in the digital lean manufacturing world. In D. Y. Kim, G. von Cieminski, and D. Romero (Eds.), *IFIP Advances in Information and Communication Technology*, Vol. 664. Berlin: Springer, pp. 575–585.

Saabye, H. and Powell, D. J. (2022). Fostering insights and improvements from IIoT systems at the shop floor: A case of industry 4.0 and lean complementarity enabled by action learning. *International Journal of Lean Six Sigma.* https://doi.org/10.1108/IJLSS-01-2022-0017.

Spenhoff, P., Wortmann, J. C., and Semini, M. (2021). EPEC 4.0: An Industry 4.0-supported lean production control concept for the semi-process industry. *Production Planning & Control*, 33(14), 1337–1354.

Tortorella, G., Saurin, T. A., Fogliatto, F. S., et al. (2022). The impact of Industry 4.0 on the relationship between TPM and maintenance performance. *Journal of Manufacturing Technology Management*, 33(3), 489–520.

Trebuna, P., Pekarcikova, M., and Edl, M. (2019). Digital value stream mapping using the Tecnomatix plant simulation software. *International Journal of Simulation and Modeling*, 18(1), 19–32.

Umeda, Y., Ota, J., Shirafuji, S., Kojima, F., Saito, M., Matsuzawa, H., and Sukekawa, T. (2020). Exercise of digital kaizen activities based on "digital triplet" concept. *Procedia Manufacturing*, 45, 325–330.

Yilmaz, A., Dora, M., Hezarkhani, B., and Kumar, M. (2022). Lean and industry 4.0: Mapping determinants and barriers from a social, environmental, and operational perspective. *Technological Forecasting and Social Change*, 75, 121320.

Żywicki, K., Rewers, P., and Bożek, M. (2017). Data analysis in production levelling methodology. *Recent Advances in Intelligent Systems and Technologies*, 571, 460–468.

14 Impact of Lean and Industry 4.0 on sustainability: a Delphi study-based identification and assessment

Fabian Dillinger, Fabian Formann, Kai Magenheimer,
Gunther Reinhart and Guilherme Tortorella

Introduction

Digitization and sustainability represent the two megatrends of today's economy (Kutzschenbach, 2020, p. 203). The disruptive nature of both drivers is leading to structural change in the industry (Werder & Rukwid, 2021). Therefore, technological and societal changes significantly impact manufacturing companies (Corejova & Chinoracky, 2021).

The current digital development is causing a fundamental disruption in value creation structures (Foit, 2018, p. 2). As a result, future-proof companies must combine innovative technologies and sustainability-oriented practices to meet the challenges of a digitized and sustainable society (Kutzschenbach, 2020, p. 204). The use of digital technologies in the context of Industry 4.0 is leading to disruptive changes in existing lean production systems. Digital networking enables the efficient exchange of data between internal and external actors, machines, and products (Dahm & Holst, 2020, p. 227; Dillinger et al., 2022a). Value chains are further developed into flexible and transparent value networks (Foit, 2018, p. 2).

In producing goods, more than profitability is necessary for long-term corporate success (Steven & Klünder, 2018, pp. 206f.). Profitability must be supplemented by economic, ecological, and social sustainability, which contribute significantly to the value orientation of the economy (BMWI, 2020). Regulatory requirements and increased customer demands for resource-efficient manufacturing of products put more pressure on companies to create sustainable value chains (Brüssel, 2018, pp. 22f.). On the one hand, sustainability aspects must be integrated into companies' digitization strategies, while on the other hand, Industry 4.0 offers considerable potential for implementing sustainability in production (BMWI, 2020). Sustainability is part of the strategic orientation of companies and represents the core driver in the upcoming structural change of industry (Piller et al., 2021).

Therefore, this chapter provides a systematic approach to identifying the influences of Lean and Industry 4.0 elements on sustainability dimensions in manufacturing. It provides transparency and supports companies in addressing upcoming challenges.

Basic definitions

Lean production

According to Ohno (2013, p. 28), lean production's fundamental idea is to increase production processes' efficiency by consistently eliminating waste. The aim is to improve performance while reducing the use of resources (Dennis, 2016, p. 19). Due to the manifold interactions between the underlying principles, methods, and corporate objectives, lean production is a holistic system that needs to be implemented at all levels of an organization to create a corporate culture of continuous improvement and striving for maximum value creation (Liker, 1997, p. ix). In the context of manufacturing companies, the 18 most appropriate lean methods were selected by Aull (2012, pp. 52ff.), based on the analysis of various production systems from the industry. The results of Aull were confirmed by additional expert interviews and supplemented by shopfloor management and value stream management. The 20 methods are subdivided into logistics-, employee-, and quality-oriented areas (see Figure 14.1).

Industry 4.0

Implementing Industry 4.0 in existing production systems entails an immense potential for improvement along the entire value chain (Ramsauer, 2013). The main goal is to holistically increase productivity and thus competitiveness (Roth, 2016, p. 5). Significant increases in productivity, product quality, and shortened product development cycles can be achieved through targeted information processing, transparency optimization, and process linking (Steven, 2018, p. 63). Industry 4.0 technologies form the basis for holistic networking, data processing, autonomous control, and monitoring in digitized produc-

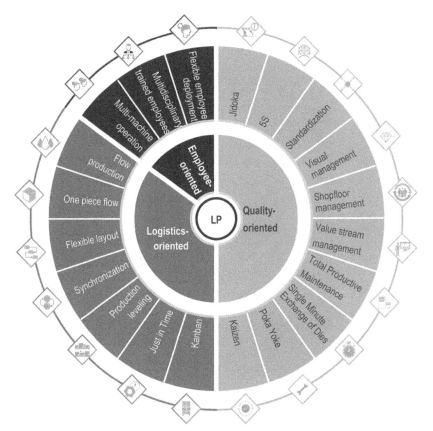

Figure 14.1 Classification of lean production according to Aull (2012, pp. 52ff.) and Dillinger et al. (2022a)

tion (Reinhart, 2017, p. xxxiv). Therefore, Industry 4.0 can be assigned to nine fundamental technology fields: Internet of Things (IoT), Big Data and Analytics, Simulation, Additive Manufacturing, Cloud, Cybersecurity, Assistance Systems, and Horizontal and Vertical Integration (Dai et al., 2020). The Industry 4.0 technology circle, according to Dillinger et al. (2021), visualizes a selection of 26 Industry 4.0 technologies and their classification into the nine technology fields. The classification is based on a co-occurrence analysis of 4,087 publications carried out with the software VosViewer (see Figure 14.2).

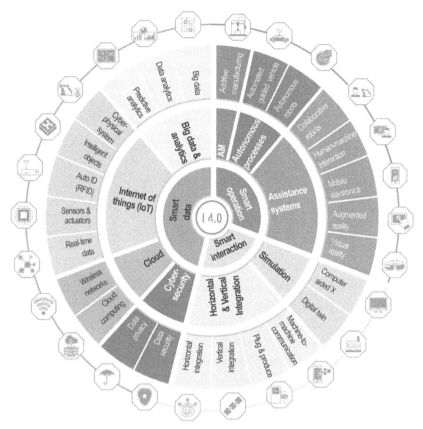

Figure 14.2   Industry-4.0 technology circle according to Dillinger et al. (2021)

Sustainability

Sustainability consists of three main pillars: social responsibility, economic performance, and environmental protection. Therefore, it affects all levels of society, from consumers and individuals to companies and NGOs to politics and international markets (Foit, 2018). Manufacturing companies that rely on raw materials are particularly affected. In addition, large amounts of pollutants are emitted due to the production and transportation of goods. Production-integrated measures can reduce or avoid resource consumption, energy requirements, and emissions in the manufacturing process (Schuh & Schmidt, 2014, p. 16). To implement sustainable development, corporate strategies must be aligned with sustainability aspects in the long term (Hofmann et al., 2018). According to the triple-bottom-line, sustainability can be divided into the economy, ecology, and social dimensions, which provide the conceptual framework of this study (Savitz & Weber, 2013). Varela et al. (2019) use a comprehensive literature analysis to break down the three dimensions into 18 specific sustainability subdimensions for the manufacturing firms (see Figure 14.3).

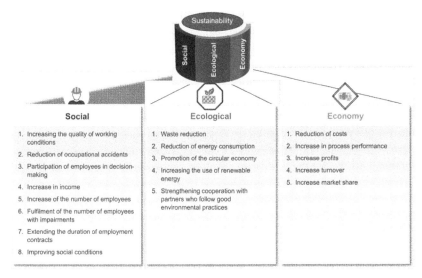

Figure 14.3 Subdimensions of the triple-bottom-line according to Varela et al. (2019)

Influences of lean production and Industry 4.0 on sustainability

As part of a scientific literature analysis, the influences of lean production and Industry 4.0 on sustainability in production were analyzed. In the following, the focus is on the production approaches' emerging impact on sustainability.

The lean production approach leverages a sustainable production environment (Varela et al., 2019). The lean methods are important to improve the economic aspects of a company, for example by reducing costs and increasing profits. In addition, environmental factors can be improved by avoiding non-value-adding activities and optimizing the use of resources. Moreover, social aspects are strengthened through the improvement of the working environment by employees (Abualfaraa et al., 2020; Dillinger et al., 2022b). Lean production emphasizes the involvement of employees in the continuous improvement process, enabling them to overcome obstacles, such as resistance to change or innovation, which can hinder the promotion of environmentally friendly practices and thus affect companies' performance (Chen et al., 2020). Adopting lean production offers multiple benefits for companies, including a safer working environment, high productivity, improved product quality, and less waste. Through consistent waste prevention, lean production creates the basis for higher resource efficiency. Moreover, the systematic implementation of lean production supports companies' organizational development into economic and environmentally oriented units (Afum et al., 2021). Bertagnolli (2020, pp. 304ff.) argues that Lean production positively impacts all pillars of sustainability. In the economy, there is a shorter payback period, and the energy requirement per manufactured product is reduced. The reuse of materials and energy recovery has a positive impact on ecology. In the social sphere, all ergonomics-related issues are relevant. Despite some trade-offs between lean production and sustainability, the synergies achieved through the combined application are paramount (Kabzhassarova et al., 2021).

In addition, Industry 4.0 creates the basis for overcoming the challenges posed by competition or short product life cycles and thus contributes significantly to the sustainable development of an organization (Jayashree et al., 2021). Bai et al. (2020), Dillinger et al. (2022b), and Jamwal et al. (2021) point out the potential of Industry 4.0 to significantly support all dimensions of sustainability. In particular, the positive impact of Industry 4.0 on resource efficiency in production is highlighted by Demartini et al. (2019). Also, Industry 4.0 opens up the possibility of linking technology with resources and capabilities in terms of sustainability benefits and can reduce the environmental impact of a process (Ejsmont et al., 2020). Cochran and Rauch (2020) consider the comprehensive implementation of Industry 4.0 as a lever for sustainable production. According to Bai et al. (2020), the shortening of set-up times, the reduction of labor costs, and the resulting increase in profits improve economic sustainability. From an environmental perspective, Industry 4.0 technologies can reduce energy and resource consumption by increasing transparency in production and supply chain processes (Jayashree et al., 2021). Also, digital technologies protect workers' health and safety by minimizing monotony and repetitive tasks and leading to social sustainability (Bai et al., 2020). Rakic et al. (2021) point out that there might also be negative effects on sustainability. It must be taken into account that using Industry 4.0 technologies leads to increased energy consumption, e.g., the usage of energy-consuming additive manufacturing processes, and that humans may become partially redundant as workers.

Based on the scientific literature analysis, the relevance of a detailed analysis of the influences of single lean production and Industry 4.0 elements on sustainability's subdimensions becomes clear. There needs to be a more in-depth analysis of the impact of lean methods and Industry 4.0 technologies on sustainability.

Impact of lean and Industry 4.0 on sustainability: a Delphi study

A methodical approach is presented to identify the influence of lean production and Industry 4.0 elements on sustainability. The targeted correlation matrix should include lean methods, Industry 4.0 technologies, and sustainability aspects of considerable importance for manufacturing companies. Moreover, the study concept development will be based on a proven and methodical research procedure used by Kuß et al. (2018), who developed a phase model to underline the important steps of a research study.

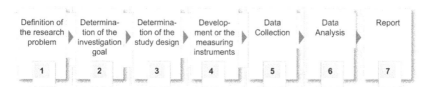

Figure 14.4   Seven phases of the market research study according to Kuß et al. (2018)

The procedure is divided into seven phases (see Figure 14.4). In the first phase, the research problem is specified, and a literature analysis is conducted to identify the relevant research questions (Kuß et al., 2018, p. 9). The study's objectives and scope are defined and clarified in the second phase. Within the third phase, the study design is selected. Therefore, it must be clarified whether the research objective can be achieved by using adequate processing and analysis of existing data or a new data collection is required (Olbrich et al., 2012, p. 54). A Delphi method is conducted for phases four to six to collect and analyze new data. The Delphi study is an iterative feedback technique with a panel of five to twenty experts, and the feedback is provided anonymously to prevent group dynamics (Grime & Wright, 2014). Consequently, individual panelists do not have a potentially disproportionate influence on the results (Schmidt, 1997). Moreover, the panelists should be composed heterogeneously to avoid biases (Nakatsu & Iacovou, 2009). The collected data are analyzed and transferred to a final report.

Table 14.1   Anonymized overview of the panelists

Experts	Job	Company	Field
1	Scientist	A	Research
2	Scientist	A	Research
3	Scientist	A	Research
4	Consultant	B	Consultancy
5	Senior Consultant	B	Consultancy
6	Senior Consultant	B	Consultancy
7	Manager	B	Consultancy
8	Senior Expert	B	Consultancy
9	Consultant	C	Consultancy
10	Consultant	D	Consultancy
11	Vice President Operations & Sustainability	E	Automotive
12	Vice President Global Supply Chain & Plant	F	Automotive
13	Manager	G	Engineering
14	Head of Electronic Operations	H	Engineering
15	VP Production Controlling & Lean Expert Manager Digital Industries	I	Automation & digitalization

Table 14.2   Likert scale for assessing the impact between the domains

Impact	Description
-3	Strong negative
-2	Medium negative
-1	Low negative
0	Neutral
1	Low positive
2	Medium positive
3	Strong positive

After carrying out the first three phases of the research procedure according to Kuß et al. (2018) a Delphi study was conducted to evaluate the influences of lean and Industry 4.0 on sustainability. Therefore, the necessary experts require in-depth knowledge of all three areas. This limits the potential participants to management executives from the industry, consultants, and scientists. In total, 15 experts could be acquired for the Delphi study. Table 14.1 provides an overview of the participants specified by their job, company, and occupational field.

According to Gordon and Pease (2006, pp. 328–331), using a two-dimensional questionnaire enables the assessment of the interrelationships between two or more dimensions. Therefore, the investigation was realized with the help of a two-dimensional matrix. The experts' assessment was based on a seven-point Likert scale, shown in Table 14.2.

Figure 14.5 shows the conceptual design of the matrix to investigate the influence of the 20 lean and 26 Industry 4.0 elements (see Figures 14.1 and 14.2) on the 18 subdimensions of sustainability (see Figure 14.3). In total, 782 possible interdependencies have been analyzed by experts using the Delphi study method.

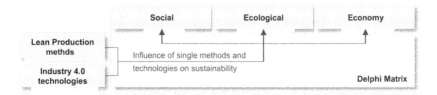

Figure 14.5   Exemplary section of the Delphi matrix

Therefore, three rounds of the Delphi study have been conducted. The experts received the questionnaire for their evaluation in the first round. At the end of the planned three-week period, all completed questionnaires were collected and combined to generate a group result. The combined matrix was then returned to the experts in the second round. The panelists were asked to reflect on their previous assessments and make adjustments if necessary. This round aims to reduce the dispersion of answers to increase the certainty of judgment (Niederberger & Renn, 2019, pp. 118ff.). The reduction was confirmed by the decreasing standard deviation (S) between the rounds, which measures the spread of values of a characteristic around its average (Bortz & Schuster, 2010, p. 31). The results of the calculation of the overall standard deviations based on the given answers of the experts per round are listed below:

- 1st round: $S = 0.65$
- 2nd round: $S = 0.62$
- 3rd round: $S = 0$

In the context of the Delphi procedure, the survey ends with the completion of the third run. This includes sending the final group result from the second round and its confirmation by the panelists.

Results of the Delphi study

Number and type of interactions

The Delphi study includes 782 possible interactions between the 20 lean methods, 26 Industry 4.0 technologies, and 18 sustainability aspects in production. Of these, 644 (82.4%) are positive interactions, 57 (7.3%) are negative interactions, and 81 (10.4%) are neutral interactions. The positive assessed interactions can be subdivided into 21 (2.7%) strongly positive, 168 (21.5%) moderately positive, and 455 (58.2%) slightly positive interactions. On the side of negative interactions, no strongly negative, 3 (0.4%) moderately negative, and 54 (6.9%) slightly negative correlations occur. Eighty-one (10.4%) of all evaluations are assigned no reciprocal interrelationships. The top three methods and technologies for each sustainability dimension are presented in the following.

Influences on the triple-bottom-line

Specific lean methods and Industry 4.0 technologies have a more decisive influence on sustainability in production. Table 14.3 visualizes the impact of the top three lean methods and Industry 4.0 technologies on the triple-bottom-line.

Overall, Kaizen, Total Predictive Maintenance, and Shopfloor Management have the most positive influence on the elements of the triple-bottom-line. The methods have in common that they involve employees of all hierarchical levels, which enables manufacturing companies to solve problems effectively, create a safer working environment, and reduce the amount of waste. The integration of Total Predictive Maintenance practices for example results in a higher overall equipment efficiency, which leads to a decrease of emissions while also improving productivity and efficiency (Abdallah & Sabra, 2019). Concerning Industry 4.0, the technologies of Predictive Analytics, Data Analytics, and Horizontal Integration obtain the most significant potential. The use of data-driven predictive analytics tools can, for example, improve the economic and ecological aspects through intelligent utilization of production capacities and targeted planning of maintenance work (Kim & Jeong, 2019). Considering the triple-bottom-line, both lean production and Industry 4.0 exert a highly positive influence on economic sustainability. Regarding the environmental pillar, the top three Industry 4.0 technologies have higher positive potential than the three most effective lean methods. Regarding social aspects, the lean methods Kaizen, Shopfloor Management, and Multi-discipline trained employees show significantly greater effectiveness than the Industry 4.0 tech-

IMPACT OF LEAN AND INDUSTRY 4.0 ON SUSTAINABILITY 237

Table 14.3   Average influences of lean methods and Industry 4.0
technologies on sustainability

Lean Production		Industry 4.0	
Social, economy, ecology sustainability	∅	Social, economy, ecology sustainability	∅
1. Kaizen	0.99	1. Predictive Analytics	1.09
2. Total Productive Maintenance	0.89	2. Data Analytics	1.05
3. Shopfloor Management	0.84	3. Horizontal Integration	0.75
Economy	∅	Economy	∅
1. Value Stream Management	1.36	1. Predictive Analytics	1.69
2. Kaizen	1.33	2. Data Analytics	1.68
3. Single-Minute Exchange of Die	1.33	3. Vertical Integration	1.43
Ecology	∅	Ecology	∅
1. Value Stream Management	0.83	1. Predictive Analytics	1.21
2. Total Productive Maintenance	0.79	2. Data Analytics	1.2
3. Kaizen	0.75	3. Horizontal Integration	0.95
Social	∅	Social	∅
1. Kaizen	0.92	1. Predictive Analytics	0.56
2. Shopfloor Management	0.89	2. Human-Machine-Interaction	0.53
3. Multidisciplinary trained employees	0.81	3. Sensoric & Actoric	0.52

nologies Predictive Analytics, Human Machine Interaction, and Sensors &
Actuators.

In addition to the average overarching effectiveness, the influence of lean
methods and Industry 4.0 technologies on sustainability aspects have been
analyzed. In the following, the three methods and technologies with the
most significant impact on sustainability aspects are presented in each case.
Particular attention is paid to contexts with a rating greater than or equal to 1.5

Table 14.4   Influence of lean and Industry 4.0 elements on economic sustainability

Economic	Lean Production	∅	Industry 4.0	∅
Reduction of costs	Total Productive Maintenance	2.1	Predictive Analytics	2.4
	Single-Minute Exchange of Die	2.1	Data Analytics	2.3
	Kaizen	2.1	Autonomous Robot	1.9
Increase process performance	Value Stream Management	2.3	Predictive Analytics	2.2
	Single-Minute Exchange of Die	2.2	Data Analytics	2.2
	Total Productive Maintenance	2.1	Vertical Integration	2.1
Increase profits	Kaizen	1.7	Predictive Analytics	1.8
	Value Stream Management	1.5	Data Analytics	1.8
	Autonomation	1.5	Vertical Integration	1.6
Increase turnover	Value Stream Management	0.7	Data Analytics	1.2
	Autonomation	0.7	Predictive Analytics	1.2
	Kaizen	0.7	Big Data	1.2
Increase market share	Flexible Layout	0.6	Additive Manufacturing	1.4
	Production Leveling	0.5	Data Analytics	0.9
	Just in Time	0.5	Predictive Analytics	0.8

(see Table 14.2). These elements offer the highest potential for implementing sustainability goals in production.

Influences on economic sustainability

Table 14.4 shows the most relevant interactions with lean methods and Industry 4.0 technologies regarding economic sustainability.

The three economic aspects of reducing costs, increasing process performance, and profits can be influenced by applying lean methods and Industry 4.0 technologies. In contrast, the categories of growing sales and market share are less affected compared to ecological and social sustainability. Implementing lean methods and Industry 4.0 technologies can improve the economic pillar, and these economic potentials are significant for legitimizing change projects in the transformation process of the industry. In the field of lean production, Single-Minute Exchange of Die (SMED) for example can significantly reduce production costs by minimizing the time required for changeovers in production processes, which also reduces the downtime and improves production efficiency. Furthermore, it results in lower production costs due to reduced labor costs per unit and increased production output (Shingo, 1985). Also, data analytics can reduce costs by enabling organizations to make data-driven decisions and optimize their operations. By analyzing large and complex datasets, data analytics can help to identify inefficiencies and other areas of waste in a production process. This allows manufacturing companies to take action to improve performance and reduce costs.

Influences on ecologic sustainability

Table 14.5 outlines the methods and technologies with the most significant impact on environmental sustainability.

One of the biggest levers for implementing sustainability in production lies in the consistent avoidance of waste and emissions. The avoidance of waste is a guiding principle in the lean philosophy, which explains the high effectiveness of lean methods in this area. The lean methods of Value Stream Management, Single-Minute Exchange of Die, and Kaizen have a significant influence (highly positive) and appear as critical enablers in this context. Value Stream Mapping for example can impact waste reduction by providing a systematic approach to identify and eliminate non-value-added activities, such as excess inventory, defects, or waiting time (Rother & Shook, 1999). Also, data transparency can improve the visibility of waste and thus considerably increase the effectiveness of production processes. Predictive analytics and data analytics technologies are essential in this constellation. They can impact waste reduction by identifying non-value-added activities in real-time and optimizing processes. By leveraging data analysis and machine learning algorithms, predictive analytics can recognize patterns and anomalies in production processes. Furthermore, they predict potential issues before they occur and enable manufacturing companies to take proactive steps to prevent waste. For example, predictive analytics can be used in manufacturing processes to forecast demand and adjust production schedules, reducing excess inventory and waste from overproduction. The predictive analytics and data analytics tools are supplemented by the Digital Twin technology, which is assigned a medium positive impact on the ecological sustainability aspect described. The Industry 4.0 technology data analytics

Table 14.5   Influence of lean and Industry 4.0 elements on ecological sustainability

Ecological	Lean Production	ø	Industry 4.0	ø
Waste reduction	Value Stream Management	2.6	Predictive Analytics	2.4
	Single-Minute Exchange of Die	2.2	Data Analytics	2.1
	Kaizen	2.1	Digital Twin	1.6
Reduction of energy consumption	Total Productive Maintenance	1.3	Predictive Analytics	1.5
	Autonomation	0.9	Data Analytics	1.5
	Kaizen	0.9	Sensoric & Actoric	1.2
Promotion of the circular economy	Value Stream Management	0.5	Horizontal Integration	1.6
	Standardization	0.5	Data Analytics	0.9
	Kaizen	0.4	Intelligent Objects	0.9
Increase the use of renewable energy	Value Stream Management	0.1	Predictive Analytics	1.3
	Flexible Layout	0.1	Data Analytics	1.1
	Production Leveling	0.1	Real-time Data	0.8
Cooperation with partners who follow good environmental practices	Value Stream Management	0.3	Horizontal Integration	0.8
	Kaizen	0.2	Cloud-Computing	0.5
	Visual Management	0.1	Data Analytics	0.4

also acts as a driver for reducing energy consumption. Horizontal integration has a positive effect on promoting the circular economy. Implementing the other ecological aspects is only slightly influenced by the application of digital technologies. The other sustainability aspects are only marginally affected and do not require any special attention.

Influences on social sustainability

Table 14.6 visualizes the three most effective lean methods and Industry 4.0 technologies on the aspects of social sustainability.

Table 14.6   Influence of lean and Industry 4.0 elements on social sustainability

Social	Lean Production	ø	Industry 4.0	ø
Increasing the quality of working conditions	5S	2.2	Collaborative Robots	1.8
	Kaizen	1.9	Augmented Reality	1.5
	Shopfloor Management	1.7	Human-Machine Interaction	1.5
Reduction of occupational accidents	Standardizing	1.7	Autonomous Robots	1.5
	Visual Management	1.7	Sensoric & Actoric	1.5
	Total Productive Maintenance	1.7	Predictive Analytics	1.2
Participation of employees in decision-making	Kaizen	2.4	Real-time data	0.9
	Shopfloor Management	2.3	Computer-Aided-X	0.8
	Multidisciplinary trained employee	1.3	Digital Twin	0.8
Increase in income	Multidisciplinary trained employee	1.7	Predictive Analytics	0.4
	Flexible employee deployment	1.4	Big Data	0.3
	Multi-machine operation	0.5	Additive Manufacturing	0.3
Increase the number of employees	Multi-machine operation	-1.1	Autonomous Guided Vehicles	-1.8
	Autonomation	-0.7	Autonomous Robots	-1.8
	Multidisciplinary trained employee	-0.6	Collaborative Robots	-0.8
Fulfillment of the number of employees with impairments	Visual Management	0.3	Autonomous Guided Vehicles	0.6
	Standardization	0.2	Autonomous Robots	0.5
	Poka Yoke	0.2	Collaborative Robots	0.5
Extending the duration of employment contracts	Multidisciplinary trained employee	1.4	Mobile Electronics	0.3
	Flexible employee deployment	1.1	Predictive Analytics	0.2
	Kaizen	0.4	Data Analytics	0.2

The social sustainability aspects relate primarily to working conditions and their impact on employees in the company (Varela et al., 2019). In terms of increasing the quality of working conditions, the methods 5S, Kaizen, and Shopfloor Management have medium to strong positive effects. The 5S method proves to be a key enabler in this context, as it reduces the risk of accidents by organizing the workplace. The most effective technologies are Collaborative Robots, Augmented Reality, and Human-Machine Interaction. Collaborative Robots for example can perform dangerous and repetitive tasks, which reduces the physical strain on workers and minimizes the risk of work-related injuries (Realyvásquez-Vargas et al., 2019). Multidisciplinary trained employees promote the further development of competencies and ultimately lead to an increase in revenues. Also, Kaizen and Shopfloor Management are crucial drivers in employee participation and decision-making.

Furthermore, it must be considered that Multi-Machine Operation, Autonomy, and Multidisciplinary trained employees impact productivity and improve working conditions. There is potential for savings in the number of employees to counter the shortage of skilled professionals by using automated guided vehicles or autonomous robots. An increase in the number of employees with impairments and extending the duration of employment contracts are not directly influenced by lean methods or Industry 4.0 technologies. However, improved quality, for example, could lead to higher demand; thus, more employees are needed.

Conclusion and future research

This contribution presents a comprehensive Delphi study with a heterogeneous panel of experts. The study was conducted anonymously over several iterative feedback rounds based on a selection of lean and Industry 4.0 elements. The study identified the influences of lean production and Industry 4.0 on sustainability.

The Delphi study could confirm the potential of lean methods and Industry 4.0 technologies as drivers for implementing sustainability goals in production. Identifying particularly effective lean and Industry 4.0 elements supports manufacturing companies in improving all pillars of sustainability. The five sustainability aspects that can be most positively influenced overall by lean methods and Industry 4.0 technologies are listed below in descending order:

1. increase in process performance (economic)

2. reduction of waste (ecological)
3. reduction of costs (economic)
4. increase profits (economic)
5. increase the quality of working conditions (social)

In addition, the Delphi study provides information on correlations that are little or not at all influenced by lean production and Industry 4.0. These can be primarily neglected in investment decisions, and increasing the number of employees with impairments is almost not influenced. It should be mentioned that many lean methods and digital technologies act as support and prerequisite factors for others. Their implementation is partly necessary to integrate more effective lean methods and Industry 4.0 technologies into the production system in terms of sustainability. Taking this into account, further research should focus on three main areas:

1. The creation of a coherent implementation sequence for lean production and Industry 4.0 technologies to achieve the manufacturing companies' sustainability goals.
2. A comprehensive quantitative analysis of the impact of single lean production methods and Industry 4.0 technologies on sustainability in different industries.
3. Implementation of lighthouse projects in various manufacturing companies of different industries to analyze the influence of selected lean production methods and Industry 4.0 technologies on sustainability in production.

References

Abdallah, T. & Sabra, M. (2019). The effect of total productive maintenance (TPM) on energy conservation: A case study in a cement manufacturing plant. *Energy Reports* (2019), 118–126.

Abualfaraa, W., Salonitis, K., Al-Ashaab, A., & Ala'raj, M. (2020). Lean-green manufacturing practices and their link with sustainability: A critical review. *Sustainability*, 12(3), 981.

Afum, E., Zhang, R., Agyabeng-Mensah, Y., & Sun, Z. (2021). Sustainability excellence: The interactions of lean production, internal green practices and green product innovation. *International Journal of Lean Six Sigma*, 12(6), 1089–1114.

Aull, F. (2012). Modell zur Ableitung effizienter Implementierungsstrategien für Lean-Production-Methoden. Dissertation, Lehrstuhl für Werkzeugmaschinen und Fertigungstechnik, Technische Universität München.

Bai, C., Dallasega, P., Orzes, G., & Sarkis, J. (2020). Industry 4.0 technologies assessment: A sustainability perspective. *International Journal of Production Economics*, 229, 107776.

Bertagnolli, F. (2020). *Lean Management. Einführung und Vertiefung in die japanische Management-Philosophie*, 2nd edition. Wiesbaden: Springer.

BMWI (2020). *Nachhaltige Produktion: Mit Industrie 4.0 die Ökologische Transformation aktiv gestalten.* Plattform Industrie 4.0.

Bortz, J. & Schuster, C. (2010). *Statistik für Human- und Sozialwissenschaftler*, 7th edition. Berlin: Springer.

Brüssel, C. (2018). Kernkompetenz Nachhaltigkeit und Corporate Social Responsibility. In S. Brüggemann (ed.), *Nachhaltigkeit in der Unternehmenspraxis. Impulse für Wirtschaft und Politik*. Wiesbaden: Springer, pp. 11–24.

Chen, P.-K., Lujan-Blanco, I., Fortuny-Santos, J., & Ruiz-de-Arbulo-López, P. (2020). Lean manufacturing and environmental sustainability: The effects of employee involvement, stakeholder pressure and ISO 14001. *Sustainability*, 12(18), 7258.

Cochran, D. S. & Rauch, E. (2020). Sustainable enterprise design 4.0: Addressing industry 4.0 technologies from the perspective of sustainability. *Procedia Manufacturing*, 51, 1237–1244.

Corejova, T. & Chinoracky, R. (2021). Assessing the potential for digital transformation. *Sustainability*, 13(19), 11040.

Dahm, M. H. & Holst, C. (2020). Auswirkungen der Digitalisierung auf die Wertschöpfungsakteure. In. M. H. Dahm (ed.), *Digitale Transformation in der Unternehmenspraxis. Mindset – Leadership – Akteure – Technologien*. Wiesbaden: Springer, pp. 221–247.

Dai, H.-N., Wang, H., Xu, G., Wan, J., & Imran, M. (2020). Big data analytics for manufacturing internet of things: Opportunities, challenges and enabling technologies. *Enterprise Information Systems*, 14, 1279–1303.

Demartini, M., Evans, S., & Tonelli, F. (2019). Digitalization technologies for industrial sustainability. *Procedia Manufacturing*, 33, 264–271.

Dennis, P. (2016). *Lean Production Simplified. A Plain-Language Guide to the World's Most Powerful Production System*, 3rd edition. Boca Raton: CRC Press.

Dillinger, F., Bernhard, O., Kagerer, M., & Reinhart, G. (2022a). Industry 4.0 implementation sequence for manufacturing companies. *Production Management*, 16, 705–718.

Dillinger, F., Kophal, A., & Reinhart, G. (2022b). Analysis of the impact of lean production methods and industry 4.0 technologies on sustainability and flexibility. *CPSL Conference Proceedings*, pp. 319–328.

Dillinger, F., Messmer, C., & Reinhart, G. (2021). Industrie-4.0-Technologiekreis für produzierende Unternehmen. *Identifikation und Strukturierung relevanter Industrie-4.0-Elemente für die industrielle Produktion. ZWF (Zeitschrift für wirtschaftlichen Fabrikbetrieb)*, pp. 639–643.

Ejsmont, K., Gladysz, B., & Kluczek, A. (2020). Impact of industry 4.0 on sustainability: Bibliometric literature review. *Sustainability*, 12(14), 5650.

Foit, D. (2018). Industrie 4.0 und Nachhaltigkeit – Digitalisierung als Teil der "großen Transformation". Discussion paper, Fakultät für Wirtschaftswissenschaften, Universität Paderborn.

Gordon, T. J. & Pease, A. (2006). RT Delphi: An efficient, "round-less" almost real time Delphi method. *Technological Forecasting and Social Change*, 73(4), 321–333.

Grime, M. M. & Wright, G. (2014). Delphi Method. In *Wiley Stats Ref: Statistics Reference Online*. Chichester: John Wiley & Sons.

Hofmann, F., Zwiers, J., Jaeger-Erben, M., & Marwede, M. (2018). Circular Economy als Gegenstand einer sozialökologischen Transformation? *Jahrbuch für nachhaltige Ökonomie*, 2018/2019.

Jamwal, A., Agrawal, R., Sharma, M., & Giallanza, A. (2021). Industry 4.0 technologies for manufacturing sustainability: A systematic review and future research directions. *Applied Sciences*, 11(2), 5725.

Jayashree, S., Reza, M. N., Malarvizhi, C. A., & Mohiuddin, M. (2021). Industry 4.0 implementation and triple bottom line sustainability: An empirical study on small and medium manufacturing firms. *Heliyon*, 7(8), e07753.

Kabzhassarova, M., Kulzhanova, A., Dikhanbayeva, D., Guney, M., & Turkyilmaz, A. (2021). Effect of Lean 4.0 on sustainability performance: A review. *Procedia CIRP*, 103, 73–78.

Kim, H. J. & Jeong, J. W. (2019). A data-driven predictive maintenance approach for improving sustainability in manufacturing systems. *Sustainability*, 11(19), 5299.

Kuß, A., Wildner, R., & Kreis, H. (2018). *Marktforschung. Datenerhebung und Datenanalyse*. Wiesbaden: Springer.

Kutzschenbach, M. von (2020). Die Interdependenz von Digitalisierung und Nachhaltigkeit als Chance der unternehmerischen Transformation. In. M. H. Dahm (ed.), *Digitale Transformation in der Unternehmenspraxis. Mindset – Leadership – Akteure – Technologien*. Wiesbaden: Springer, pp. 201–217.

Liker, J. K. (1997). *Becoming Lean. Inside Stories of U.S. Manufacturers*. New York: Productivity Press.

Nakatsu, R. T. & Iacovou, C. L. (2009). A comparative study of important risk factors involved in offshore and domestic outsourcing of software development projects: A two-panel Delphi study. *Information & Management*, 46(1), 57–68.

Niederberger, M. & Renn, O. (eds.) (2019). *Delphi-Verfahren in den Sozial- und Gesundheitswissenschaften. Konzept, Varianten und Anwendungsbeispiele*. Wiesbaden: Springer.

Ohno, T. (2013). *Das Toyota-Produktionssystem*, 3rd edition. Frankfurt am Main: Campus Verlag.

Olbrich, R., Battenfeld, D., & Buhr, C.-C. (2012). *Marktforschung. Ein einführendes Lehr- und Übungsbuch*. Berlin: Springer.

Piller, F., Brachmann, D., Falk, S., Gitzel, R., Klement, P., Madeja, N., Rüchardt, D., Schiller, C., Schmidt, F., & Wegener, D. (2021). *Zehn Thesen, wie digitale Geschäftsmodelle Nachhaltigkeit in der Industrie 4.0 fördern*. Berlin.

Rakic, S., Pavlovic, M., & Marjanovic, U. (2021). A precondition of sustainability: Industry 4.0 readiness. *Sustainability*, 13(12), 6641.

Ramsauer, C. (2013). *Industrie 4.0 – Die Produktion der Zukunft*. WINGbusiness.

Realyvásquez-Vargas, A., Arredondo-Soto, K. C., Garcia-Alcaraz, J., Márquez-Lobato, B. Y., & Cruz-Garcia, J. (2019). Introduction and configuration of a collaborative robot in an assembly task as a means to decrease occupational risks and increase efficiency in a manufacturing company. *Robotics and Computer-Integrated Manufacturing*, 57, 315–328.

Reinhart, G. (ed.) (2017). *Handbuch Industrie 4.0. Geschäftsmodelle, Prozesse, Technik*. München: Carl Hanser Verlag.

Roth, A. (ed.) (2016). *Einführung und Umsetzung von Industrie 4.0. Grundlagen, Vorgehensmodell und Use Cases aus der Praxis*. Berlin: Springer.

Rother, M. and Shook, J. (1999). *Learning to See: Value Stream Mapping to Add Value and Eliminate Muda*. Boston: Productivity Press.

Savitz, A. W. & Weber, K. (2013). *The Triple Bottom Line. How Today's Best-Run Companies Are Achieving Economic, Social, and Environmental Success – and How You Can Too*. San Francisco: Jossey-Bass.

Schmidt, R. C. (1997). Managing Delphi surveys using nonparametric statistical techniques. *Decision Sciences*, 28, 763–774.

Schuh, G. & Schmidt, C. (eds.) (2014). *Produktionsmanagement. Handbuch Produktion und Management*. Berlin: Springer.

Shingo, S. (1985). *A Revolution in Manufacturing: The SMED System*. New York: Productivity Press.

Steven, M. (2018). *Industrie 4.0. Grundlagen – Teilbereiche – Perspektiven*. Stuttgart: Kohlhammer Verlag.

Steven, M. & Klünder, T. (2018). Nachhaltigkeit schlanker Industrie 4.0 – Netzwerke. In A. Khare et al. (eds.), *Marktorientiertes Produkt- und Produktionsmanagement in digitalen Umwelten*. Wiesbaden: Springer, pp. 201–222.

Varela, L., Araújo, A., Ávila, P., Castro, H., & Putnik, G. (2019). Evaluation of the relation between lean manufacturing, industry 4.0, and sustainability. *Sustainability*, 11(5), 1439.

Werder, M. von & Rukwid, R. (2021). Strukturwandel: Zukunftsangst in der Industrie. *Wirtschaftsdienst*, 101, 726–731.

Index